THE AMERICAN CENTURY SERIES

FEDERAL HILL

IN THE TWENTIETH CENTURY

THE AMERICAN CENTURY SERIES

FEDERAL HILL

IN THE TWENTIETH CENTURY

Joe Fuoco and Albert Lothrop

ARCADIA PUBLISHING

ISBN 978-0-7385-6397-8

Published by Arcadia Publishing
Charleston, South Carolina

Printed in the United States of America

Library of Congress Catalog Card Number: 2008938678

For all general information contact Arcadia Publishing at:
Telephone 843-853-2070
Fax 843-853-0044
E-mail sales@arcadiapublishing.com
For customer service and orders:
Toll-Free 1-888-313-2665

Visit us on the Internet at www.arcadiapublishing.com

This book is dedicated to the memory of
Tony "Good Old Monaleek" Marrocco,
who for many years told the story of Federal Hill in the Echo *newspaper*
in his simple, straightforward, honest style.
Without Good Old Monaleek, Federal Hill would have been poorer,
for he gave it a place in history and its people a worthy nobility.

Contents

Acknowledgments

This book is the result of the cooperation and generosity of many, including some who were so forthcoming in the previous book *Federal Hill and the Mill Villages*. My gratitude goes to Antonette Marino, Isabel Micheli, Viola La Chapelle, Dorothy Potenza, Tommy Cursio, Frank Melucci, Michael Antonellli, and the essential, invaluable work of Al Lothrop, photographer, without whom this book would have been impossible.

Introduction

A long time ago, in the era of the great immigrations when hopeful people courageously sailed from Italy to the United States, Federal Hill was the place of gathering and of coming together. In those days, fifty-four thousand or so Italian Americans lived on the Hill. As it approaches the third millennium, the year 2000, Federal Hill is now home to less than six thousand Italian Americans. Hyphenation of group names, like Italo-Americans and Irish-Americans, is now perceived as an anomaly; people are no longer a hyphenated people—they are one people joined on the Hill.

True, the Federal Hill ethos is still embellished by a nostalgia for a past that will never come again, for a time when two languages only were spoken on the Hill, when hundreds of pushcarts fed the population, when three- and four-story tenement houses embraced the throng, and when the churches seemed indestructible. Many of those things are gone and will never return as they once were.

Today, Federal Hill is home to a variety of peoples, and on any given day, a walk down its most famous street, Atwells Avenue, brings the sounds of many languages to the ear, for today one encounters the new immigrants, the new entrepreneurs, people from all over the globe who have come to the Hill because it has always been the place to come. Japanese, Thai, Chinese, Portuguese, Caribbean, Russian, Ukrainian, Bellarussian, African, and Hispanic—they are all here, living, working, and forging beginnings on the Hill. Tenements have been razed; derelict aggregates of houses that nearly touched each other, that stood for so long shoulder to shoulder, have been demolished, and new, bright, colorful one-family dwellings have taken their places. High-rise apartment houses stand as sentries at either end of the Hill. The look has changed, even the character of this magnet for immigrants.

Johnson and Wales University, sprawling over hundreds of acres in the city of Providence, has brought its eclectic and rich world culture to the Hill. Students from countless countries live on the Hill—the richness is a boost to a place once on the edge of cultural extinction. For as bits and pieces of a nostalgic past were being broken and lost in time, little was replacing those ethnic arts. Now the Hill is alive again, more alive than it has been in decades. Broadway, the great boulevard, has become a restored, envied thoroughfare—a perfect example of the past resurrected for the present, secured for the future. Great mansions gleam once again, and plaques tell us who lived there and when; the ages flow over the viewer, and there is a connection that is umbilical. Thousands of new trees, many saplings, will live beyond the current residents and another generation will enjoy the coolness of their shade. A progressive, uncelebrated force called the Broadway Renaissance Group has taken the boulevard and has made it again a street of great beauty.

Where a newspaper of one hundred years ago spoke in one language to immigrants, the Italian language, a resident newspaper today speaks in three languages, for new people have come.

Where once the restaurant fare, famed throughout the world, was defined by an Italian cuisine and custom, Federal Hill now offers foods of the world to those who come here. Japanese and Chinese restaurants, Portuguese and Thai, the unique cuisine of the Caribbean Islands, the foods of Hispaniola, all mingle on th avenue and its tendril streets.

Where some of the churches once stood, removed and destroyed despite the cries of people who wanted them to remain, parks have been created, small oases in a busy, noisy, again teeming place. Golden street lights have replaced garish white, and the light is softer, a welcoming light.

Yet, some things do not change and will move into the year 2000 stronger, for they have endured. Old names of old eating places, decades in the growing, are still here. Tenements remain on many streets, and movie directors come for an ambience still linked to the days of struggle and denial, of hope and success, and have brought the name of Federal Hill to the corners of the earth. Some of the businesses have been given to sons and daughters, the gift of honest toil, and they have kept the family names alive. Not all have left the Hill affluent, seeking the suburban quiet and affirmation of success, of "having made it"; some have remained, even the young, and have kept promises—promises to stay, to work, and to live on the Hill.

The great welcoming arch has not changed and cannot ever change. It invites the world and its variety to Federal Hill. It endures, as if realizing that things must be lost for things to be gained. The suspended pine cone, "La Pigna," says what it has always said, and what it must continue to say into the year 2000 and beyond: "You are welcome, come to this place. All are welcome."

One

The Turn of the Century

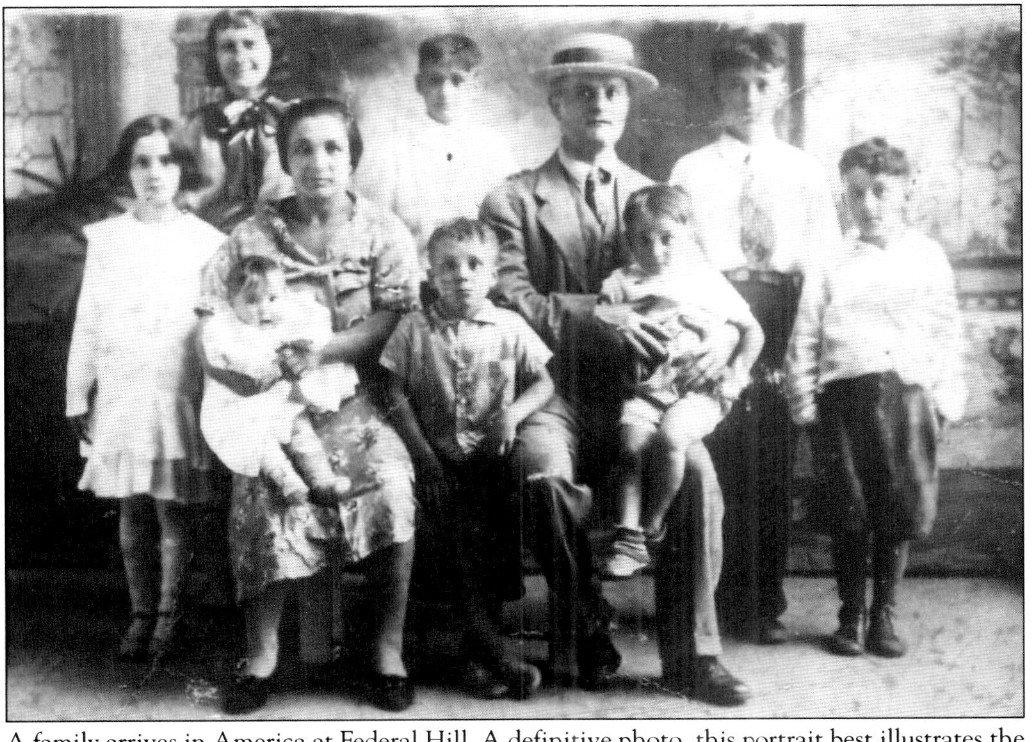

A family arrives in America at Federal Hill. A definitive photo, this portrait best illustrates the look of the immigrant family. All are here—father, mother, brothers, sisters, and children. A new world had beckoned. Photo courtesy of Isabel Micheli.

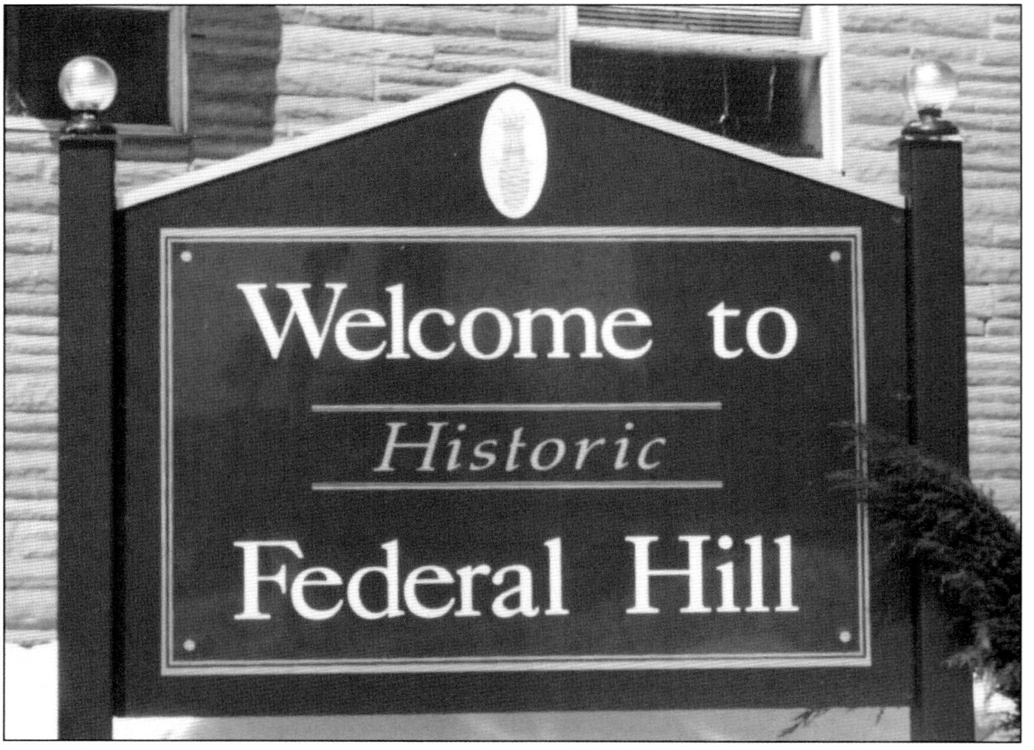

This is an invitation to the Hill. A new sign welcomes visitors, tourists, and all interested in experiencing the special ambience of Federal Hill.

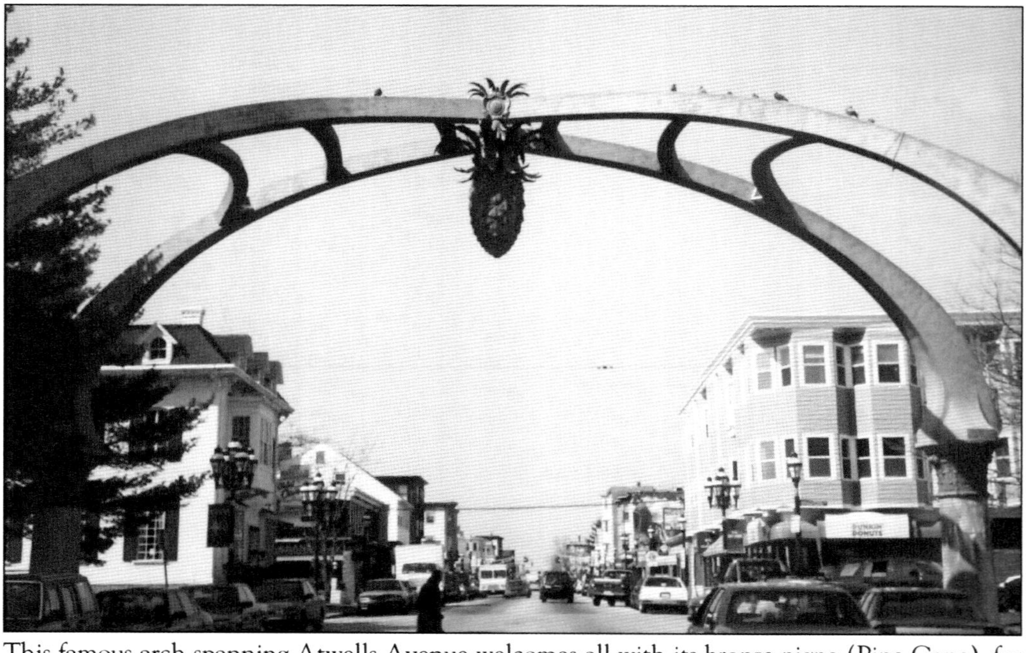

This famous arch spanning Atwells Avenue welcomes all with its bronze pigna (Pine Cone), for the pine cone is the symbol of hospitality. Through the arch, one can see old and new buildings.

The Italian-American family had arrived, and here is an example of one family ensconced on Federal Hill at the turn of the century. A remarkable photo, this picture shows the impeccable dress of the children and the elegance of the father and mother. Photo courtesy of Viola La Chapelle.

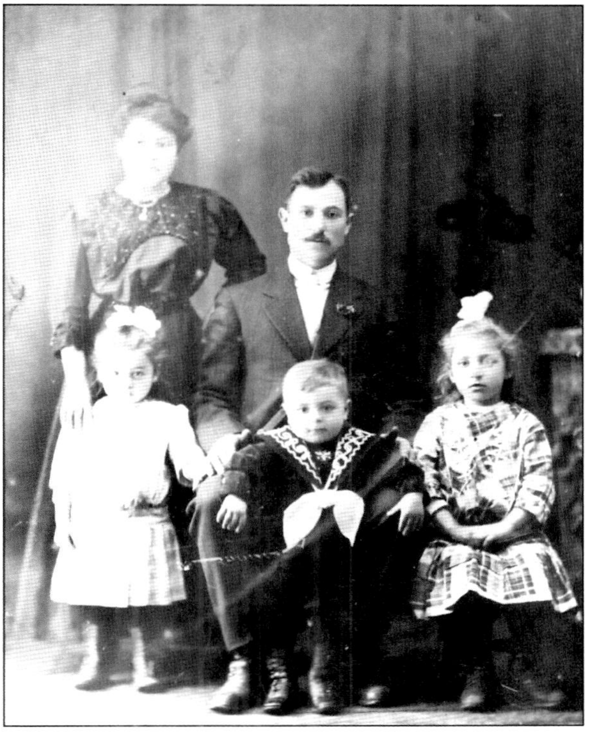

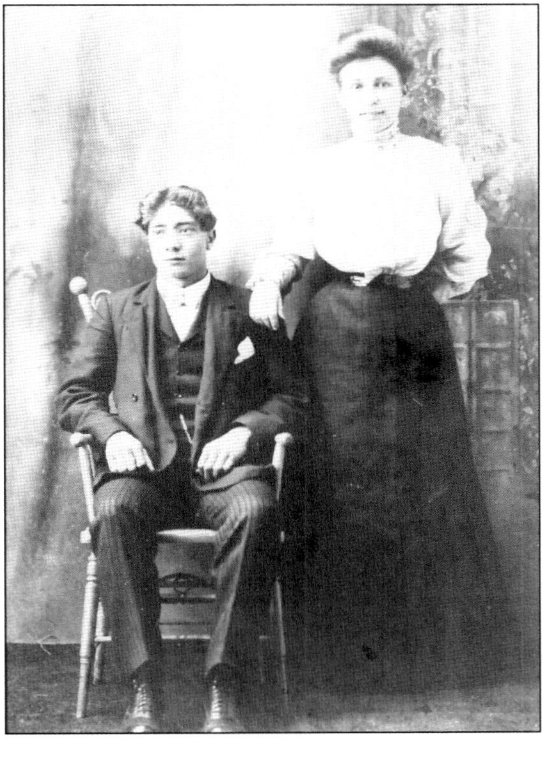

Stoic and determined, the young couple, as yet unmarried, posed in a Westminster Street photo studio in the teens. Photo courtesy of Viola La Chapelle.

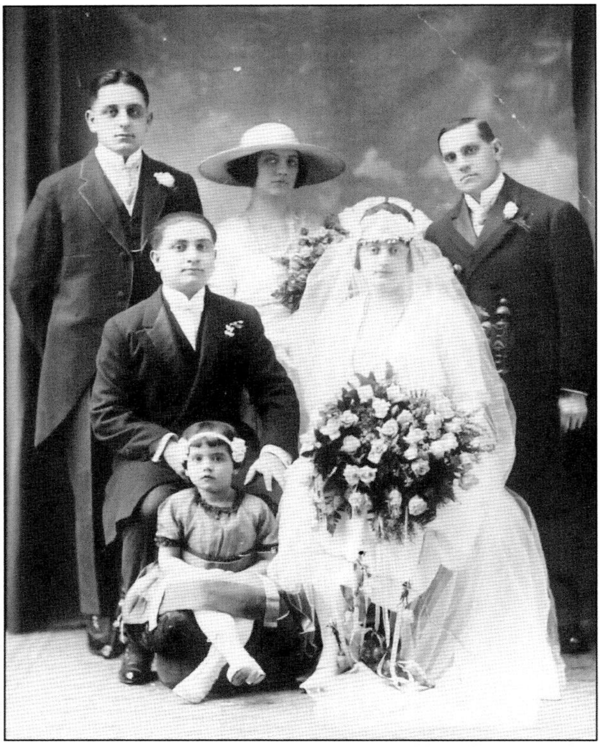

Where there were immigrants, there had to be weddings. This is the wedding of Emma Tella to Mr. La Banca. Emma became a schoolteacher and died young. The gentleman in the top row on the left had the looks of a movie star of the era. Photo courtesy Viola La Chapelle.

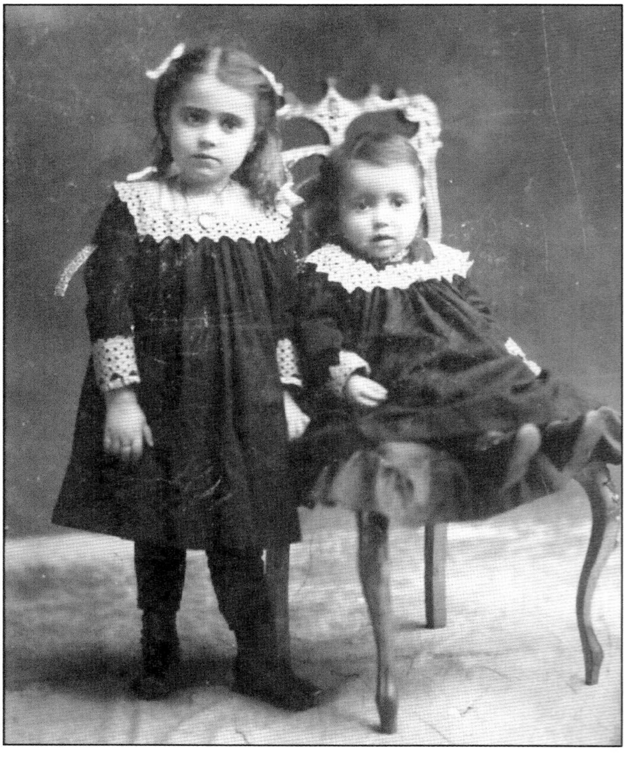

The children of Italian immigrants experienced hardship on Federal Hill, but they were always neatly dressed and beautifully groomed. Notice the heart-shaped locket about the older sister's neck, a familiar decoration of the time. Photo courtesy of Viola La Chapelle.

We know her as Mrs. Cambio, as an adult, but that is all. Immigrant children, like Mrs. Cambio, did not eschew education. In fact, their parents insisted on it, realizing that education was the key to success in a new country. Photo courtesy of Viola La Chapelle.

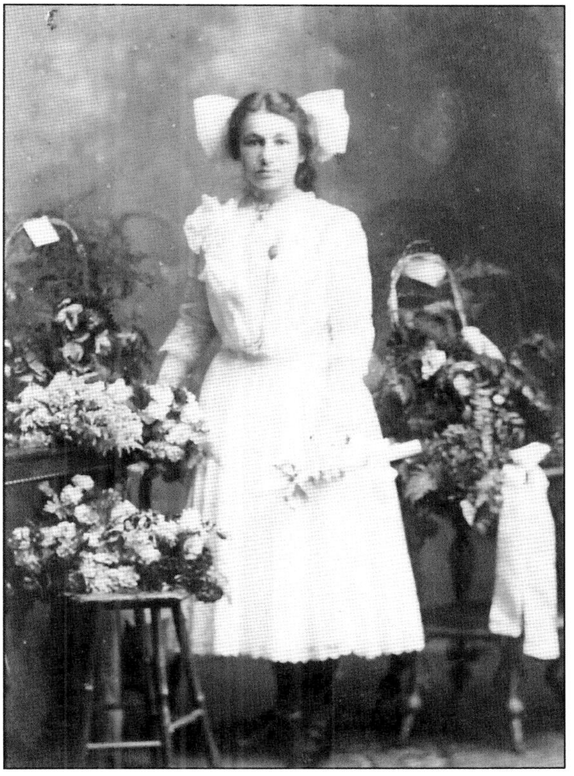

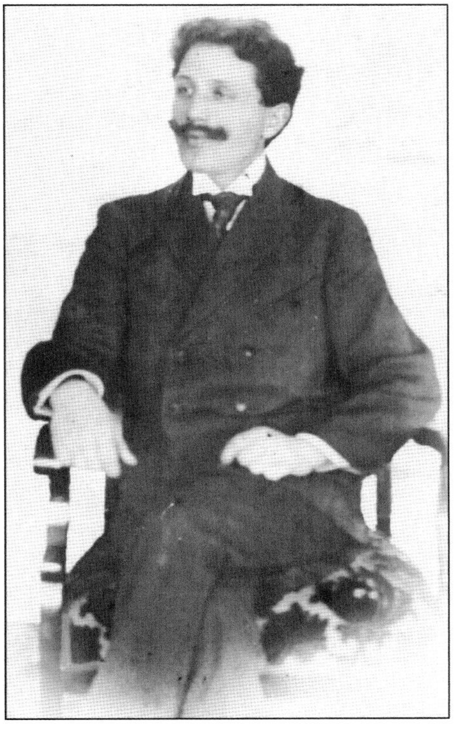

We do not know who this man is, but he is definitely dignified, a little aloof, and in complete possession of himself. Such men, Dons or near Dons, were characteristic of the Hill at the turn of the century. Photo courtesy Viola La Chapelle.

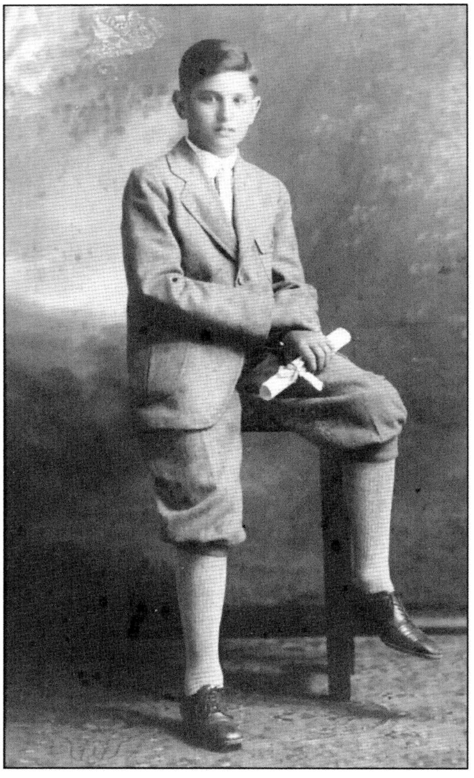

Young Freddie Martelucci proudly holds his rolled diploma. This photo was taken at the Outlet Studio in downtown Providence. Photo courtesy of Viola La Chapelle.

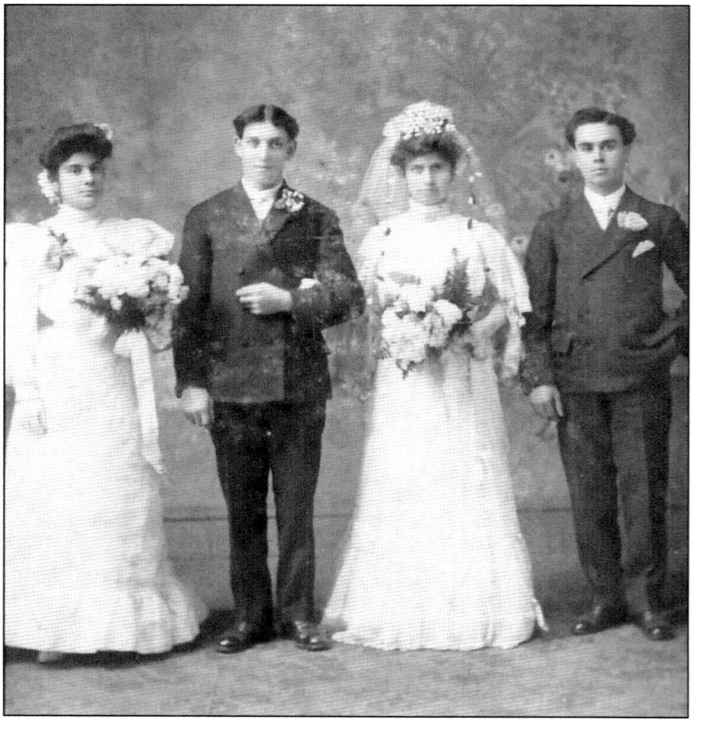

This is a picture of another wedding, this of John Parillo to Jennie Marotta. Nobody knew her by that name, however. Everybody called her by Jennie Marriot. The Anglicizing of Italian names was quite common. Photo courtesy of Viola La Chapelle.

This is an equal time for the girls. Here, Eva Mancuso looks with quiet satisfaction at her diploma. Such events were beautifully posed before mock-ups of walls of books and with bouquets of beautiful flowers. Photo courtesy of Viola La Chapelle.

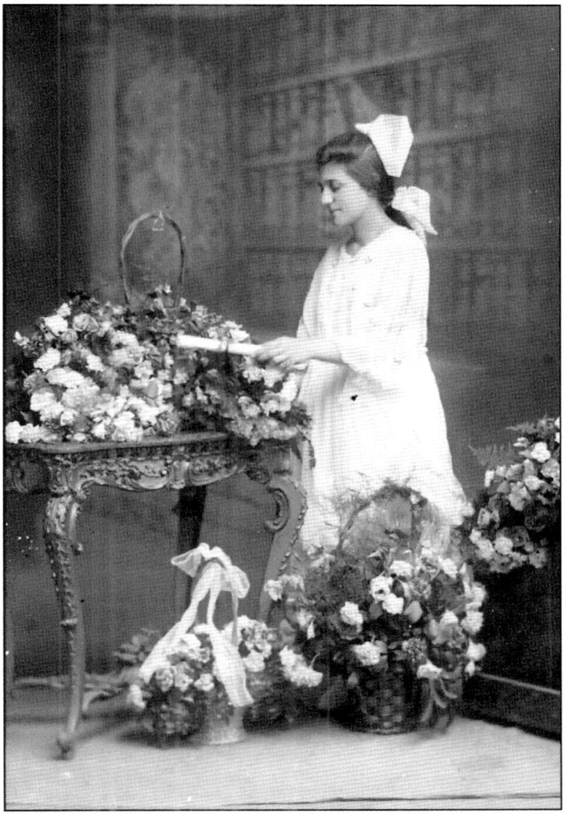

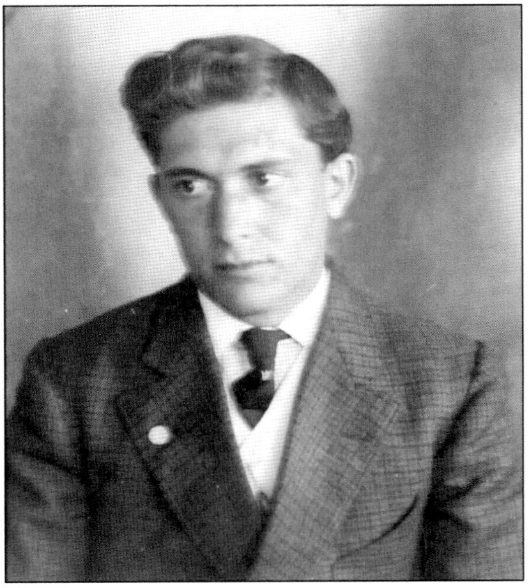

This is a picture of Vincent Tella. His family of several brothers and sisters was well known. A brother opened one of the early bars on Federal Hill. Photo courtesy of Viola La Chapelle.

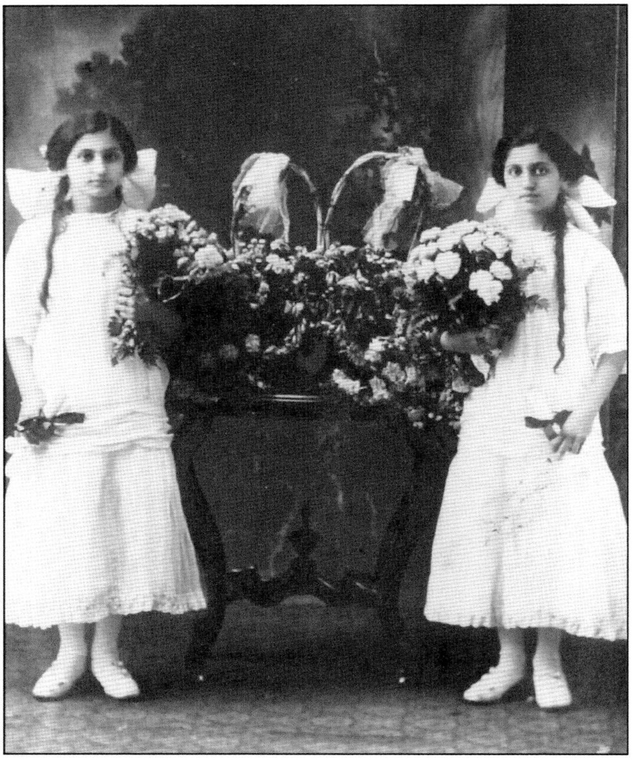

The Perry twins are shown here graduating. They were known as the Perrys, but the name was Parillo. Identical twins, they were virtually indistinguishable, eccentric, colorful, and close in later years. Photo courtesy of Viola La Chapelle.

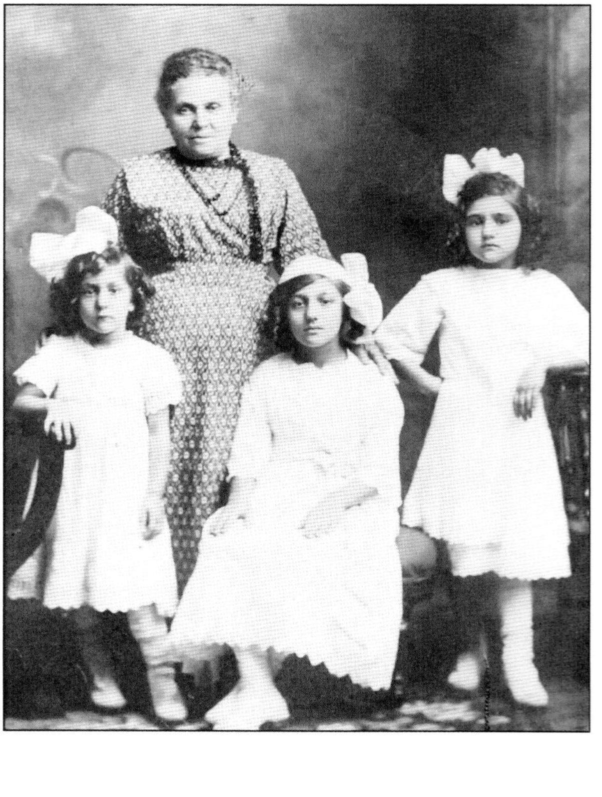

A Grand Dame in her own right, Philomena Tella ruled her family wisely, if rigidly. Here she stands with her granddaughters: (from left to right) Irene, Eva, and Emily, now all deceased. Photo courtesy of Viola La Chapelle.

This wedding photo taken in a studio on 183 Atwells Avenue called the International Photo Studio of Ansaldi & Caiazza is so beautiful that it is a tragedy we do not know who the people are. Photo courtesy of Viola La Chapelle.

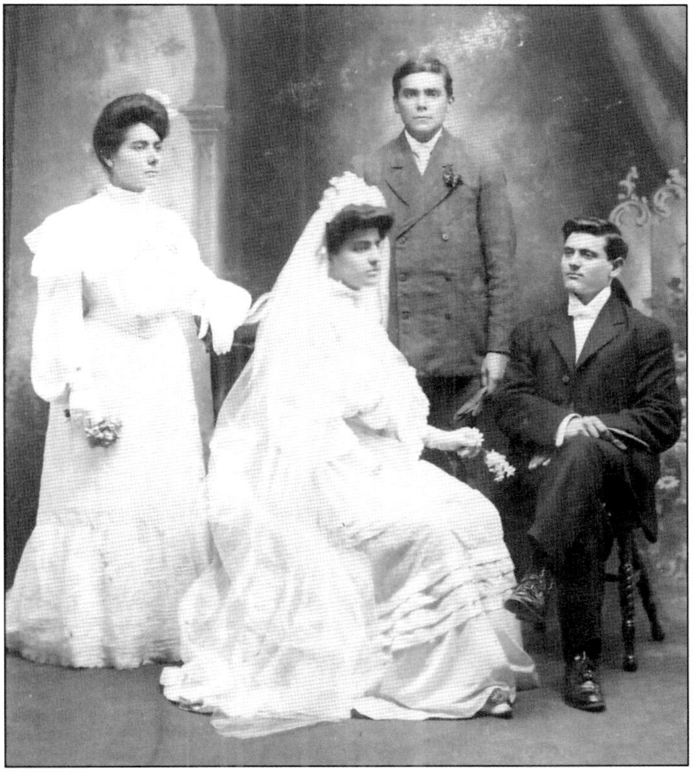

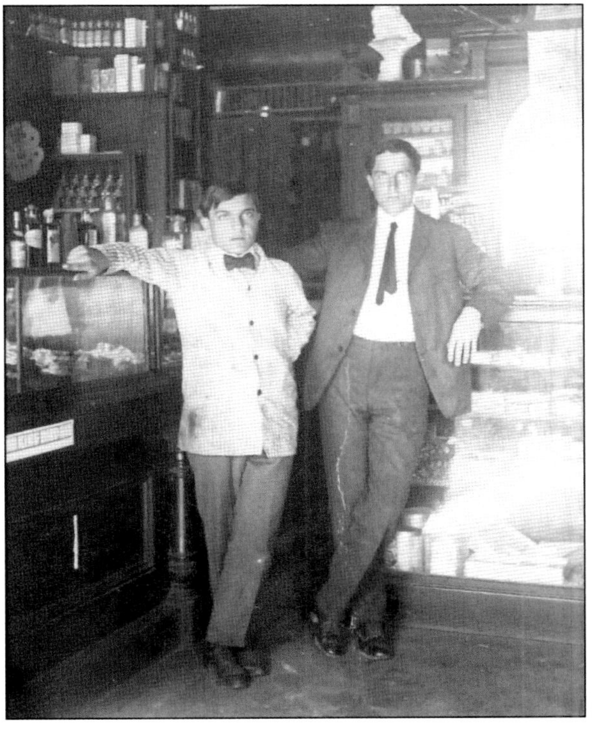

Pasco Tella, on the left, is pictured in his store. Here he sold cigars, as well as tooth powder. In fact, Pat, as he was called, sold just about everything. Photo courtesy of Viola La Chapelle.

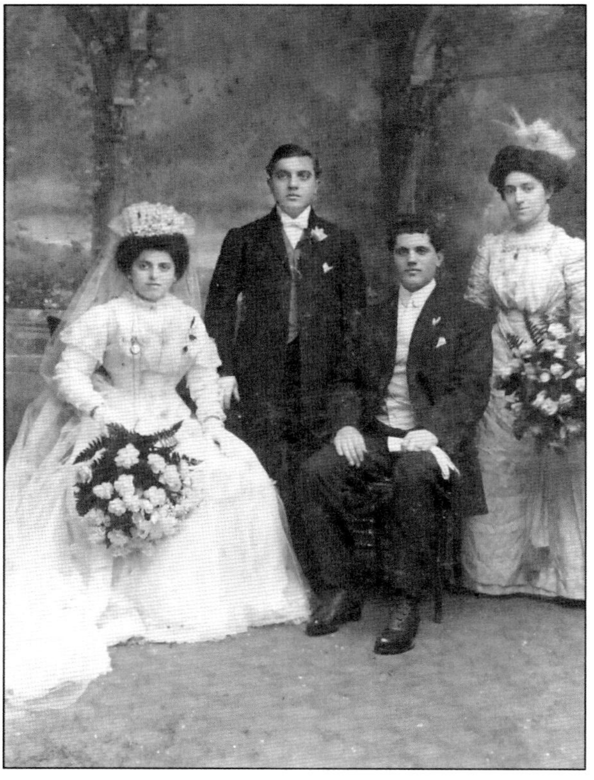

At a wedding on the Hill, Pasco Tella and Viola Tella, son and daughter of the matriarchal Philomena, stand next to the bride and groom. Photo courtesy of Viola La Chapelle.

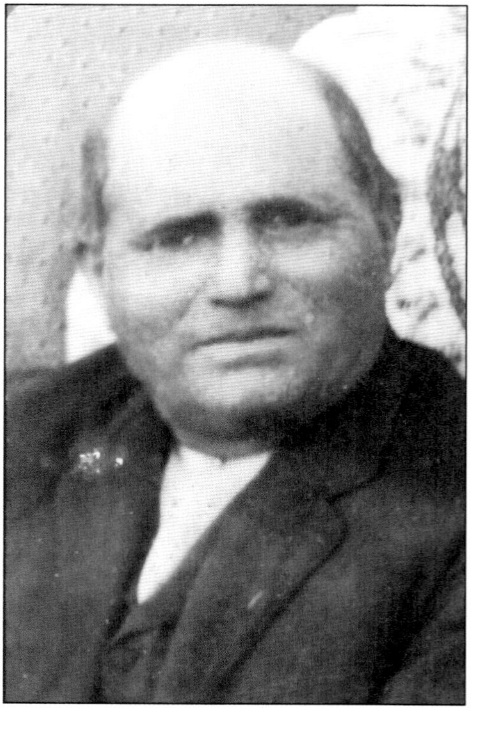

Gaetano (Danny) Tella was a kind, gentle man and the father of enterprising sons like the dapper Pasco and the sportsman John. Photo courtesy of Viola La Chapelle.

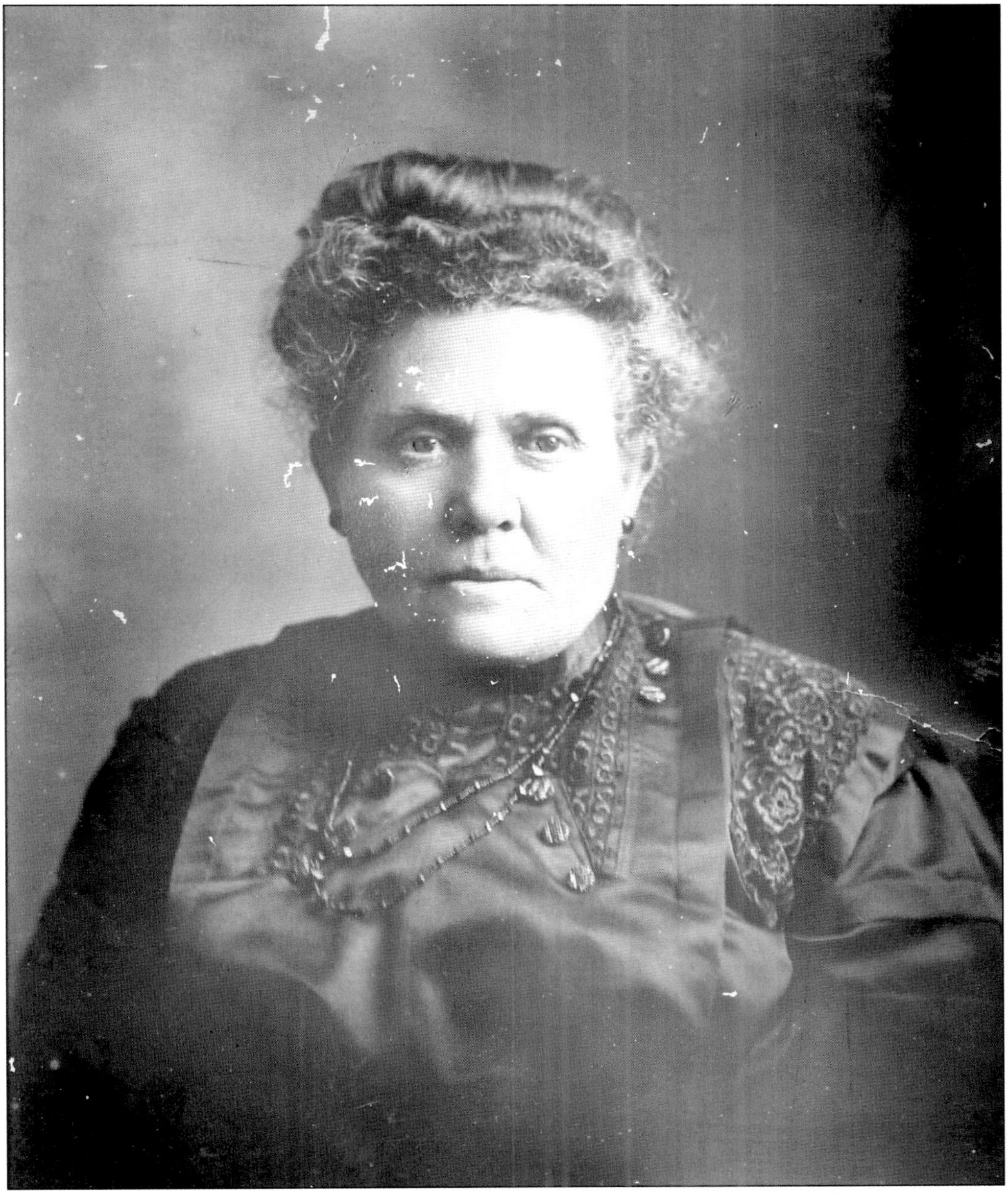

Here she is, dispelling the old cliche about the poor, worn-out, overwhelmed immigrant mother. True, there were those as well, but here Philomena Tella illustrates dramatically that she was someone to contend with, a great, memorable character. The Tellas were one of the five founding families of Federal Hill. Photo courtesy of Viola La Chapelle.

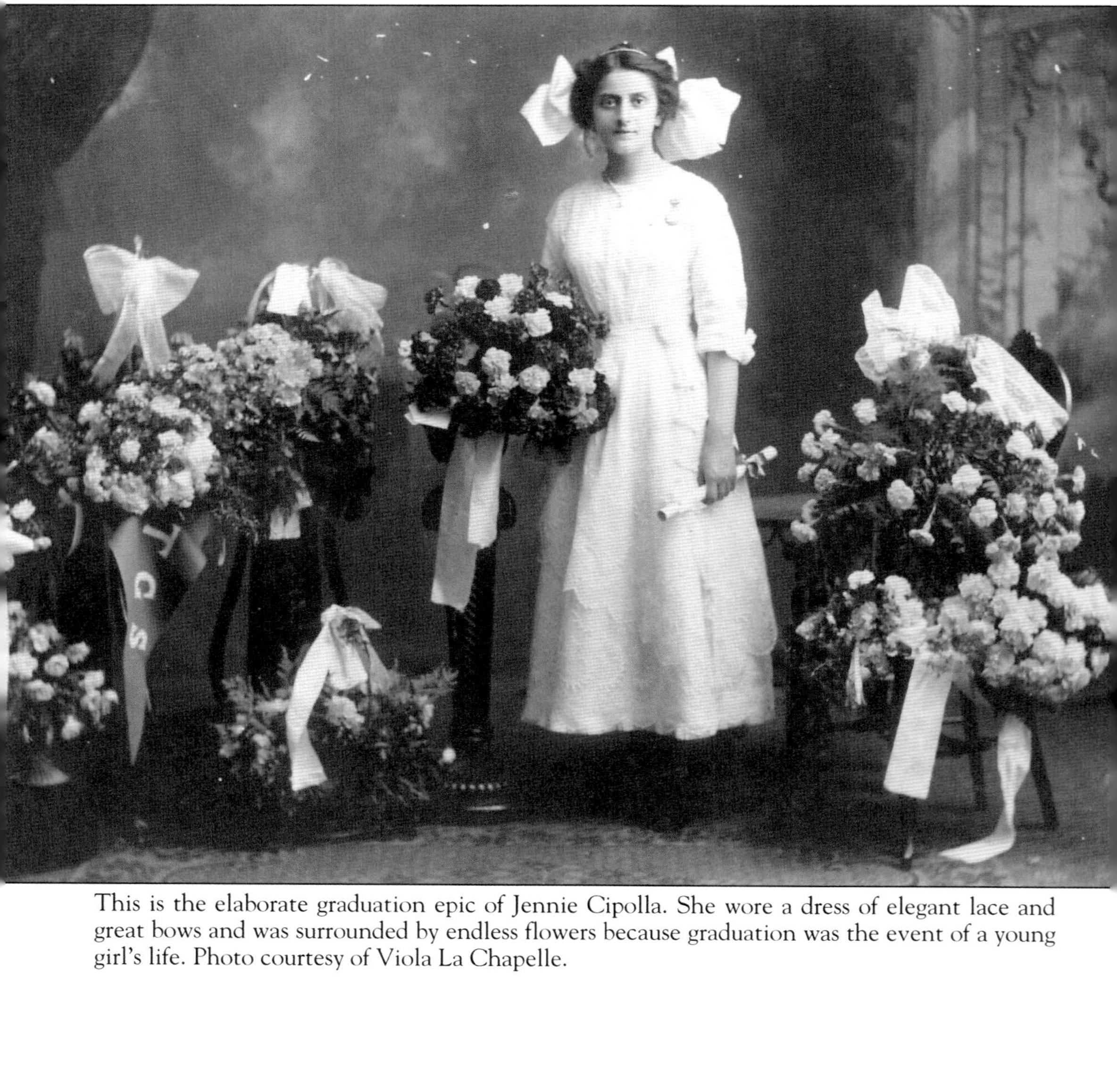

This is the elaborate graduation epic of Jennie Cipolla. She wore a dress of elegant lace and great bows and was surrounded by endless flowers because graduation was the event of a young girl's life. Photo courtesy of Viola La Chapelle.

Two

The Family, the Community

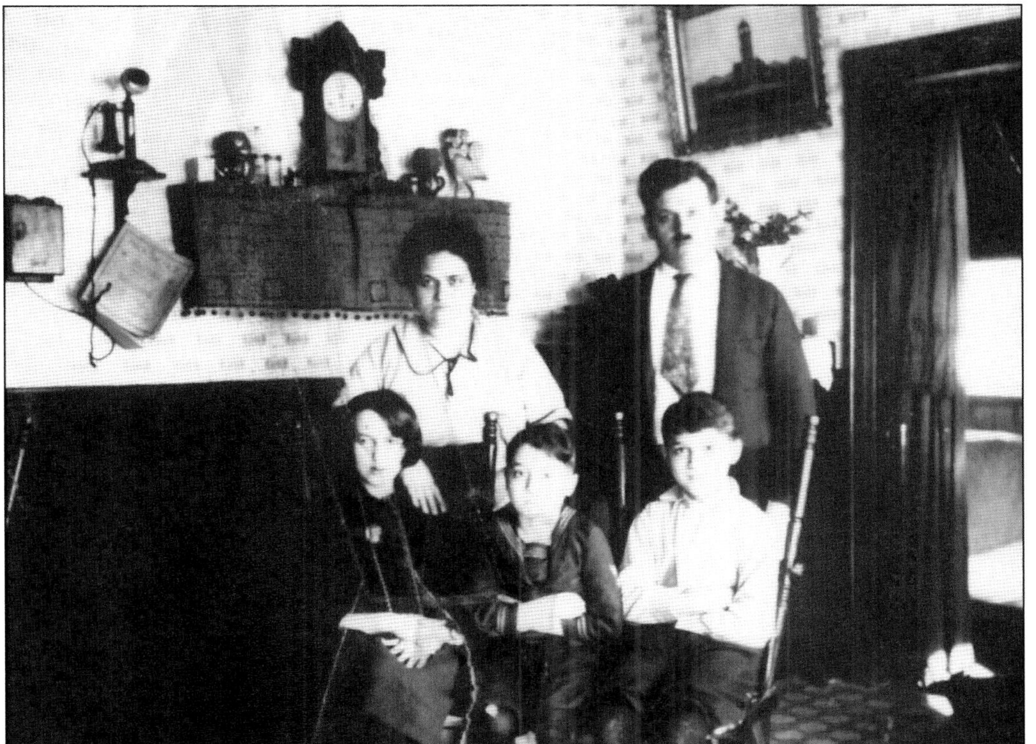

The Gallo family, mother, father, sister, and two brothers, of Federal Hill are shown here in 1924. This is a beautiful photograph that says something about endurance and closeness. Photo courtesy of Antonette Marino.

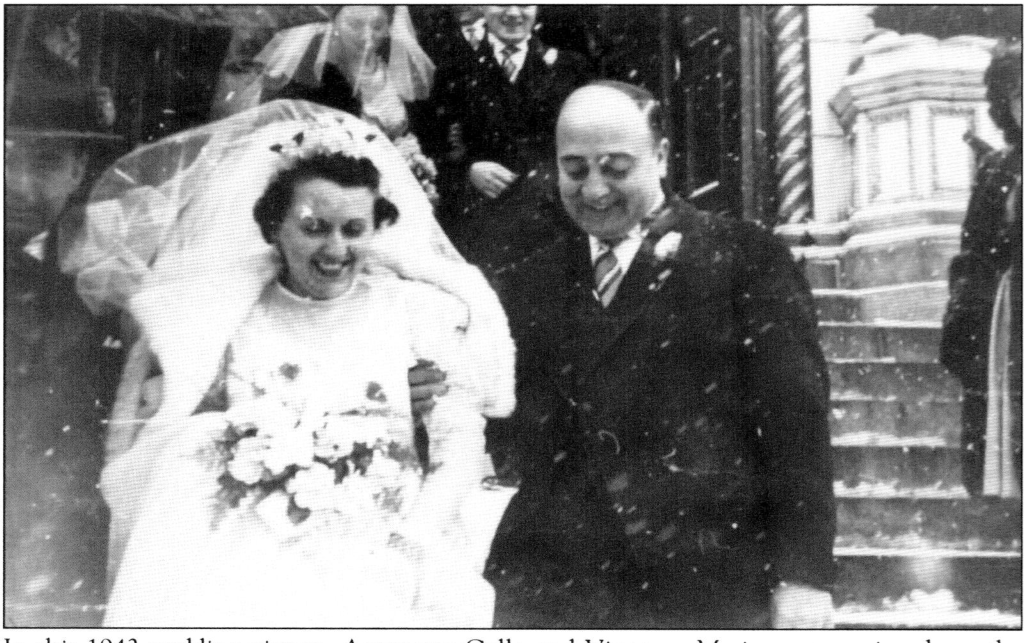

In this 1943 wedding picture, Antonette Gallo and Vincenzo Marino are coming down the stairs of the historic Holy Ghost Church. Vincenzo lived a few days short of his 100th birthday. Photo courtesy of Antonette Marino.

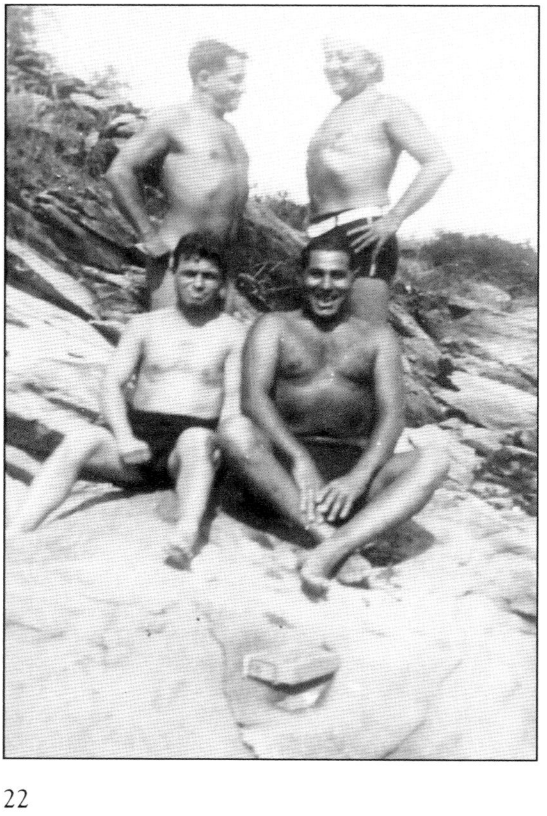

Who said people didn't know how to enjoy themselves then? At the beach and pushing out his chest is Vincenzo Marino (top right). Photo courtesy of Antonette Marino.

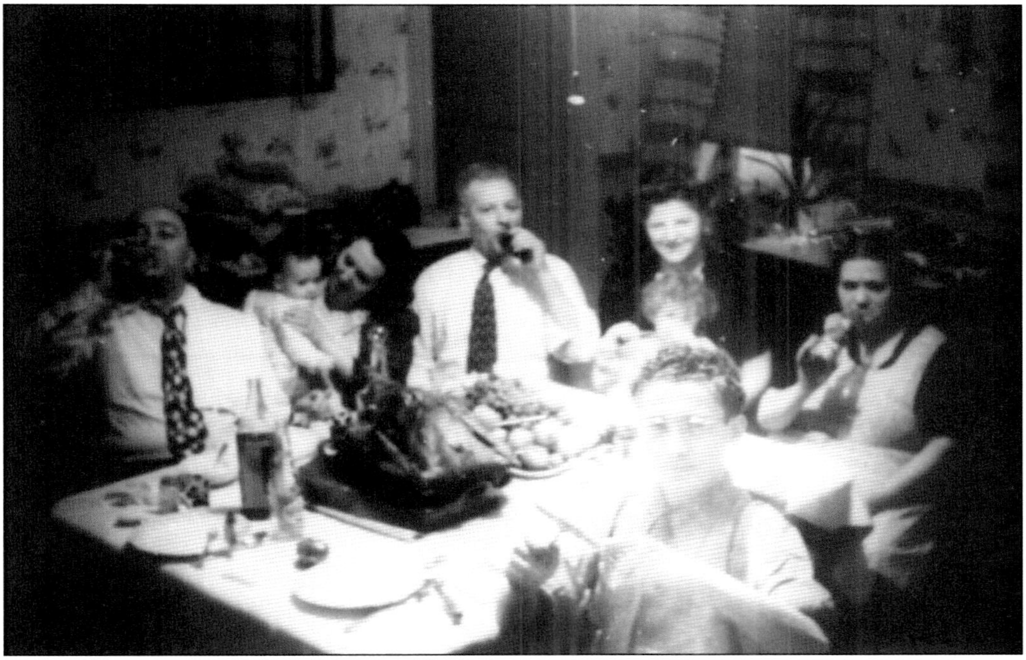

This is a family gathering in the Marino household. The table is full, the wine is there, and the closeness of the family is lit by a wonderful light. Photo courtesy of Antonette Marino.

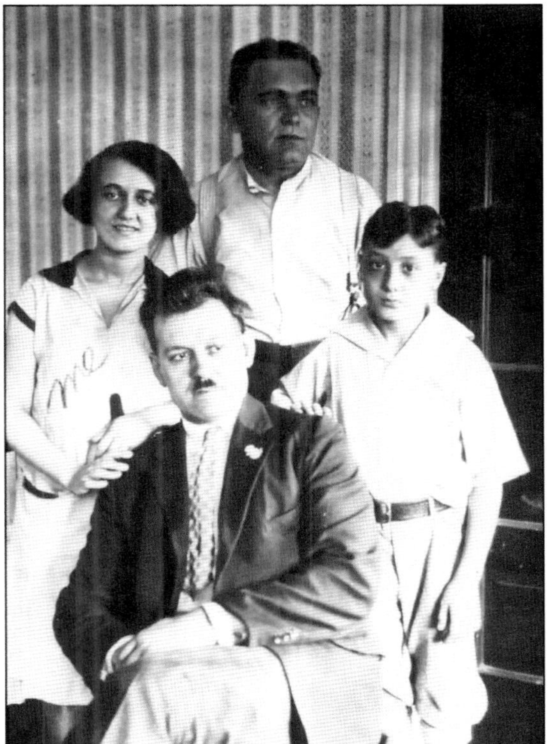

The Gallo family is pictured here in the 1930s. Antonette was the only daughter. Photo courtesy of Antonette Marino.

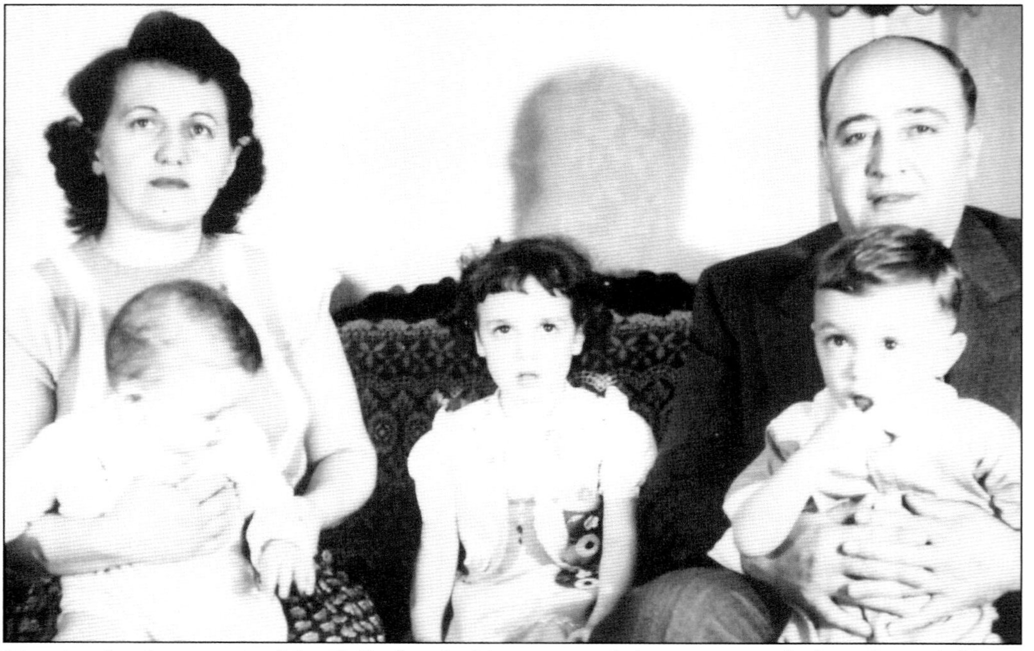

Here is a family portrait of the Gallo family, Vincenzo and Antonette, with their three children. Notice the delicate, beautiful doily on the back of the couch. Photo courtesy of Antonette Marino.

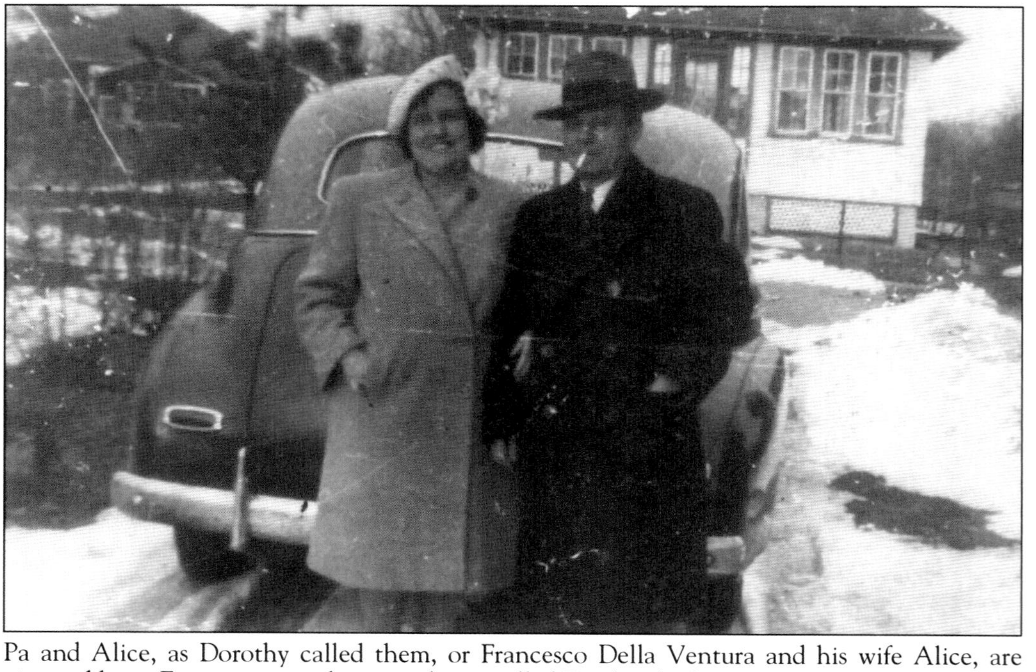

Pa and Alice, as Dorothy called them, or Francesco Della Ventura and his wife Alice, are pictured here. Francesco, a tailor, was always called Frank. The bungalow behind them is right out of the late 1920s, but the car informs the viewer that it is possibly two decades later. Photo courtesy of Dorothy Potenza.

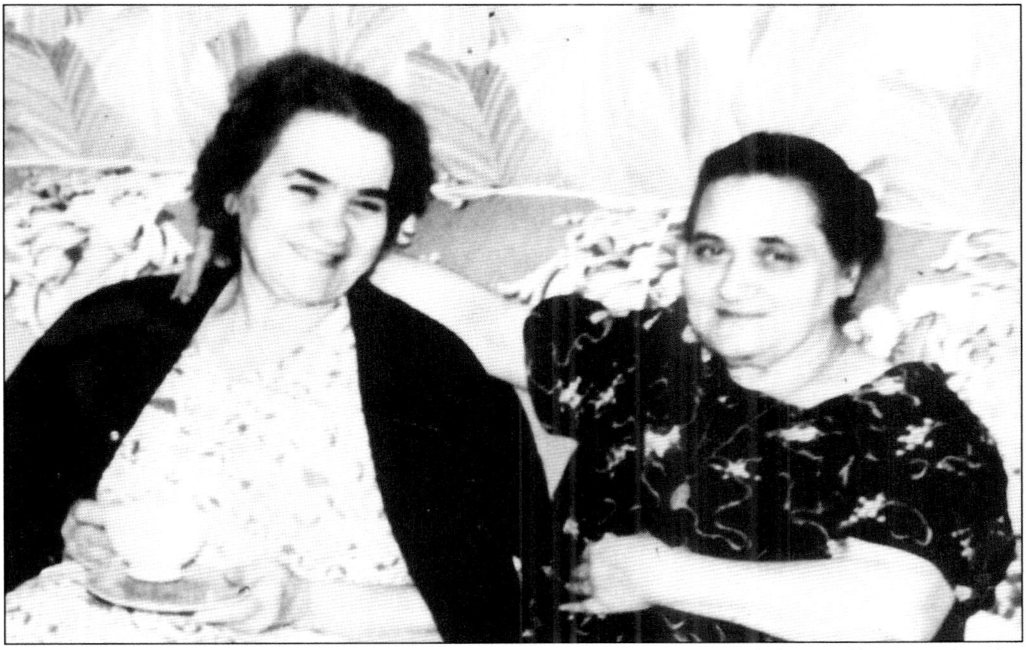

What a picture! Two friends of many years share a cup of coffee and share affection. On the left is Eliza Petrarca, who had fourteen children; on her right is Josephine Gallo, mother of Antonette Marino. Photo courtesy of Antonette Marino.

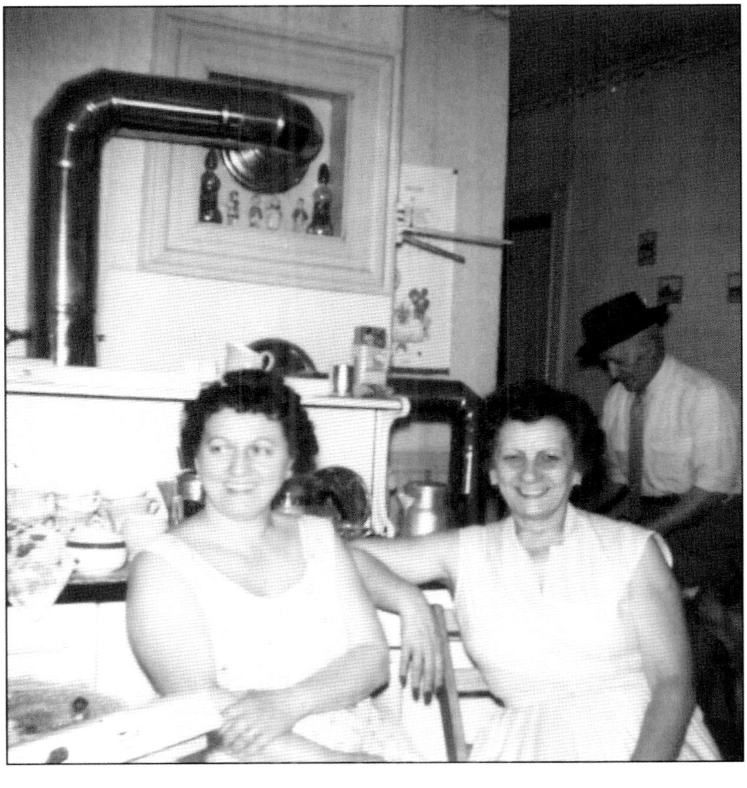

They don't make kitchens like this any more. Sitting in the close warmth of a kitchen with the requisite stove pipe are Carmella Ferro (left) and Antonette Marino (right). Notice the extent of pipes in the room. Photo courtesy of Antonette Marino.

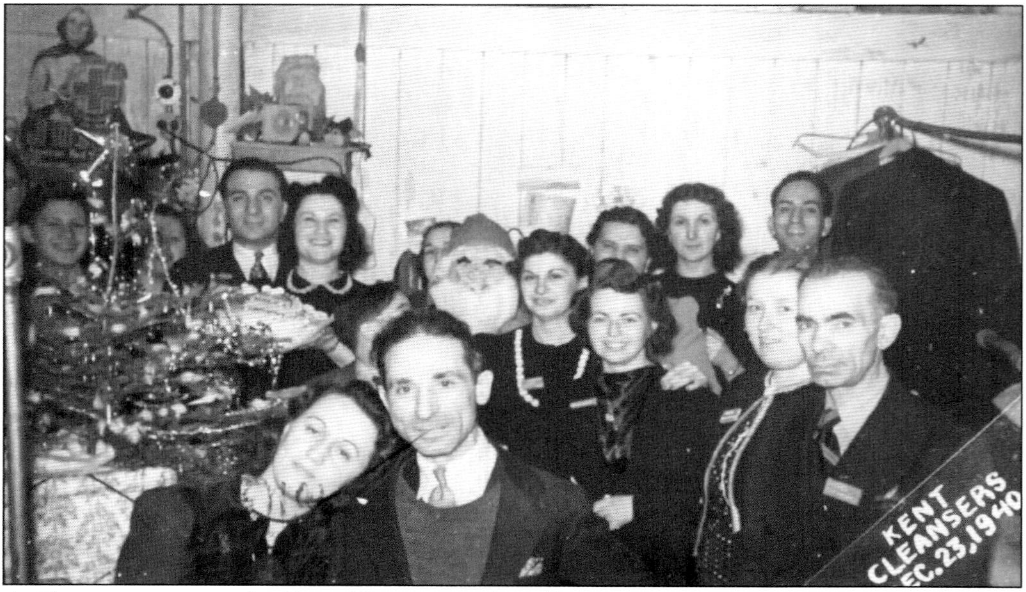

A Christmas party at the Kent Cleaners on Atwells Avenue in 1940 looks as if it was quite a party, if the drowsy expression on the girl at the left is any indication—actually, it was, according to Antonette, who was that girl at the left. Photo courtesy of Antonette Marino.

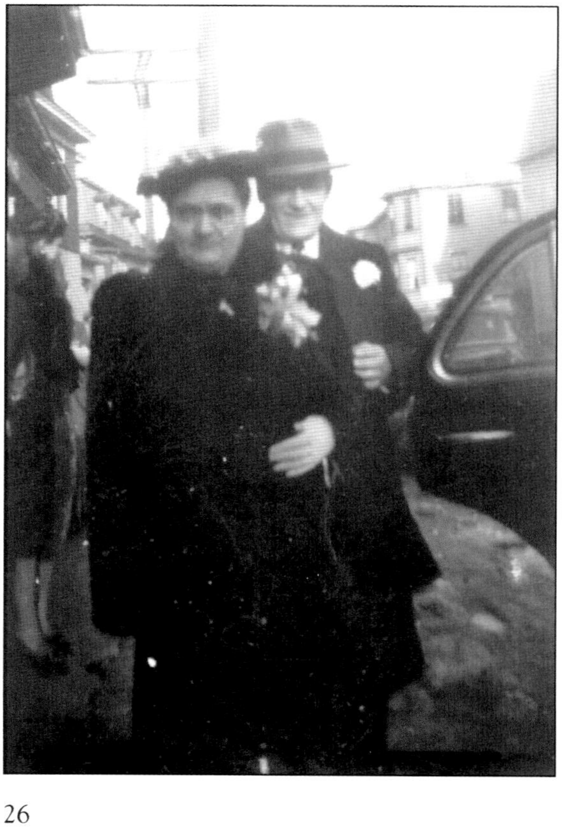

Mr. and Mrs. Gallo are shown in their later years. Yes, this is the couple in the photo of 1924. They, like some of Faulkner's solid-rock characters, endured. Photo courtesy of Antonette Marino.

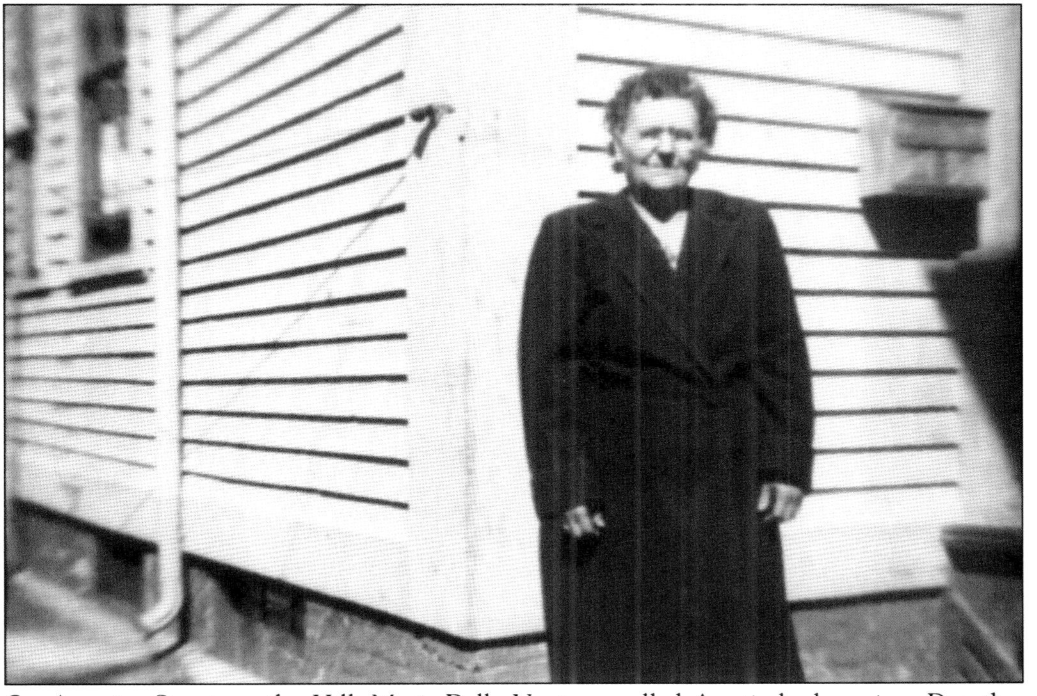

On America Street on the Hill, Maria Della Ventura, called Auntie by her niece Dorothy, poses for this photograph. Photo courtesy of Dorothy Potenza.

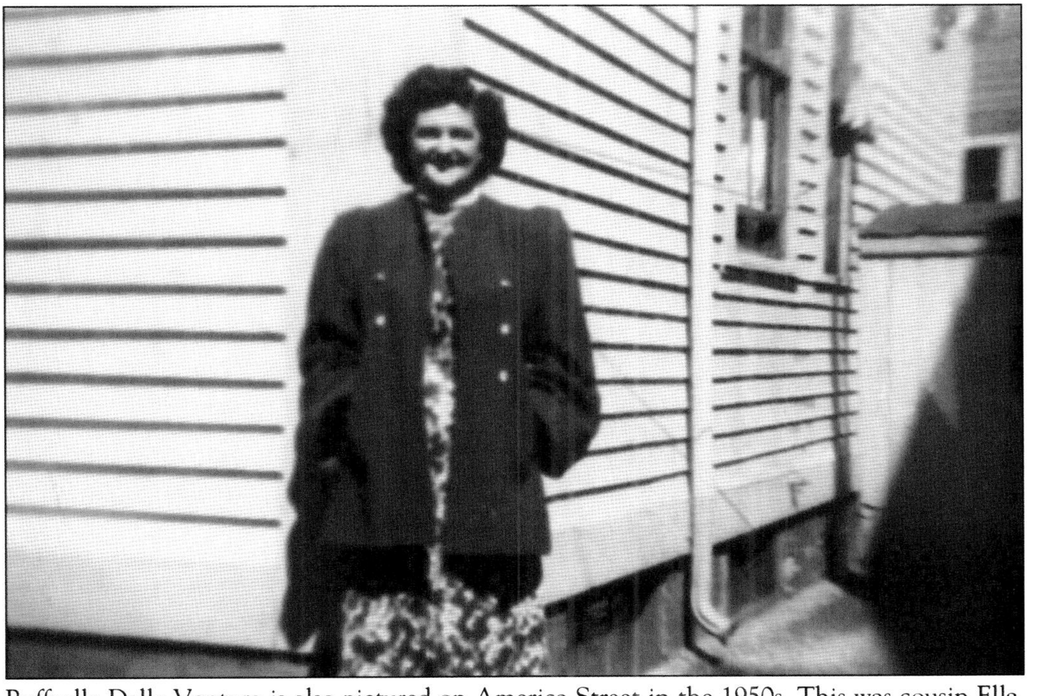

Raffaella Della Ventura is also pictured on America Street in the 1950s. This was cousin Ella. Photo courtesy of Dorothy Potenza.

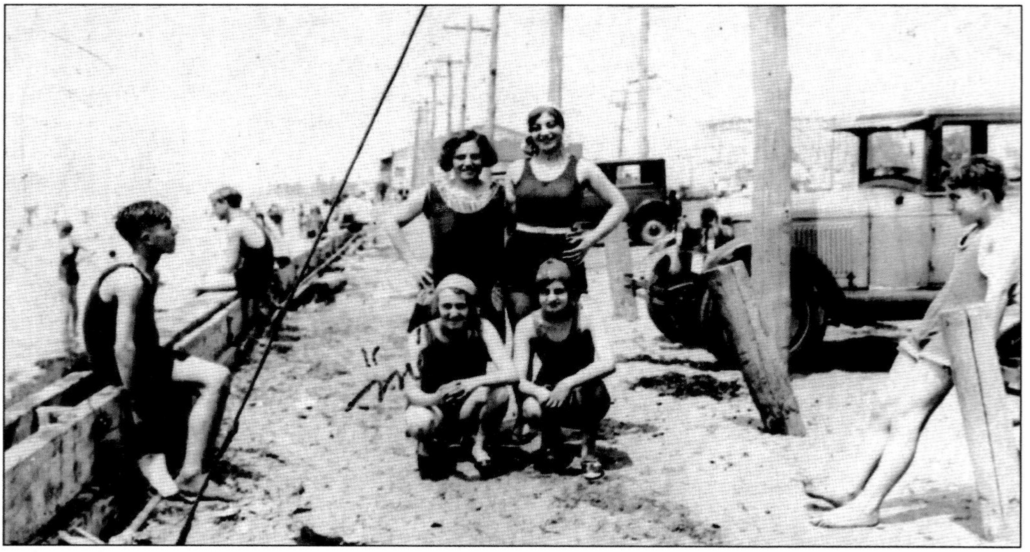

What a day at Oakland Beach, this was one of the best known and attended amusement parks in Rhode Island. A group of Federal Hill-ites enjoys the day, July 10, 1929. Oakland Beach was destroyed in the Great Hurricane of 1938 and never recovered. Photo courtesy of Antonette Marinio.

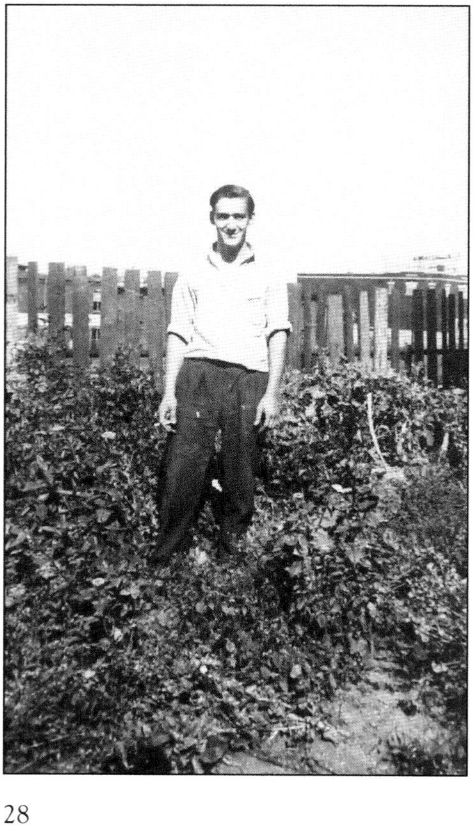

The young man of the neighborhood shown here later became the owner of a well-known market. Rudolph Micheli stands in an overgrowth on Federal Hill. He was later to go to the war. Photo courtesy of Isabel Micheli.

Successful as a businessman, Rudy Micheli decided to run for public office. Here he stands before a sign asking constituents to "Let's rock." Photo courtesy of Isabelle Micheli.

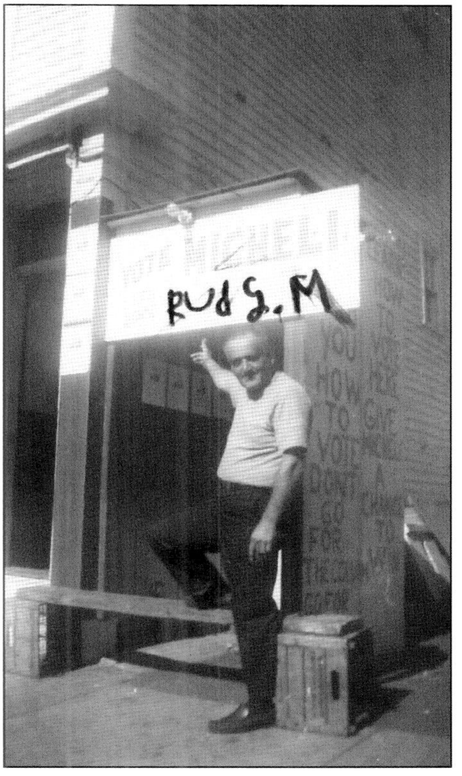

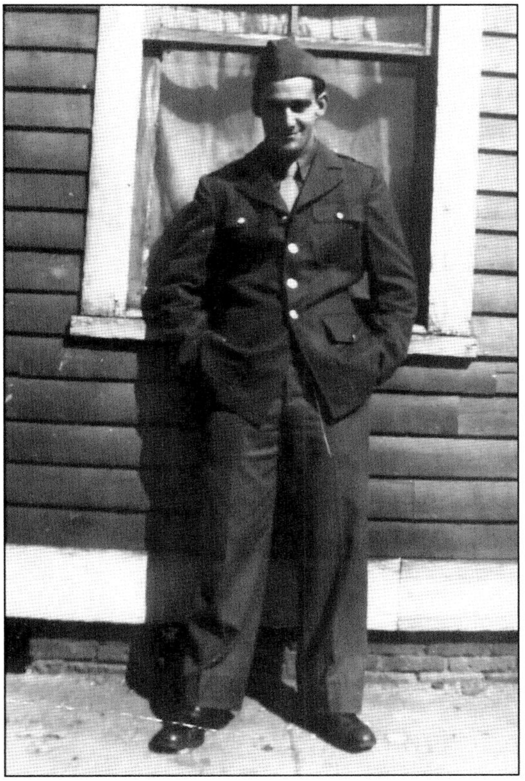

In uniform, with his customary smile, Rudy Micheli is a soldier during the Second World War. He epitomizes the Federal Hill youth who went off to war, were lucky enough to return, and who did something with their lives. Photo courtesy of Isabelle Micheli.

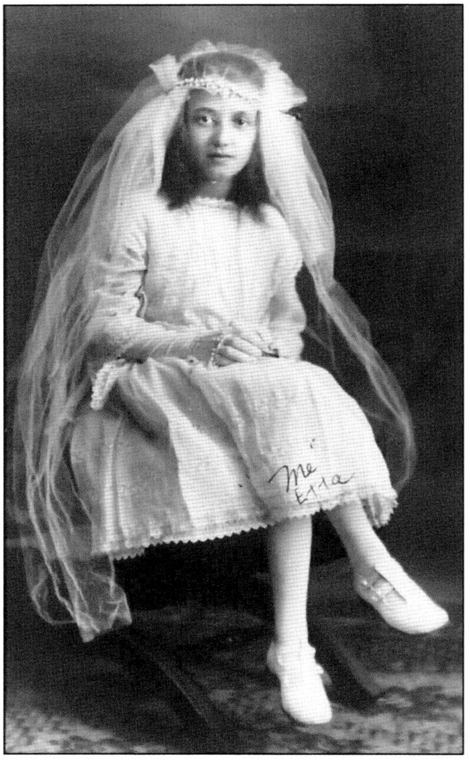

This is the first Communion of eight-year-old Antonette Marino, who was called Etta. Her life had begun on the Hill, and her family had prospered on the Hill. Photo courtesy of Antonette Marino.

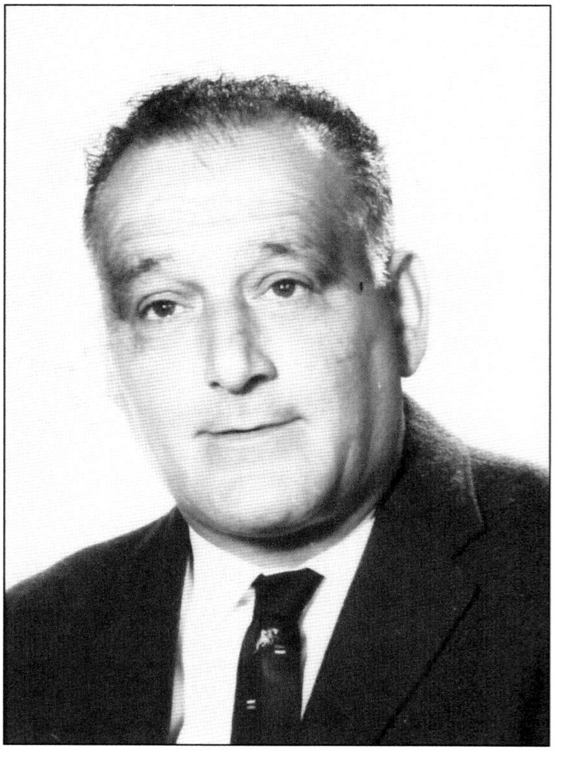

Rudy Micheli, still sporting that wry, quizzical smile, was a man who had experienced much, whose life was simple and yet grand. Though he is gone, Rudy and his market that fed so many, often gratis, are remembered on the Hill. Photo courtesy of Isabel Micheli.

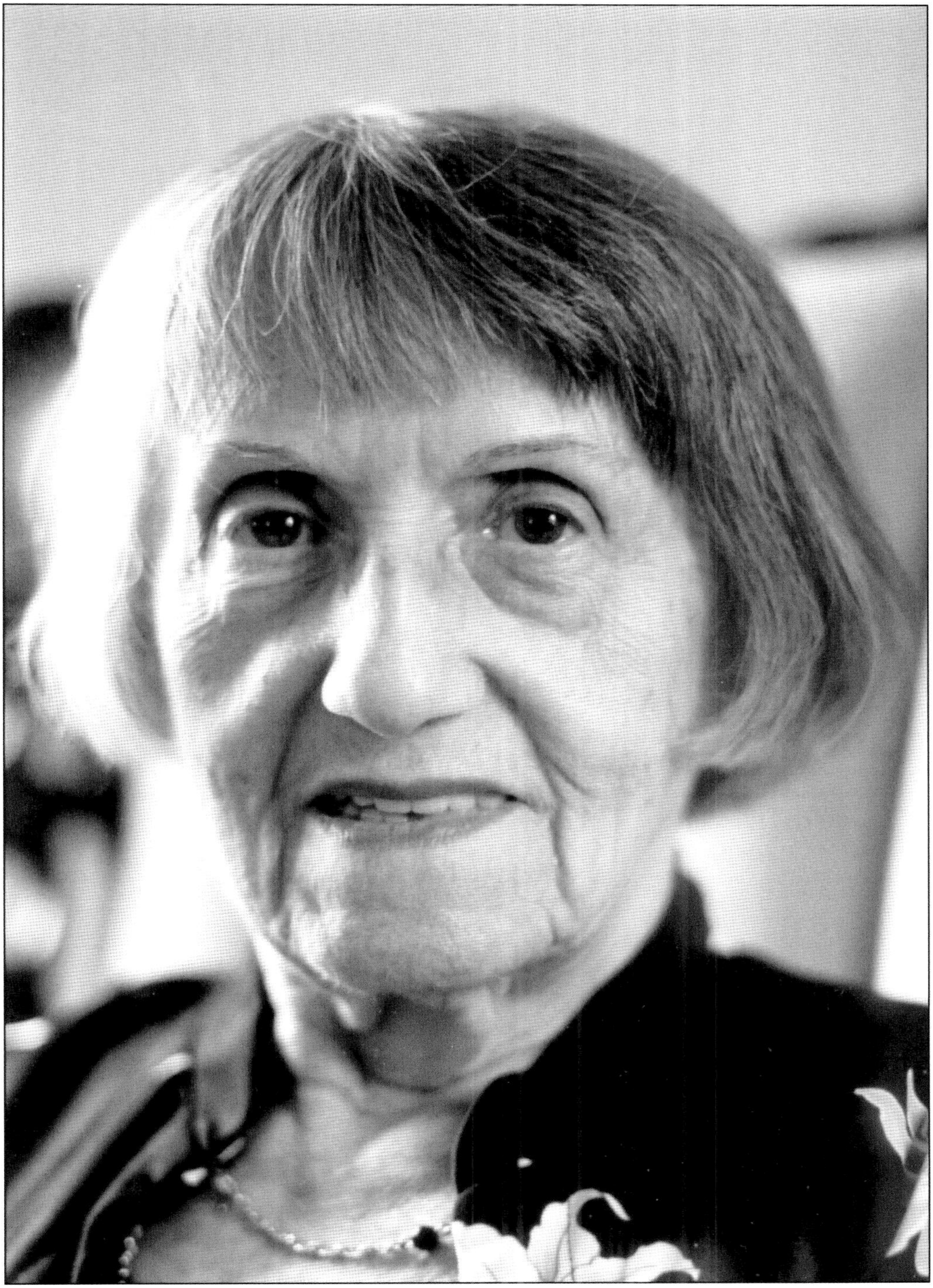
And here is Antonette today. She is a survivor with rich memories. Antonette is in some ways the definition of Federal Hill, for she has experienced many of the changes in the town. Her roots are there, and her family is forever there. Photo by Devika Daulat-Singh.

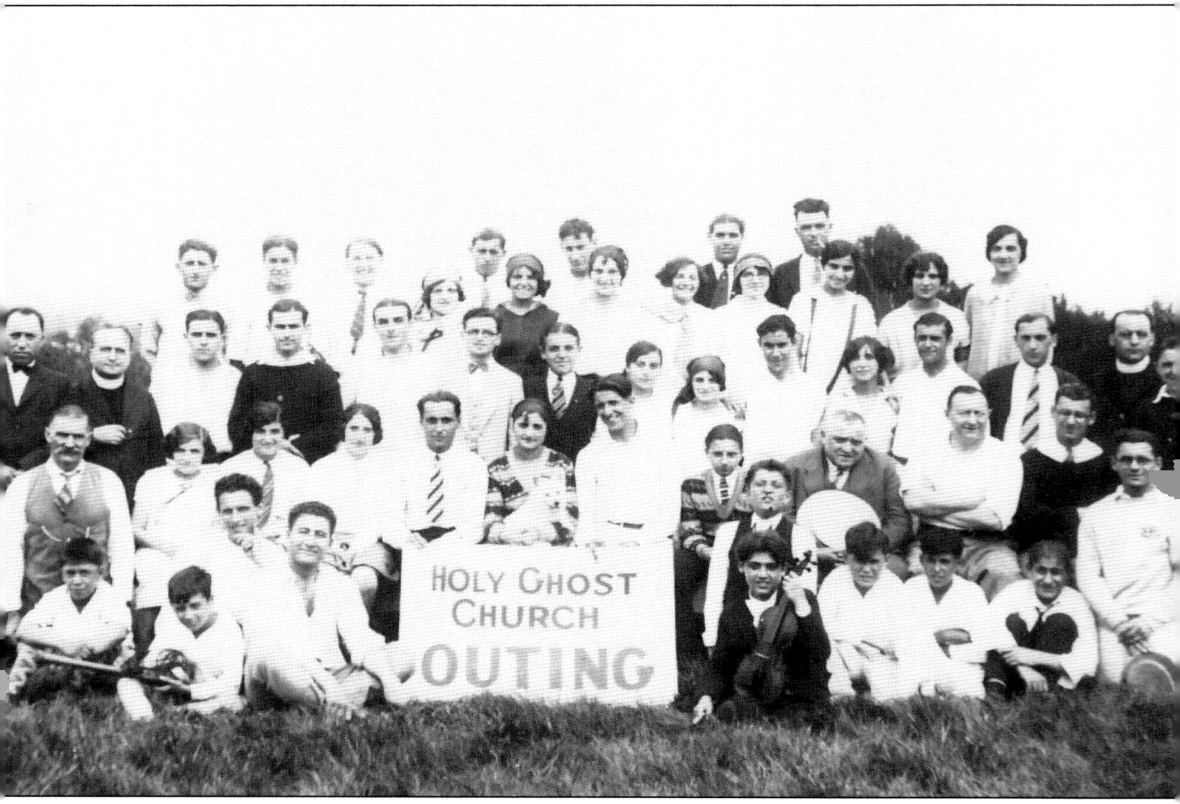

This early 1930s photograph of an outing of families from the Holy Ghost Church truly does justice to the meaning of community and family. Outings like this were very popular. They have largely vanished as a result of the separation and scattering of families to the suburbs.

Three

Churches: Then and Now

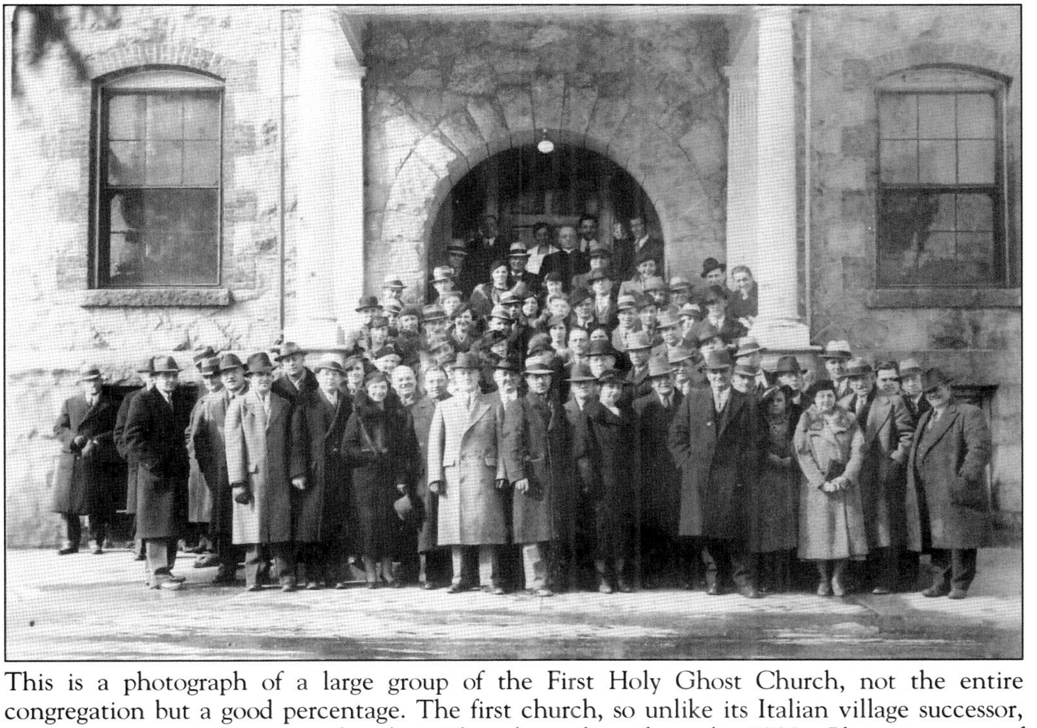

This is a photograph of a large group of the First Holy Ghost Church, not the entire congregation but a good percentage. The first church, so unlike its Italian village successor, was a monument of stone and arches. This photo dates from the 1920s. Photo courtesy of Michael Berarducci.

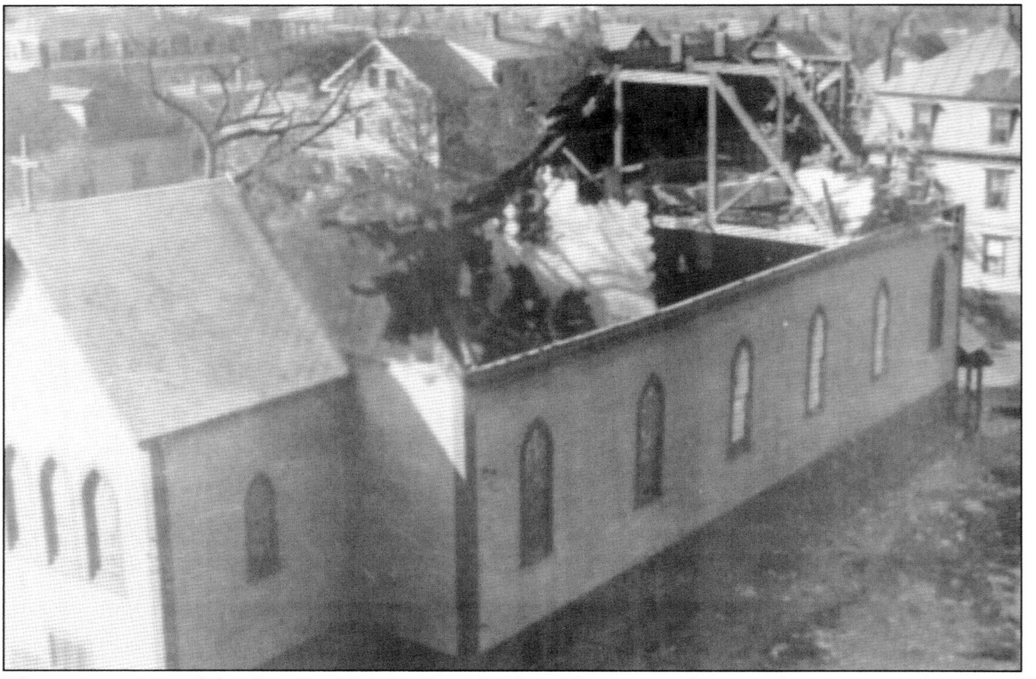

This is a picture of the first St. Mary's Church after a hurricane destroyed it in September 1938. This edifice stood just behind the magnificent stone structure (the present church), now restored. St. Mary's was the church for the Irish immigrants to the Hill. They literally built it stone by stone, purchasing each block of stone separately. Photo courtesy of St. Mary's Church.

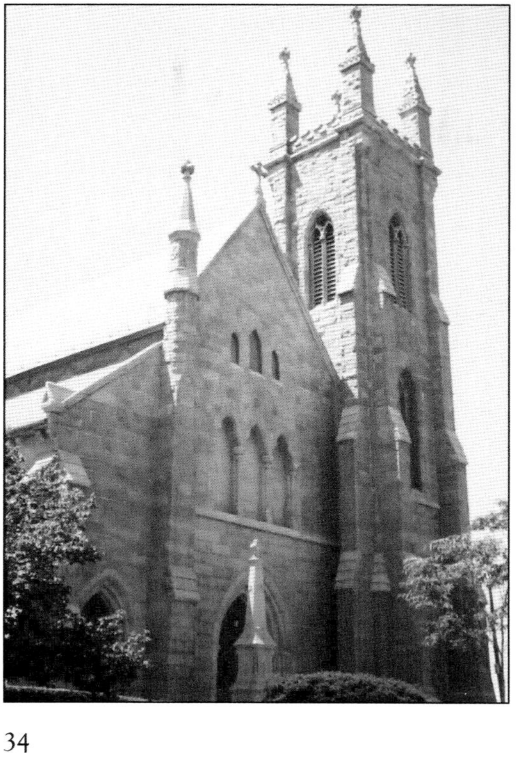

St. Mary's appears here as it looks today. This contemporary photo illustrates the picturesque qualities of this superb Gothic church on the famed Broadway Boulevard.

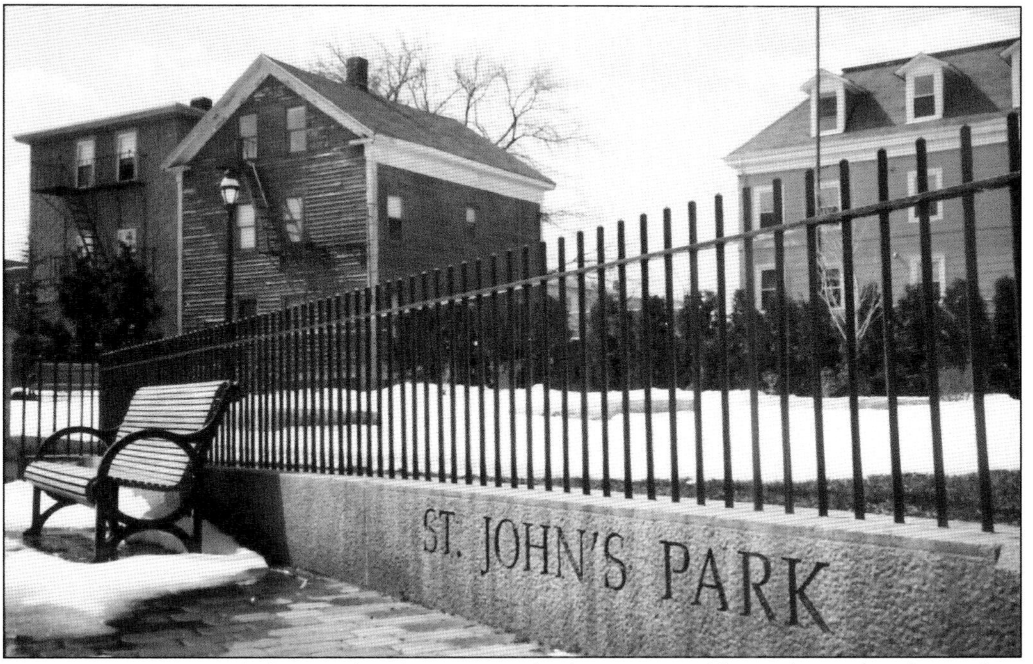

These are two views of where a church once stood. The century-old St. John's Church stood on this spot until razed a few years ago, much to the dismay of its parishioners. Today it is a park, a small oasis on Federal Hill.

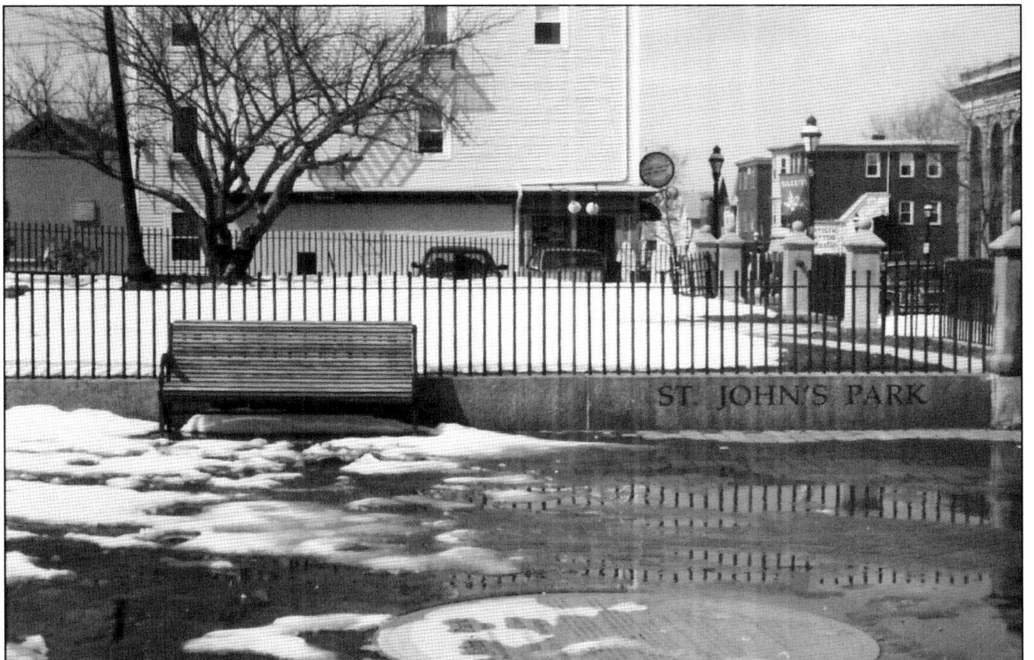

The large stone posts, the granite wainscotting, and the stairs are all that are left of St. John's Church, incorporated into the park.

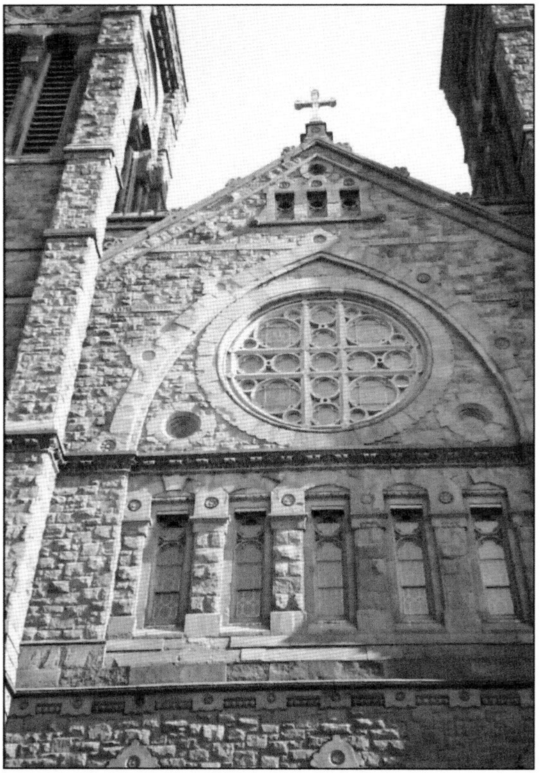

This rose window at the Cathedral of St. Peter and Paul rivals the marvels of any European churches. An edifice of stone and glass, the great rose window is one of the architectural wonders of the city.

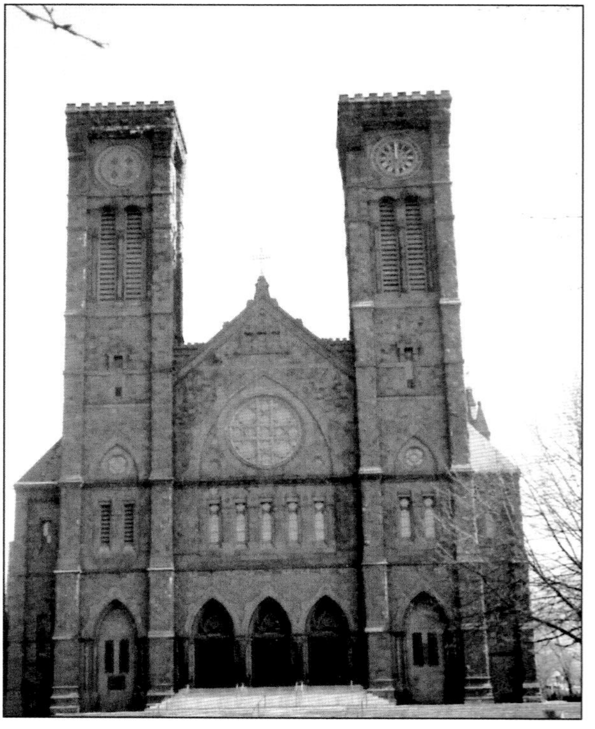

The Cathedral of St. Peter and Paul is the seat of the bishop of Rhode Island. This magnificent church, recently restored, was the "big" church, one that served for years the Irish immigrants to the Hill. Later, the area and parish were to be populated by Italian immigrants as well.

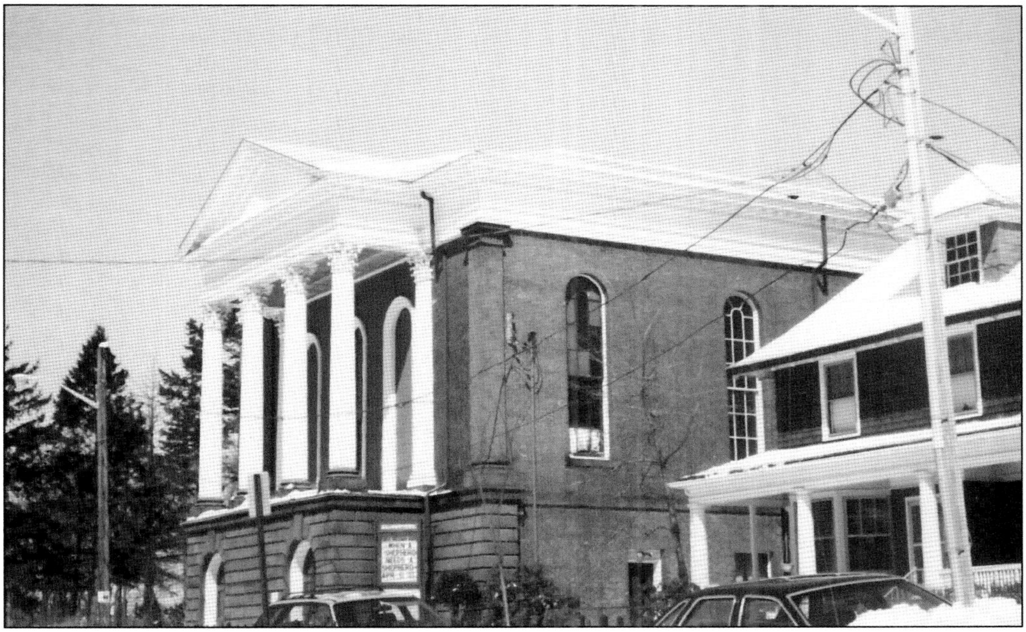

The Bell Street Chapel is a Unitarian church off Broadway (St. Mary's Roman Catholic Church is diagonal to it). This restored Greek Revival church is home to many activities and serves as a meeting hall, art gallery, etc. Unitarianism has grown on the Hill.

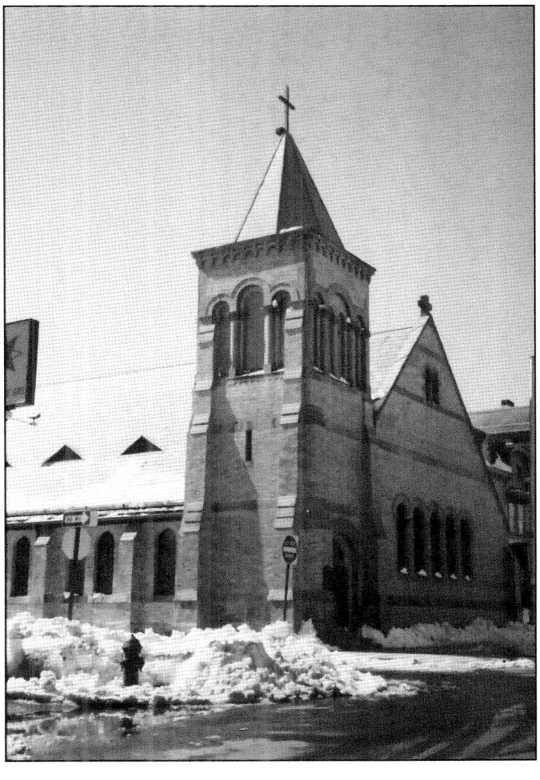

The Armenian Apostolic Church on Broadway's interior is stunning in its style of Armenian decoration, possessing a vibrant richness. All religions are now represented on the Hill.

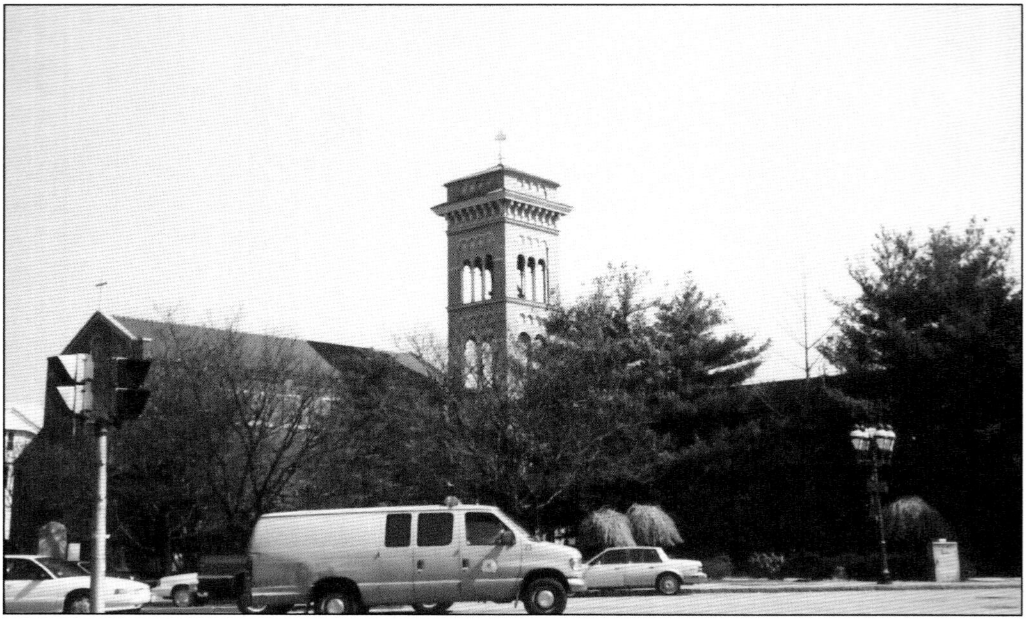

This is a view of the graceful, exquisite bell tower of Our Lady of Mt. Carmel Church off Atwells Avenue on the Hill. An active church, it now offers masses in Spanish, in accord with the great Hispanic settlement on the Hill.

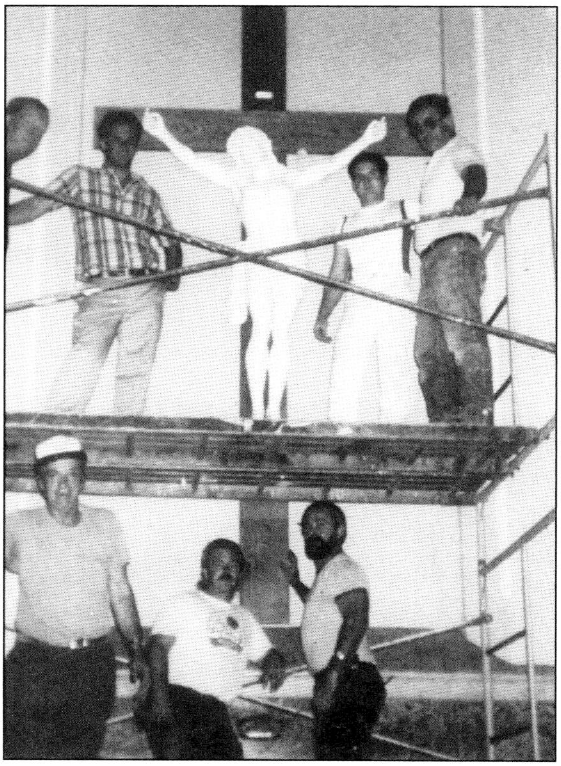

This is the restoration of a landmark. The Holy Ghost Church, over a century old, is the cornerstone of Federal Hill, actually situated where the rise of Atwells Avenue begins at its western end. This photograph shows several men restoring the great crucifix in 1989. Photo courtesy of Holy Ghost Church.

The front door of the beautiful church is removed, and the portal surrounding the doors is of mosaic, stone, and sculptured plaster. Photo courtesy of the Holy Ghost Church.

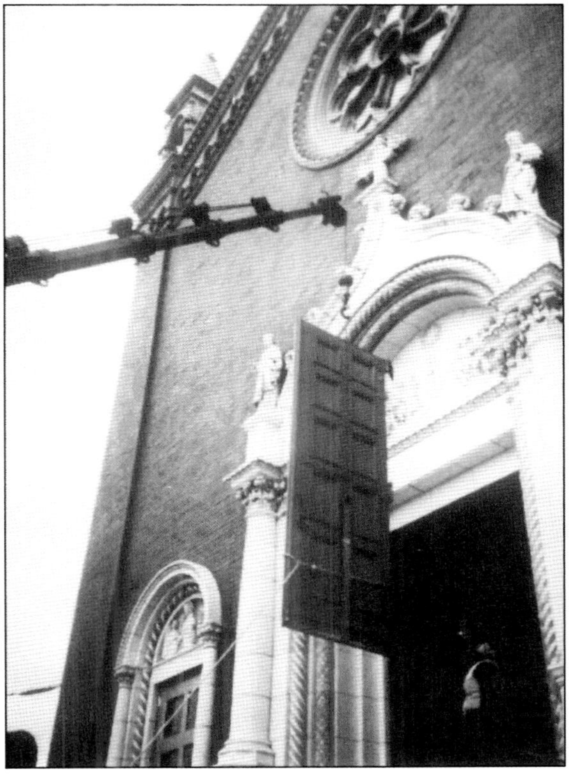

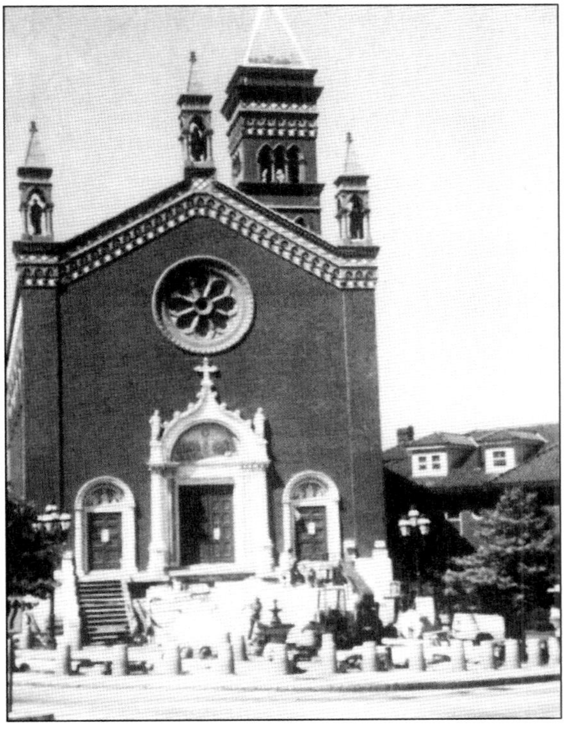

The church is under renovation in this picture. The interior as well was restored, including the murals, frescoes, and vaulting. Photo courtesy of the Holy Ghost Church.

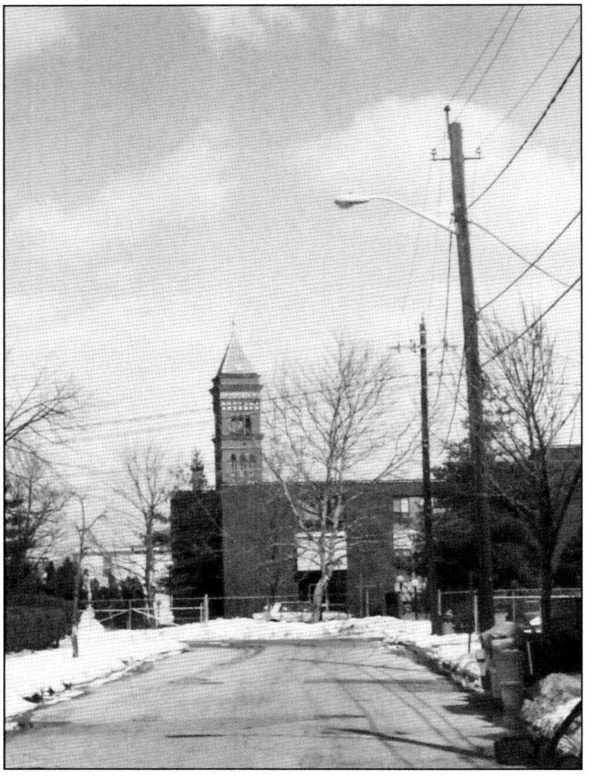

This is a view of the lofty bell tower of the Holy Ghost Church. Notice how the church itself is now obscured from this vantage point by housing for the elderly, hundreds of whom attend the church.

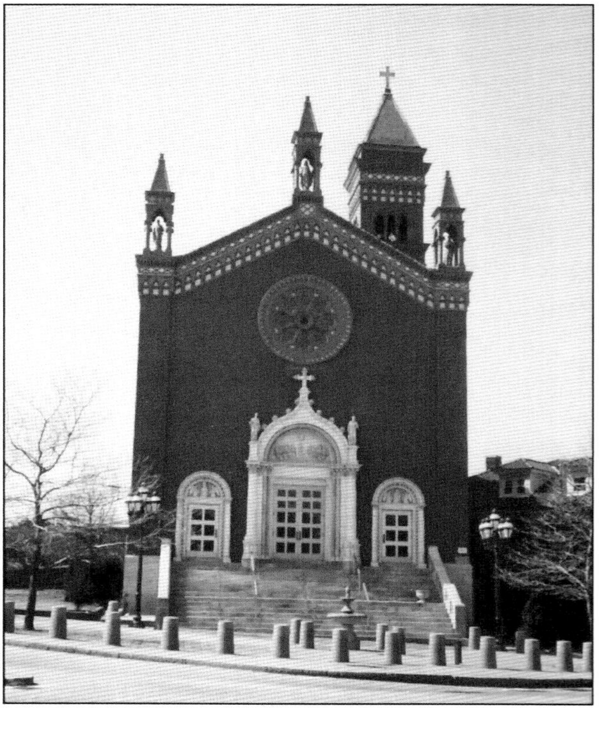

The church is shown here today. Looking absolutely pristine, the present Holy Ghost Church has been reborn to insure another one hundred years of service to the Hill.

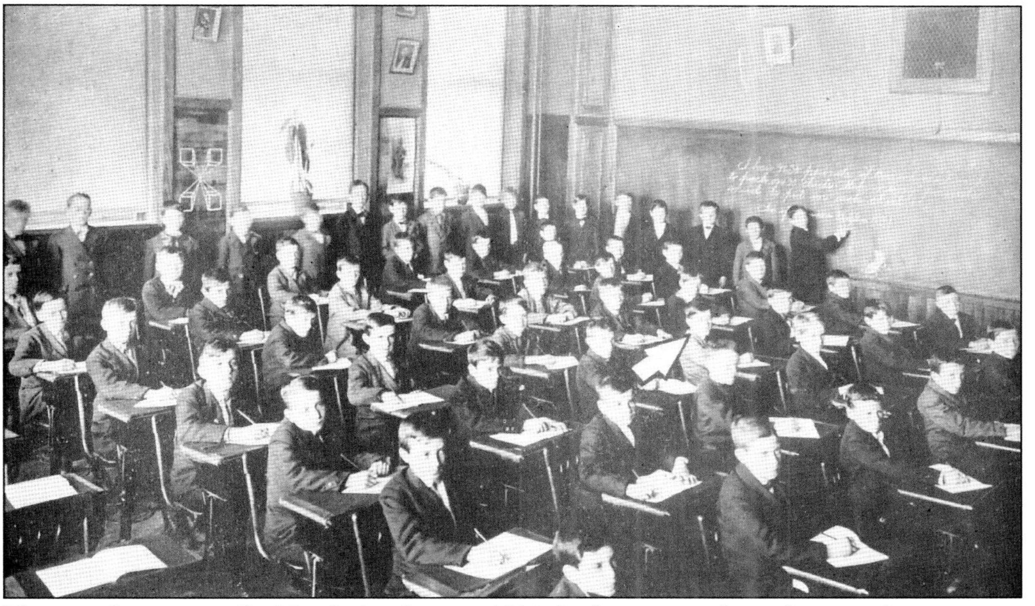

This is a classroom in St. Mary's Academy in 1914. In this very uniform class sit a future mayor, physician, and priest. The faint white arrow (appearing on the blackboard) points to the future mayor of Providence, the late Walter Reynolds. In front of him is the future Rev. Edmund Fitzgerald, and at his left is Edward T. Streker, who became a physician. Photo courtesy of St. Mary's Church.

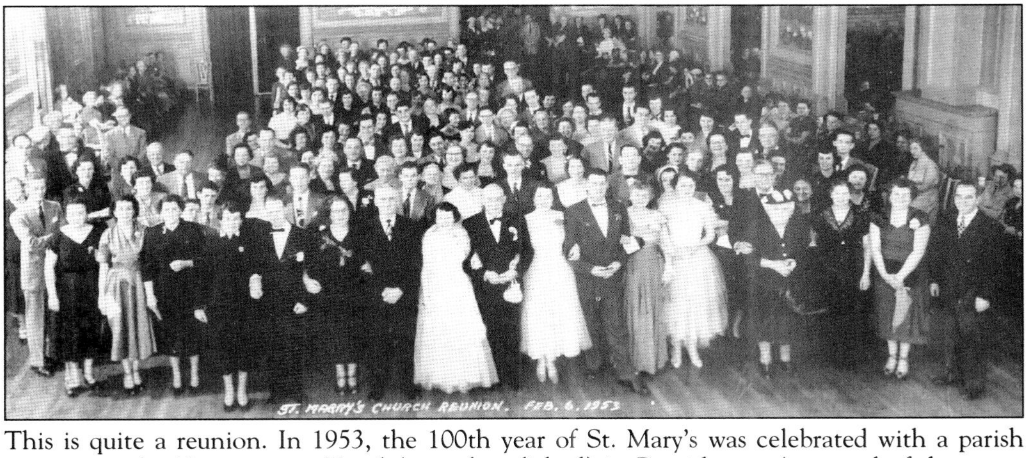

This is quite a reunion. In 1953, the 100th year of St. Mary's was celebrated with a parish reunion in the Narragansett Hotel (now demolished) in Providence. A perusal of the many names illustrates that by this time some Italian Americans were attending what had always been known as the "Irish Church." Photo courtesy of St. Mary's Church.

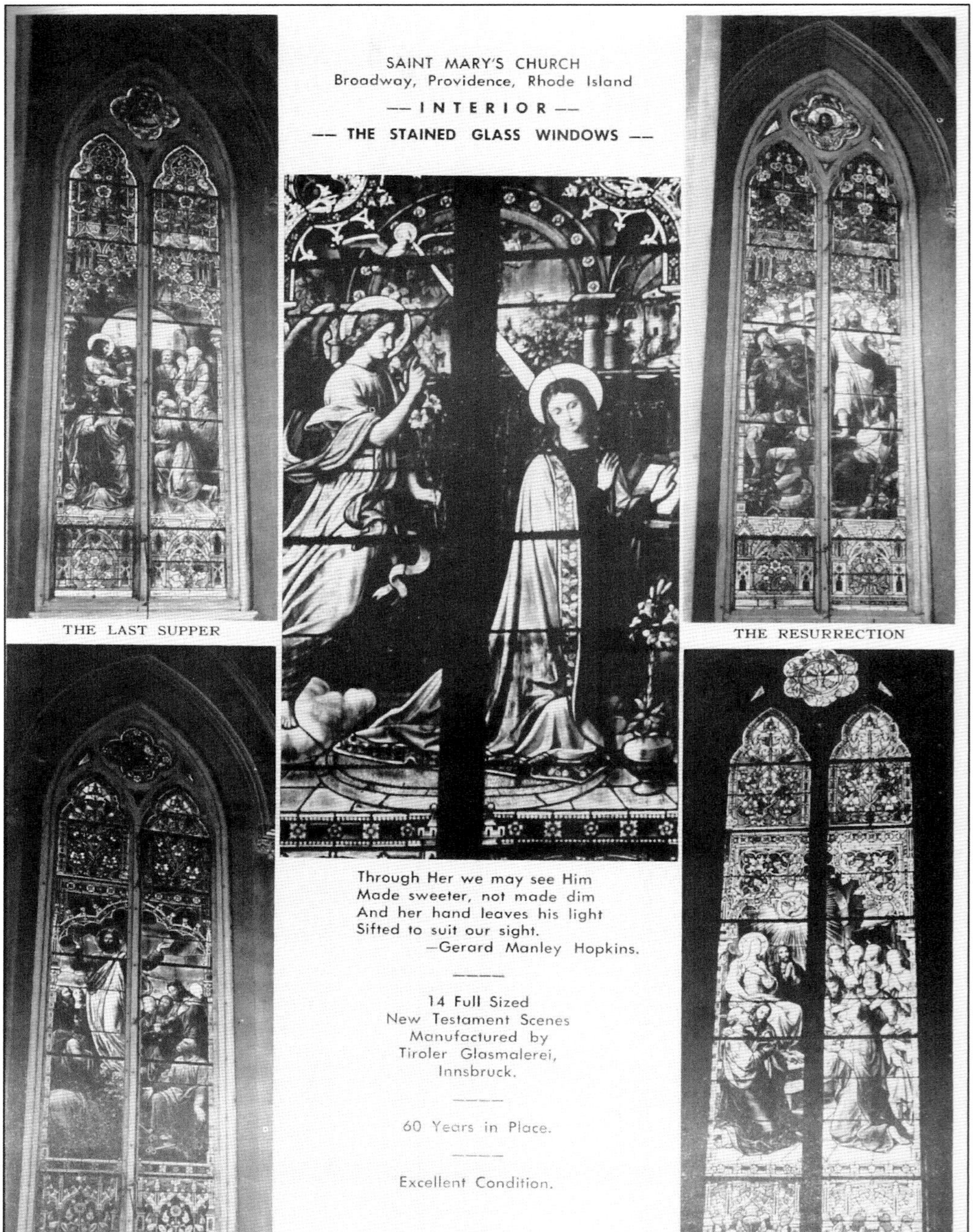

These windows are an example of the art treasures of Broadway. This elegant, wide boulevard, where St. Mary's Church sits, can boast of these magnificent stained-glass windows, a treasure that will last well into the twenty-first century as an example of artistic genius. Photo courtesy of St. Mary's Church.

Four

Blight and Renewal

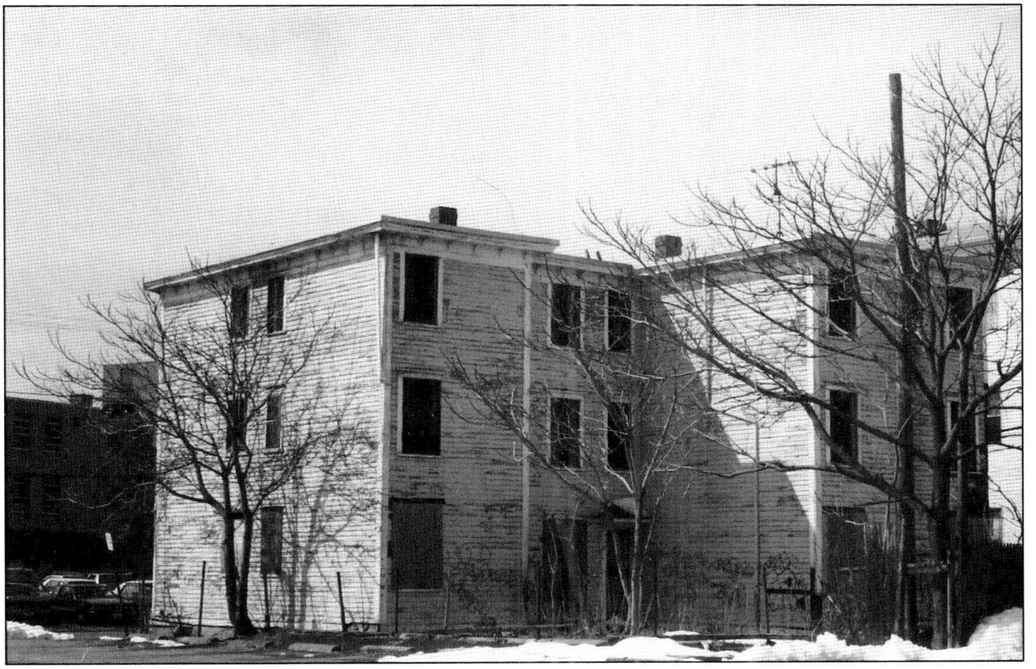

Deterioration appears here on Federal Hill. Controversy surrounds the reasons for this, but an abandoned house, once a crack house, illustrates how far the blight had gone on the Hill.

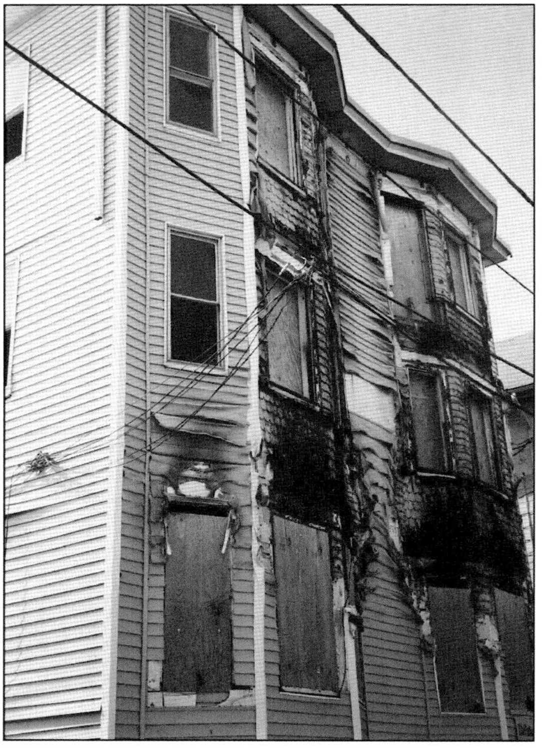

Fire has taken much of the derelict houses of the Hill. This one was lost entirely.

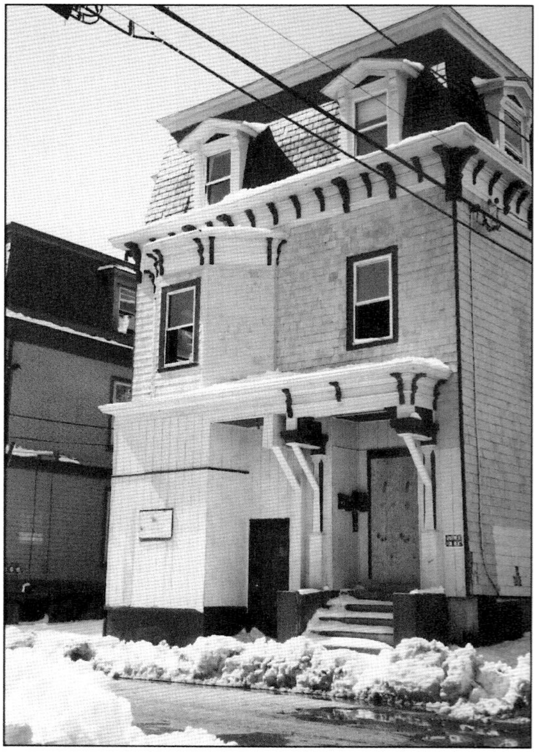

Boarded-up buildings, once storefronts and men's clubs, are products of abandonment and of absentee landlords.

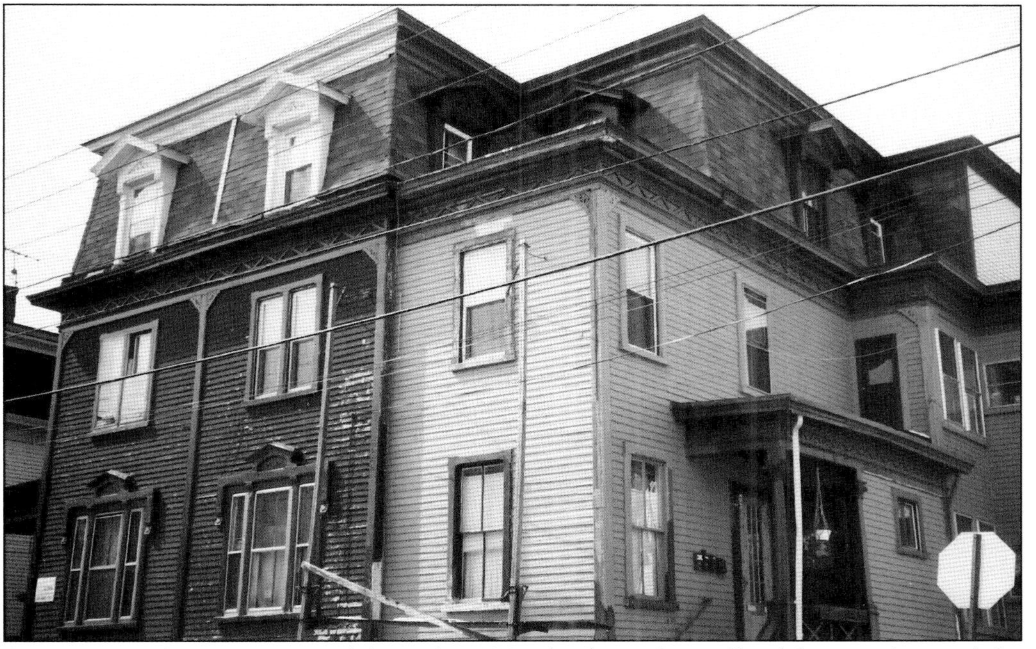

A once magnificent mansion of the early 1900s, this house has suffered from neglect and the elements. But there is hope, for it is slowly, carefully being saved.

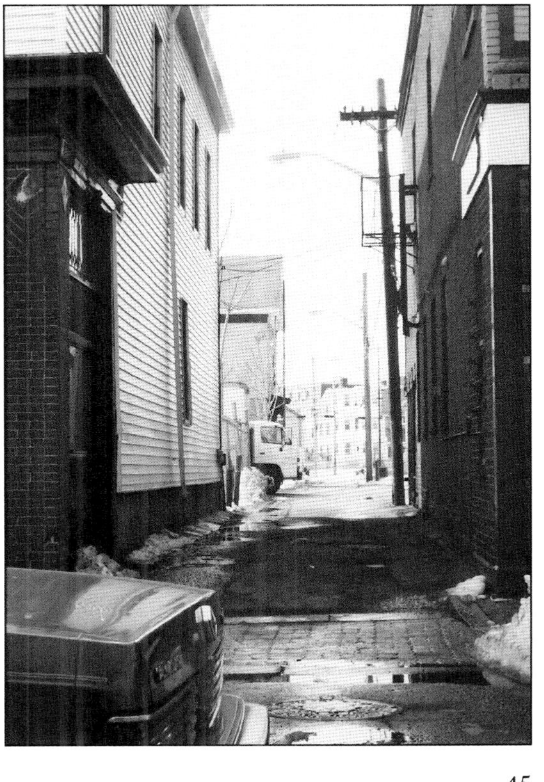

An alley on the Hill is not so much a sign of deterioration, but of congestion indicative of areas still to be reclaimed.

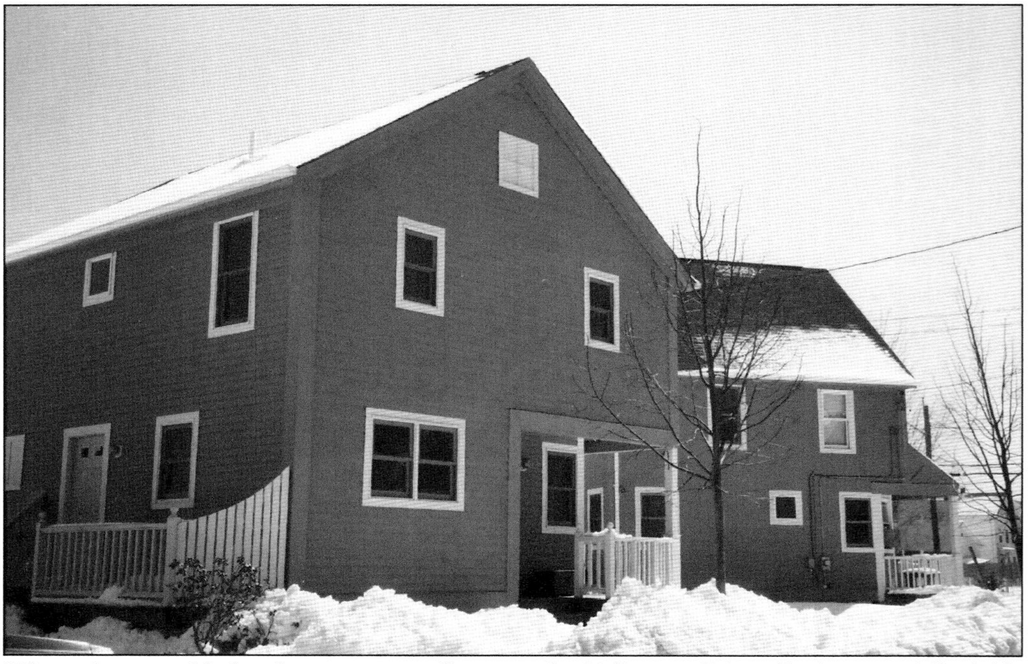

Where there was blight, there are new villages on the Hill, just off Atwells Avenue. Affordable individual houses stand where derelict crack houses and abandoned hulks once prevailed.

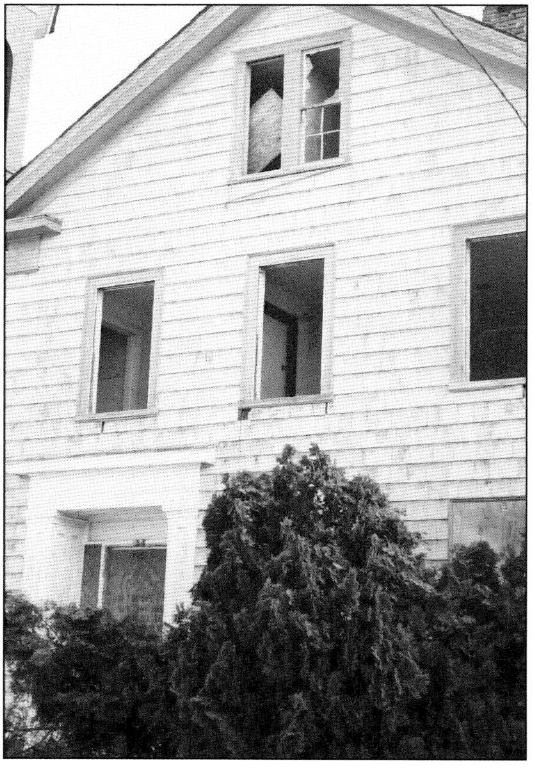

Empty, lost, uninhabitable, this building will either be razed, or restored.

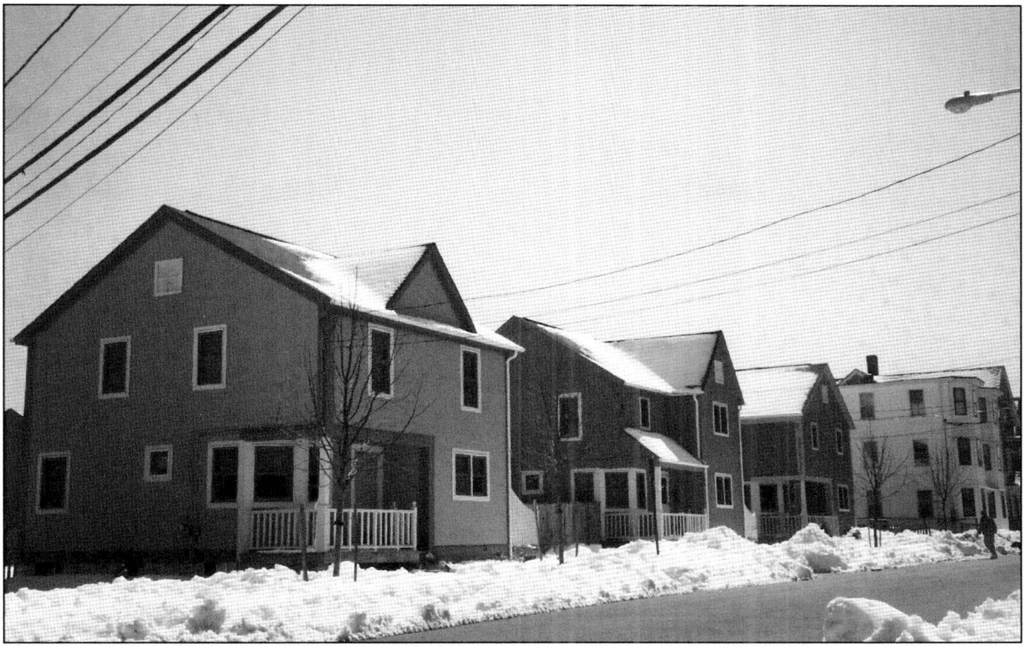

The old and the new are neighbors. These fresh looking, attractive houses edge up to old but solid and beautifully preserved tenements.

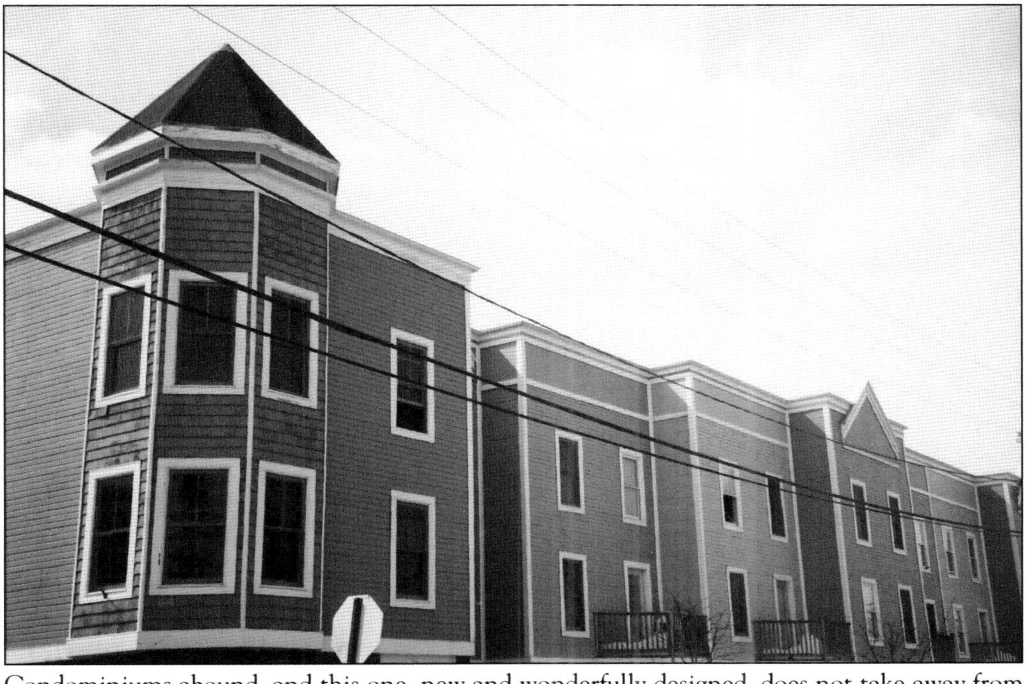

Condominiums abound, and this one, new and wonderfully designed, does not take away from the look of the Hill or from the architecture that once defined the Hill.

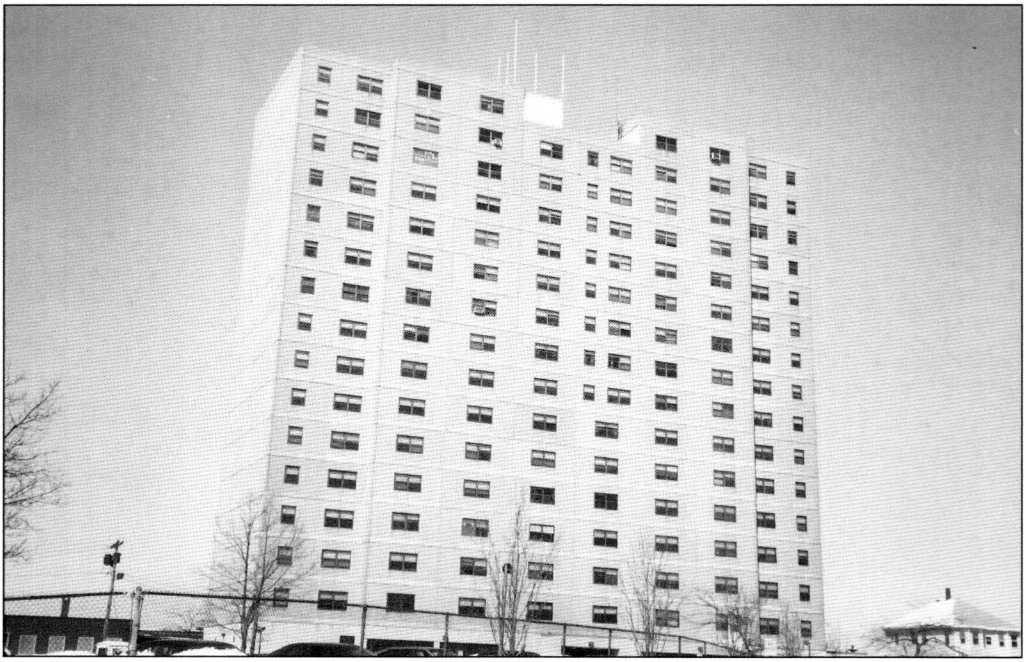

A high-rise apartment for the elderly and the disabled is located at one end of Atwells Avenue. This has not only brought in many new people to the Hill, but the proximity of stores, markets, parks, churches, etc. is a benefit for the residents.

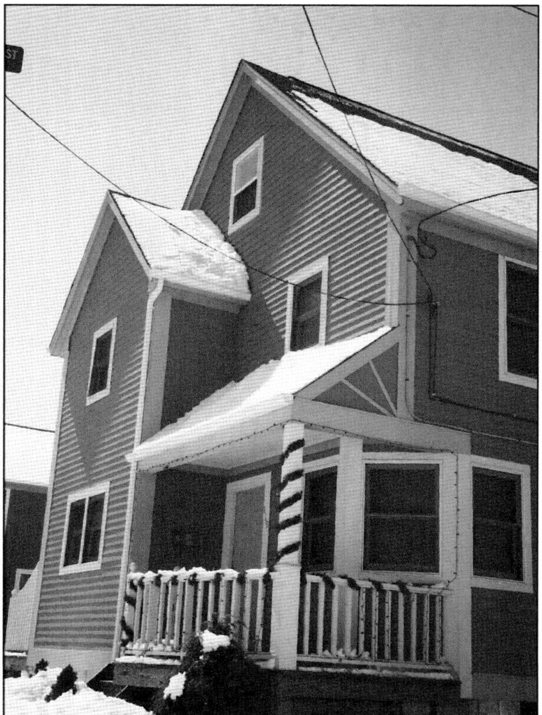

Decorated for Christmas, this single-family dwelling looks proud. This renewal, prodded by a courageous and dedicated Mayor Vincent A. Cianci Jr., stands as an example of what can be done to a disintegrating neighborhood as it moves into the twenty-first century.

Row Houses, reminiscent of apartment rows in Boston yet reflecting a contemporary design, were some of the first of the new dwellings built in the Hill area; these homes are located on Westminster Street.

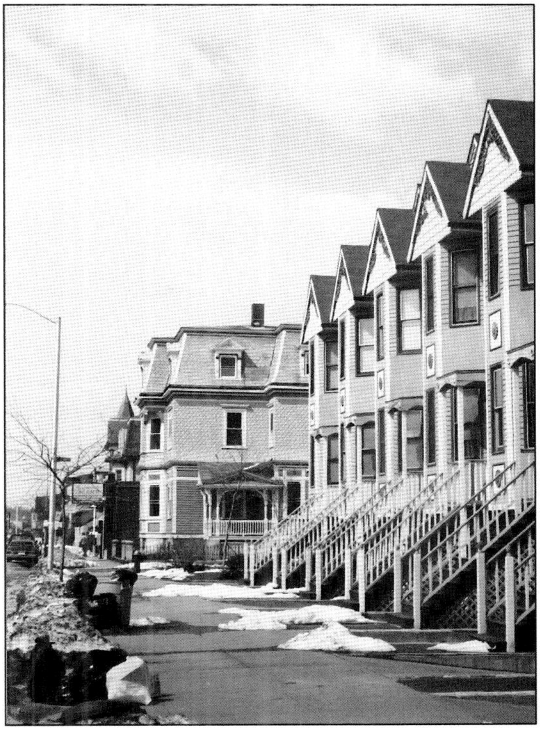

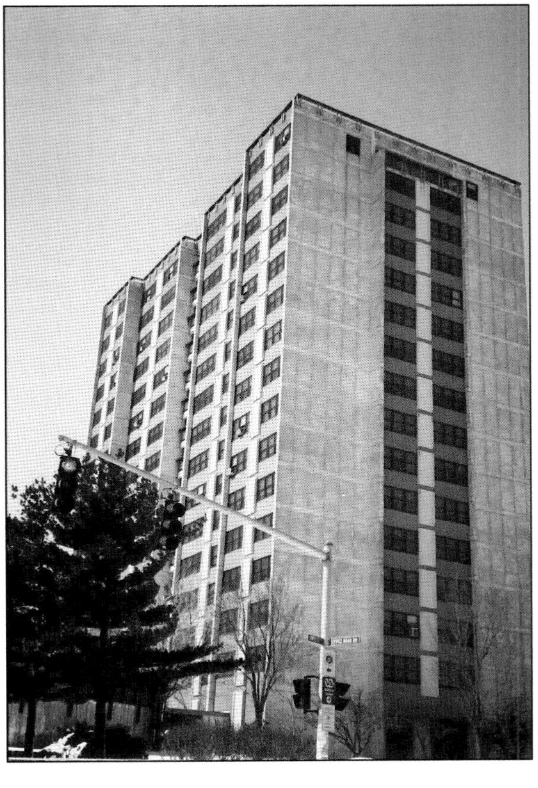

The Sister Domenica Manor is located at the other end of the Hill, beyond the arch, facing downtown Providence. It is within walking distance of the downcity area and the multitude of variety stores, restaurants, etc. on the Hill.

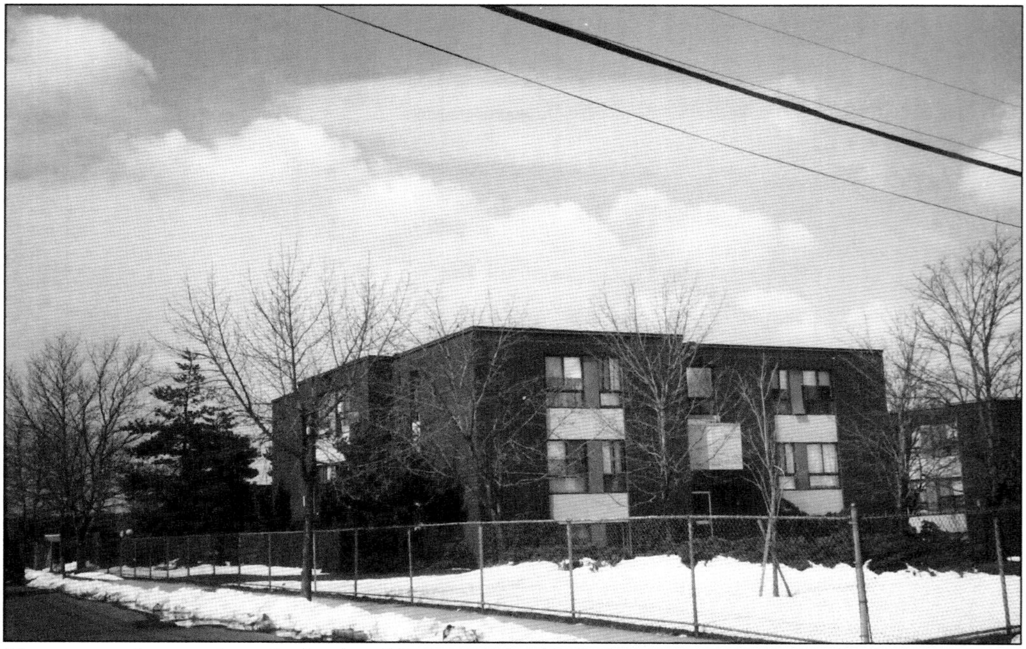

Housing in the condo style for the elderly and disabled, these attractive brick dwellings face the Holy Ghost Church. Once having sold their houses, many residents of the Hill, many of whom are widows and widowers, live here, still on the Hill, still Hill-ites.

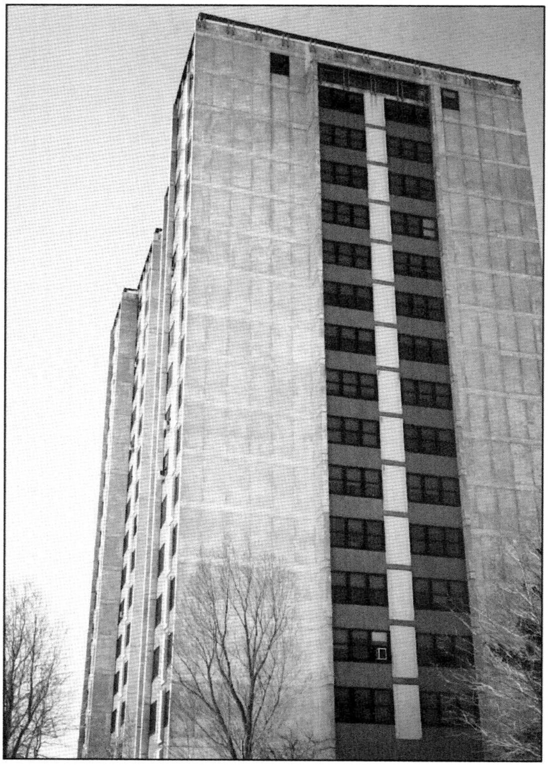

Looking like a New York high rise, this 15-story apartment house was an innovation on the Hill. Now it is a part of the ambience .

Five

Yesterday and Today

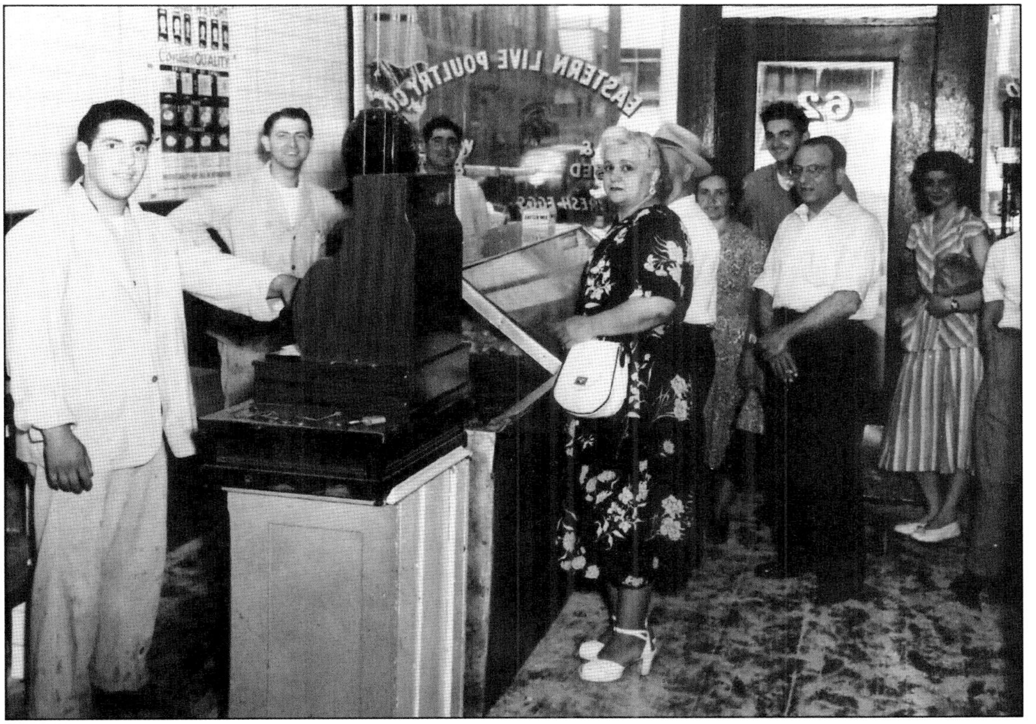

Eastern Live Poultry appears in this 1940s photograph. Here chickens, rabbits, etc. were killed and prepared in the freshest fashion for customers. Notice the old cash register; with these, you counted your own change. In those days nobody went to a supermarket for frozen fowl—it was unthinkable. Pictured are brothers Frank (left) and Mike Antonelli (right). This photograph dates from June 6, 1949. Photograph courtesy of Michael Antonelli.

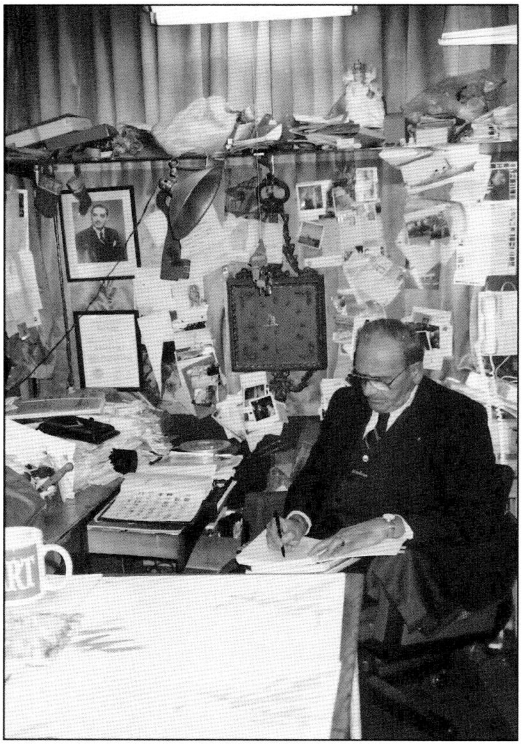

Vincent Simonelli sits where he has been sitting for decades, in the cluttered corner of the famed Simonelli's on Atwells Avenue. On the wall is beloved Governor/former Senator John O. Pastore and other icons definitive of a part of the Hill's ethos.

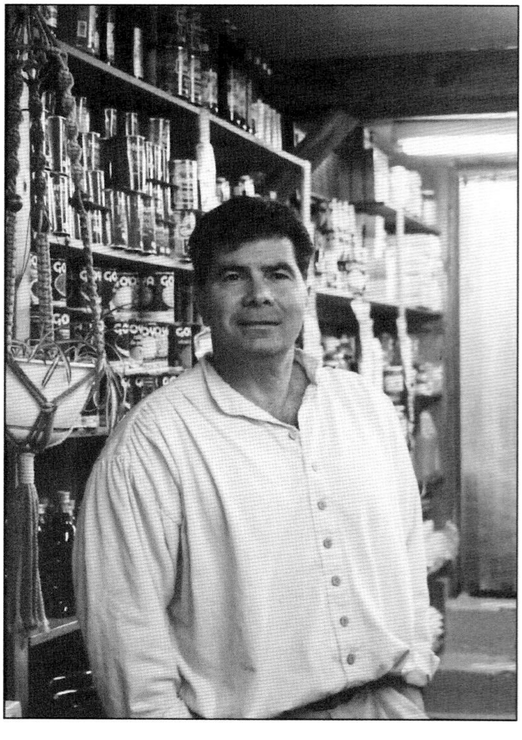

Eastern Poultry today does business under the name Antonelli's—the same fare and same way of preparing fresh fowl, rabbits, etc. Chris (Christy) Morris is the owner. Notice on the shelves the Goya products. Antonelli's now sells many items especially favored by the Hispanic community, reflecting the demographic change on the Hill.

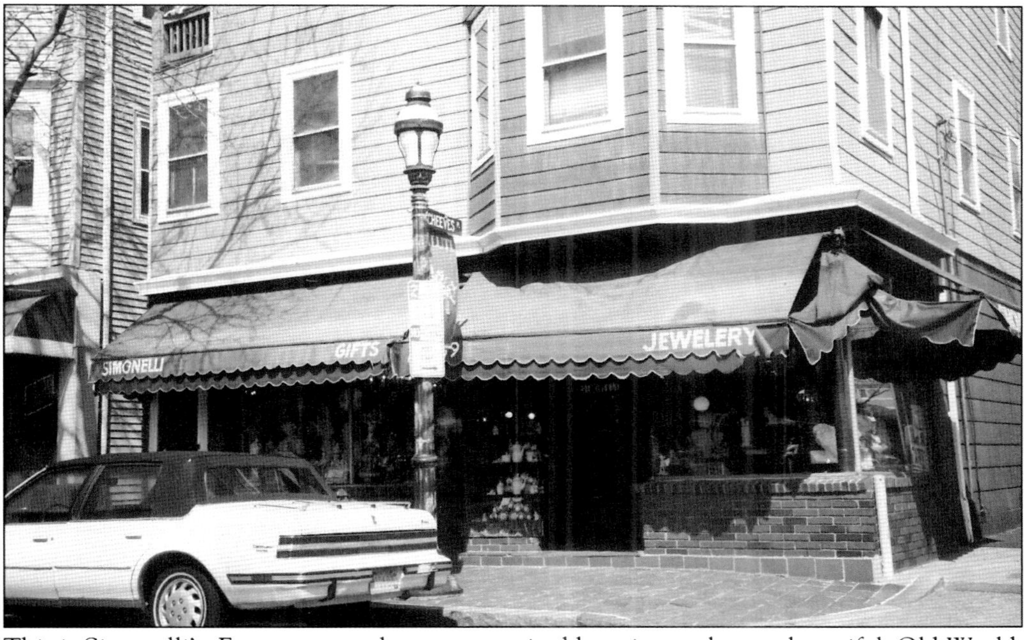

This is Simonelli's. For years, watches were repaired here in an elegant, beautiful, Old World, little room. Today, little has changed. The old awning still shades the outdoor display case. Within are statues of saints, reproductions of old masterworks—a Michelangelo here, a Rafael there—a David with a fig leaf (this is Rhode Island, after all), and the treasured Capo di Monte enamel sculptures from Italy. One cannot conceive Federal Hill without Simonelli's.

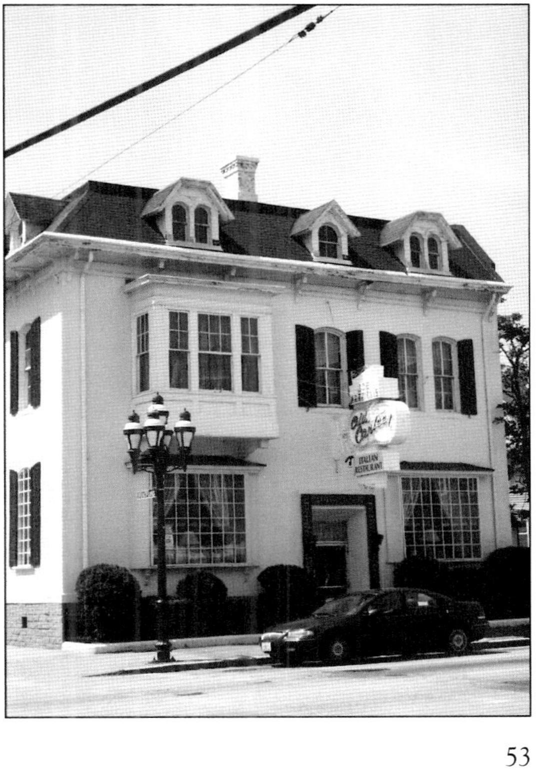

Yesterday it was Joe Marzilli's Old Canteen. Today it is Joe Marzilli's Old Canteen. Whoever has not heard of this world-famous restaurant has been living under the proverbial rock. Known for its exquisite food and wonderful warmth, the Old Canteen is where the simple and the mighty dine, from movie stars to the local neighbor. Located in what was once part of the John Nicholas Brown estate, it abuts another classic restaurant, Camille's Roman Garden.

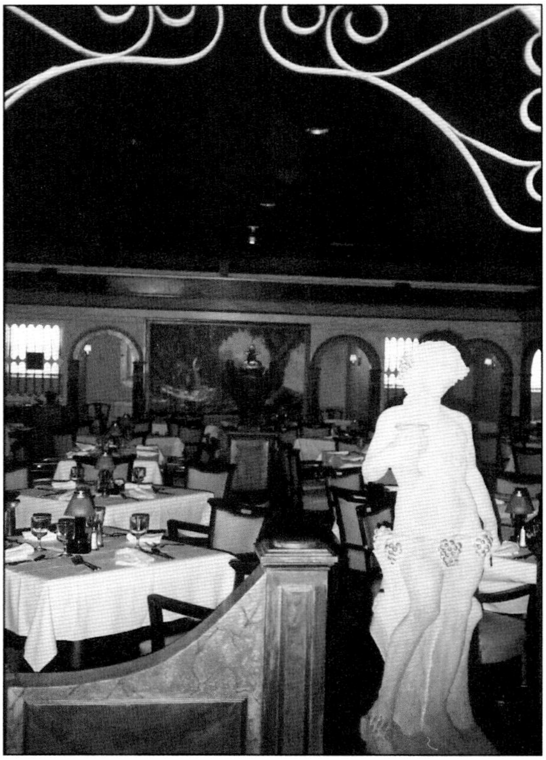

The elegant and opulent dining room of Camille's is shaped by Roman statuary, paintings, superb Roman arches, and stained-glass windows. The great vase in the center is an import from Italy.

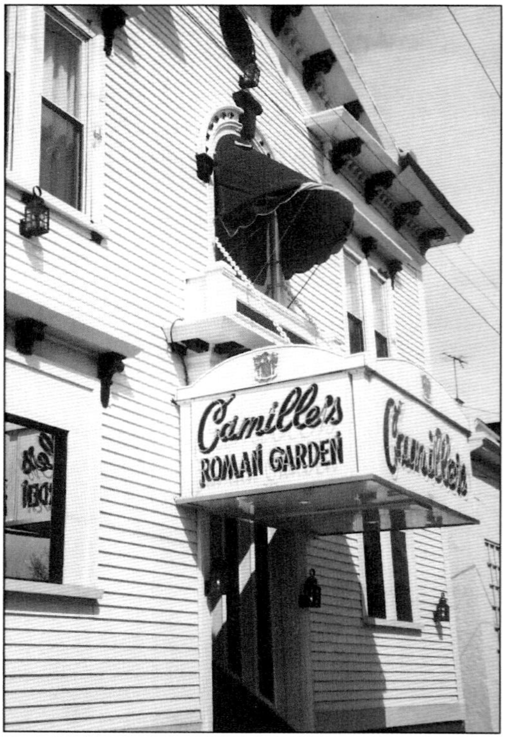

This is the entrance to Camille's Roman Garden. There is nothing quite like this extraordinary restaurant on the Hill. Created by John (Jack) Parolisi and named for his legendary wife Camille, it has served literally the famous and infamous of the planet. Everybody has been here, and they are still coming.

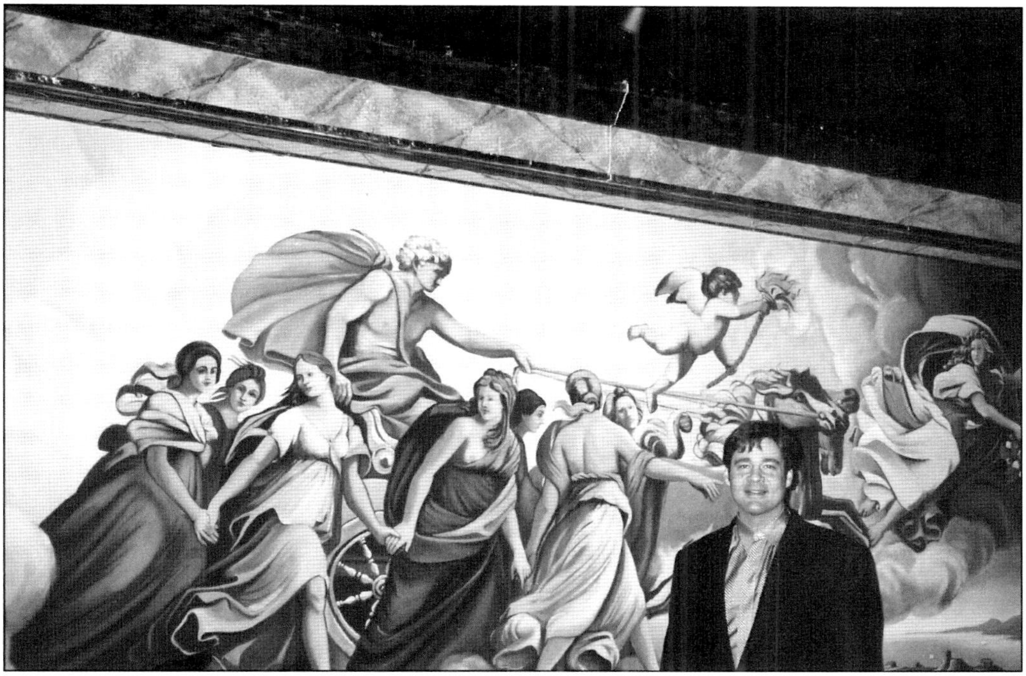

A recent restoration of Camille's, including this magnificent mural, has placed the famed restaurant, one of the jewels of the Hill, in the forefront of the march into the twenty-first century. Standing in front of the mural is current owner Gary Mantoosh, nephew of the founders of Camille's.

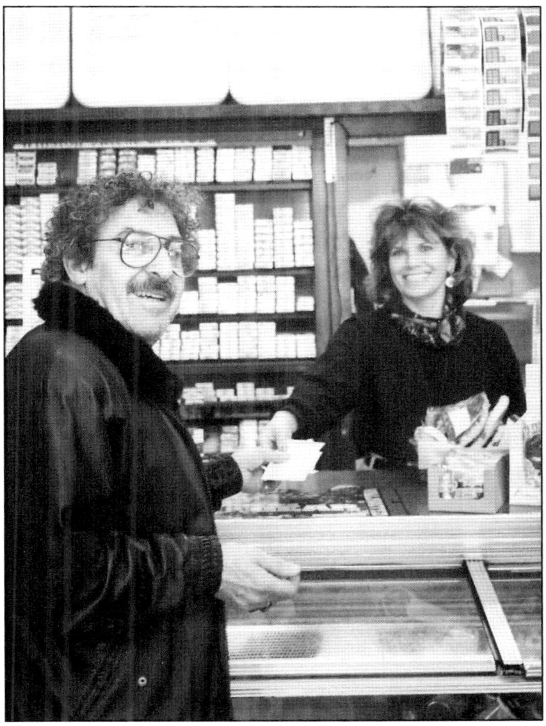

This is a look inside Braford Variety and Deli. This corner store, a sundry enterprise, has serviced the avenue for a very long time. It is a neighborhood staple. Denise Purro is behind the counter and is possibly, but only possibly, offering a winning lottery ticket to a customer.

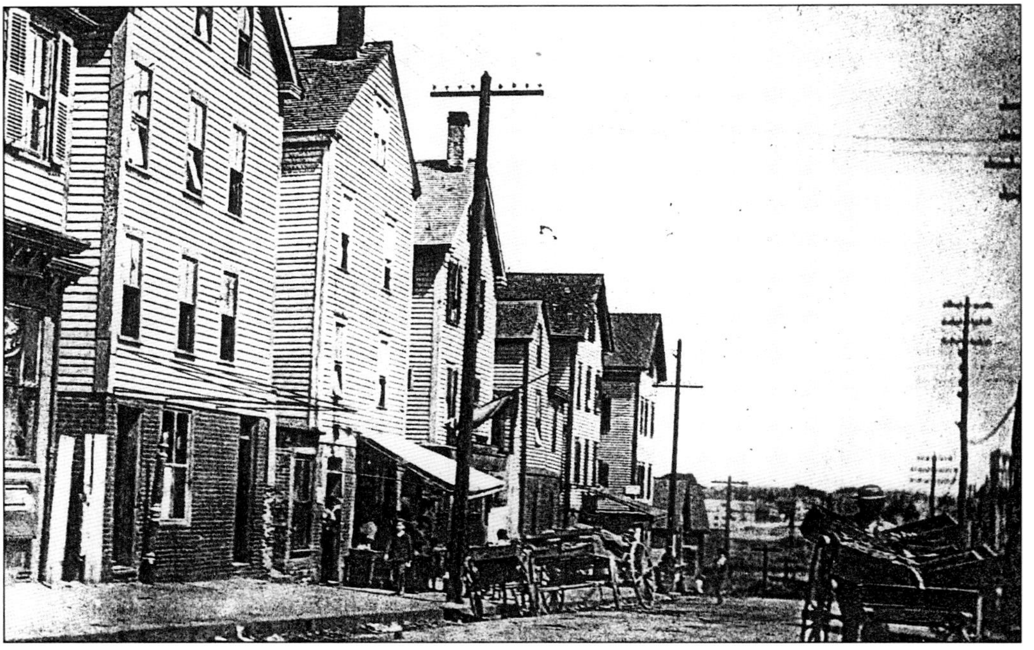

This is a historic photo of Acorn Street in 1903: a sloping street with pushcarts everywhere and creaky, yet amazingly solid buildings. Acorn Street is very different today, but the congestion of almost a century ago illustrates the way immigrants lived on the Hill.

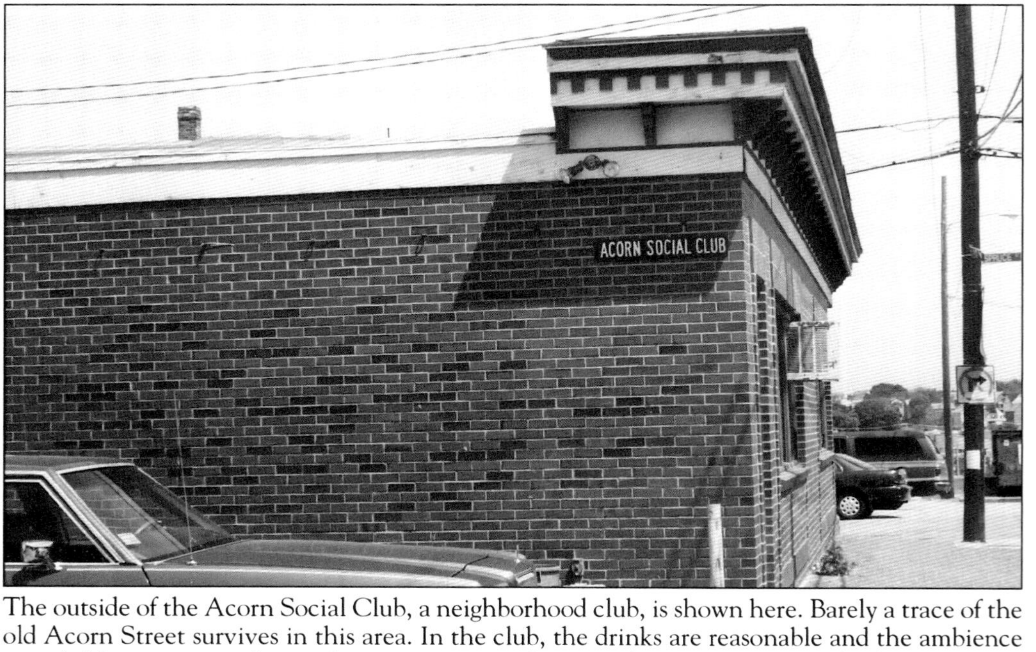

The outside of the Acorn Social Club, a neighborhood club, is shown here. Barely a trace of the old Acorn Street survives in this area. In the club, the drinks are reasonable and the ambience casual. Men come to play cards, young men to shoot pool, newcomers to ogle the treasure of old sports photographs that line the walls, and everybody to talk to owner Frank Marrapese, something of a Federal Hill legend himself, who was a famed soccer player. Photo courtesy of Frank Marrapese.

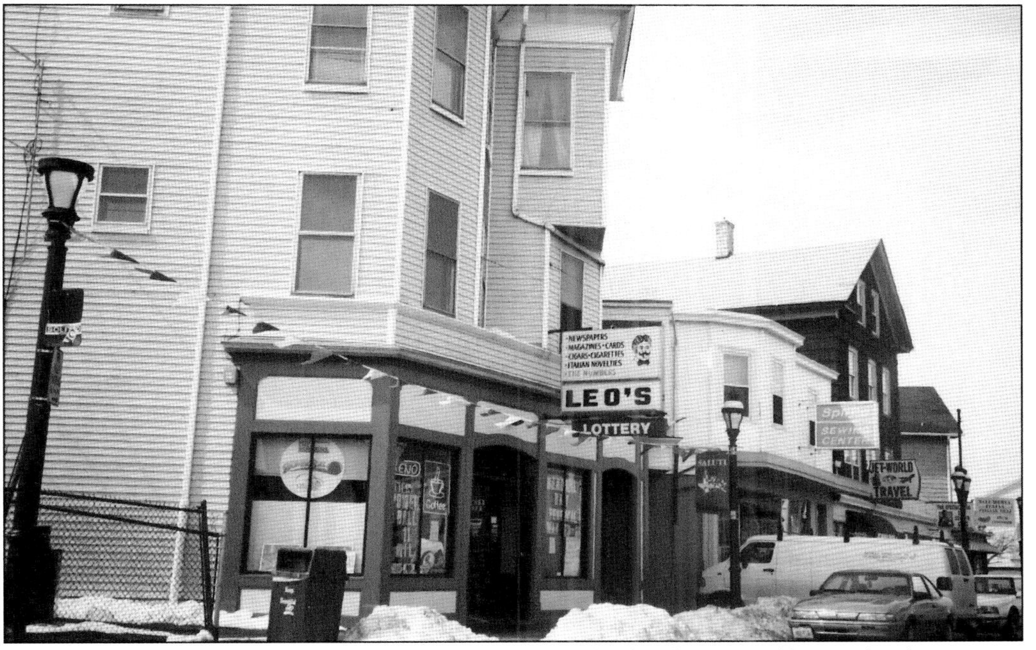

Leo's has been everywhere, even in a movie called *Federal Hill*, directed by Michael Corrente. You go into Leo's and you step back in time as you see photos of old sports figures, pencil renderings of Sinatra, pastels of John Wayne, and old family pictures decorating the big windows and the walls. Sit at a long table, have a cup of coffee, and buy a cigar or a magazine. Leo's is one of the "characters" of the Hill, truly authentic.

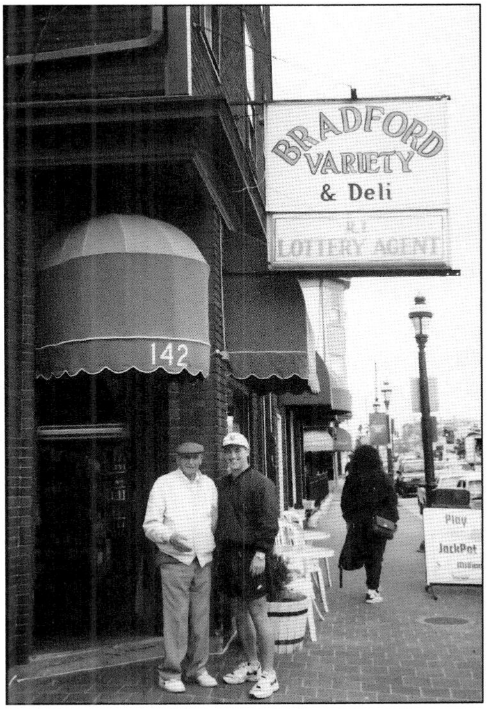

Talk about yesterday and today, outside Bradford Deli stands Joseph Rachieli, 90, with twenty-five-year-old Michael Purro, nephew of the owners of the deli store. Sixty-five years span these two Federal Hill citizens, yet both share the same feelings, the same sense of belonging to a way of life that is uniquely the Hill.

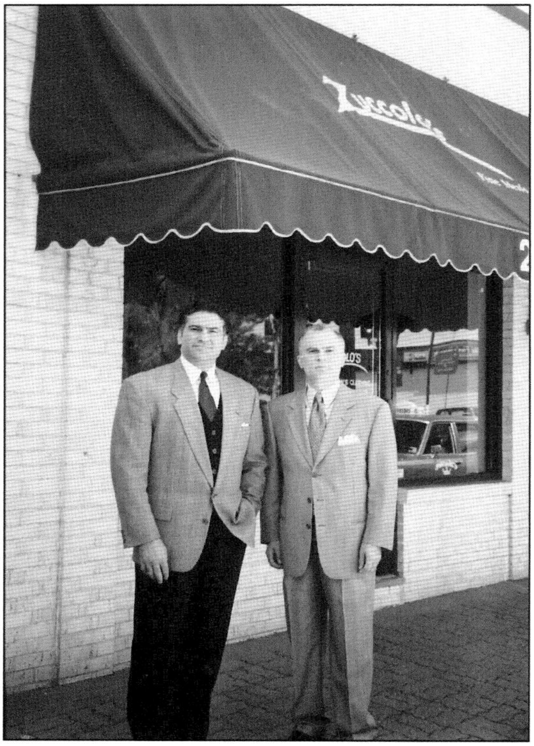

Yesterday, it was Hugo (Zook) Zuccolo who ran the very elegant and sophisticated Zuccolo's on Atwells Avenue. Today it is still Hugo (son, that is, on the right) and his son Joseph (on the left) who operate the business. Still, Zook, once called the unofficial mayor of Federal Hill, shows up, beautifully attired, as usual.

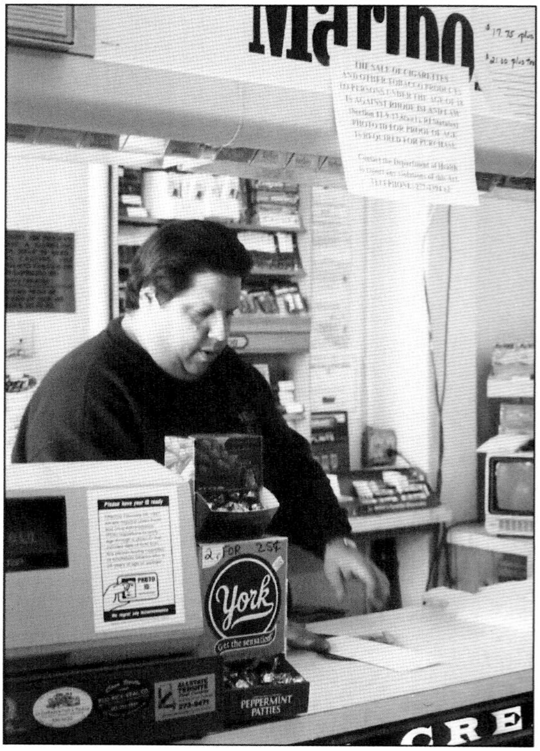

Michael Antonelli stands behind the counter in Leo's. There is little about the Hill that Michael, owner of the neighborhood store, cannot tell you.

Rudolph (Rudy) Micheli, a budding businessman in the 1940s, was the man who supplied Easter lambs to the Hill and beyond. Photo courtesy of Isabel Micheli.

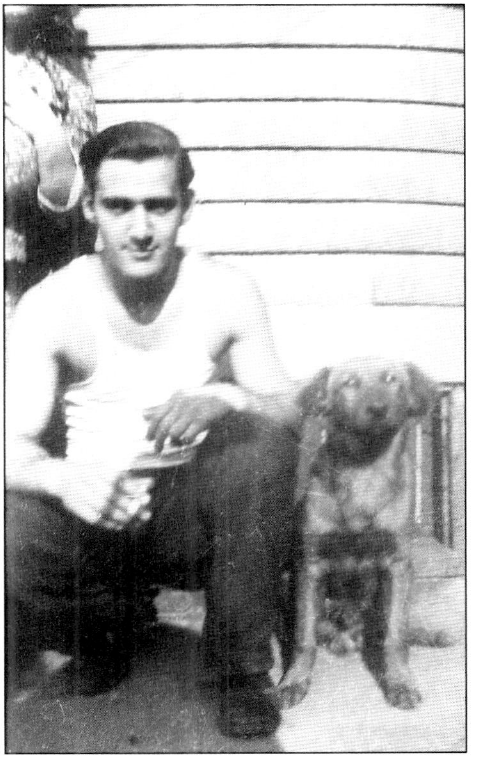

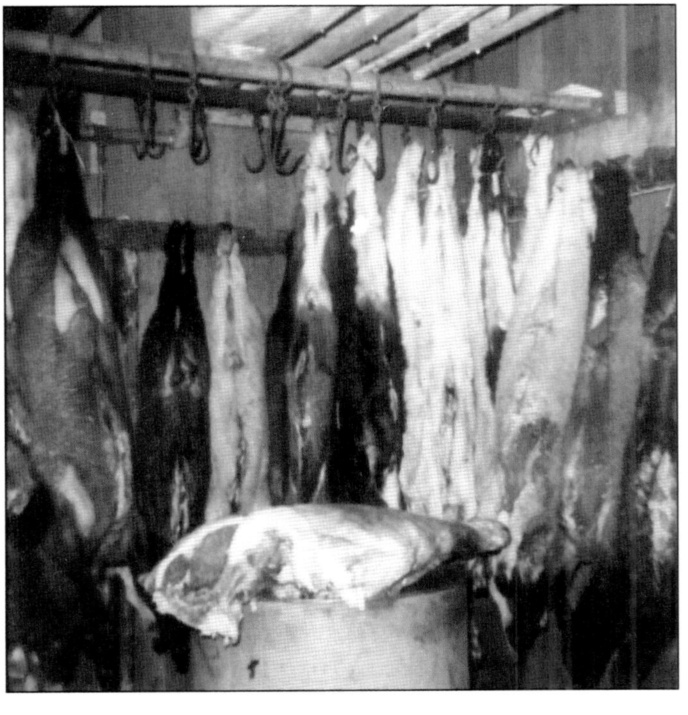

The butcher's shop is stocked for Easter. This is the market owned by Rudolph Micheli, the place where everyone went at Easter for the *agnello* (lamb) and other meats. Here thirty years ago or more, you could buy veal cutlets for $1.69 a pound or a leg of lamb for 89¢ a pound! That was yesterday; there is no today because Rudolph Micheli is gone, and the butcher shop is closed. Photo courtesy of Isabel Micheli.

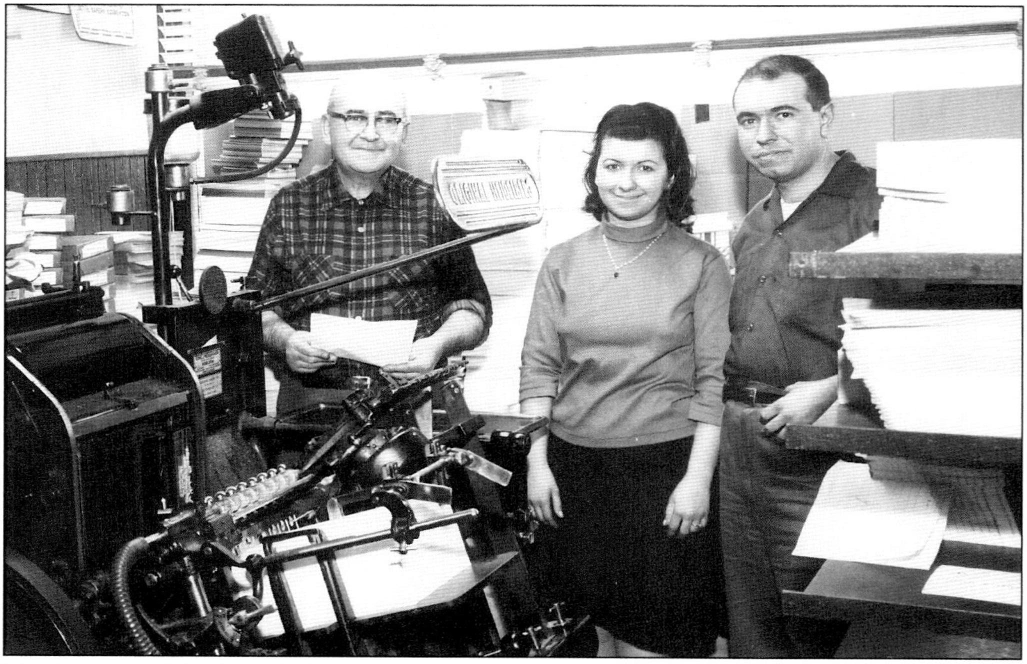

The interior of the Bradford Press appears here in the 1950s. From left to right are Rudolph Sigismondi Sr., daughter Pauline Sigismondi, and son Rudolph Sigismondi Jr. The brother and sister are still a team, running the Bradford Press at the beginning of Atwells Avenue. Notice the formidable printing press. Photo courtesy of the Sigismondi family.

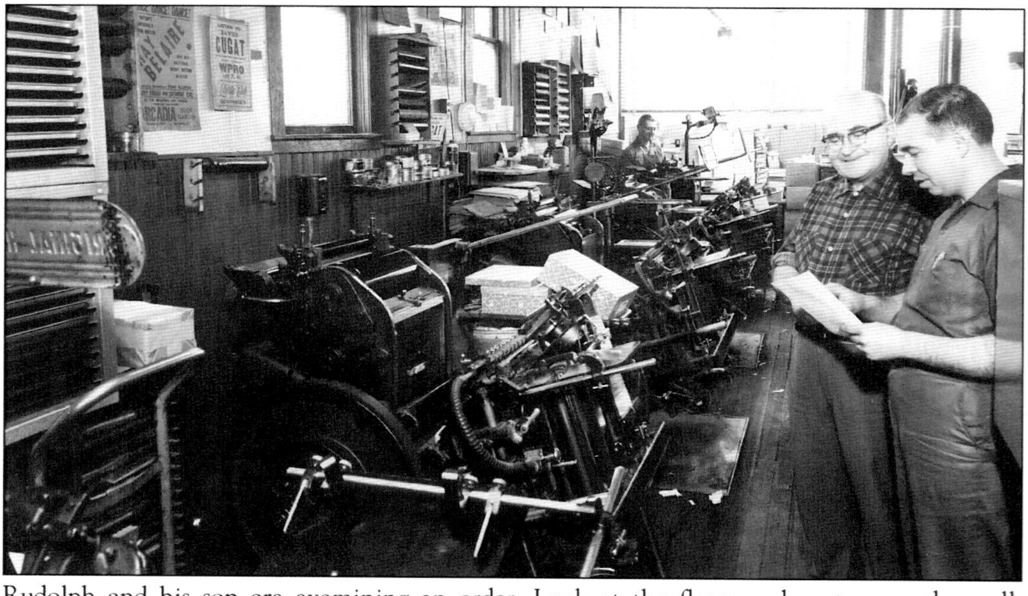

Rudolph and his son are examining an order. Look at the flyers and posters on the wall, all printed here. The fact that "Xavier Cugat" was still big and local musician Ray Belair was playing at the Arcadia gives some indication of the era. The Arcadia Ballroom is now gone, and Cugat has long departed to that rumba heaven in the sky. Photo courtesy of the Sigismondi family.

And here is Mary standing in the style of the 1920s near her home on Penn Street on the Hill. There seems to be a real animal on her right shoulder, which was the style of the time. The fur came head and all. Photo courtesy of the Sigismondi family.

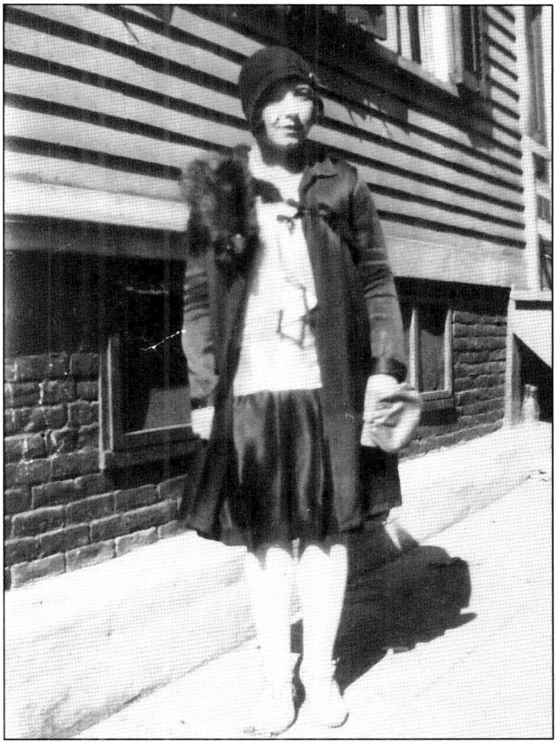

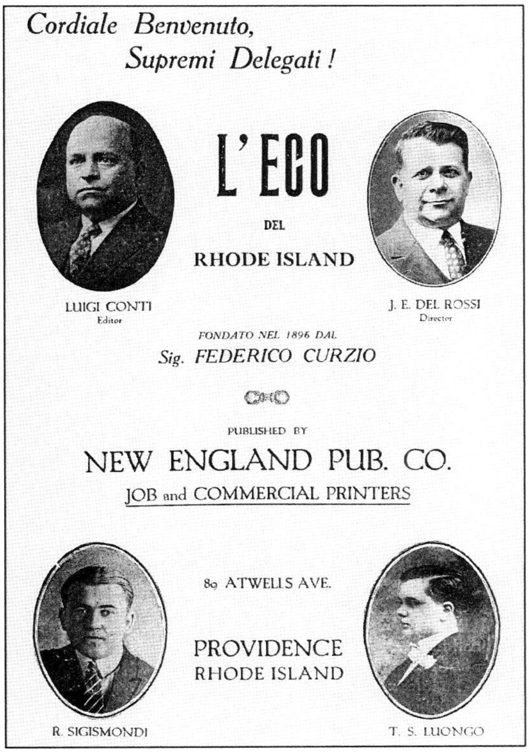

Cordiale Benvenuto,
Supremi Delegati !

L'ECO
DEL
RHODE ISLAND

LUIGI CONTI
Editor

J. E. DEL ROSSI
Director

FONDATO NEL 1896 DAL
Sig. FEDERICO CURZIO

PUBLISHED BY
NEW ENGLAND PUB. CO.
JOB and COMMERCIAL PRINTERS

89 ATWELLS AVE.
PROVIDENCE
RHODE ISLAND

R. SIGISMONDI

T. S. LUONGO

This is an example of the front page of the over-100-year-old newspaper, *L'Eco* (the Echo, now defunct) printed by the New England Publishing Co. on 89 Atwells Avenue. The gentleman in the lower left oval is Rudolph Sigismondi, founder of the Bradford Press. Photo courtesy of the Sigismondi family.

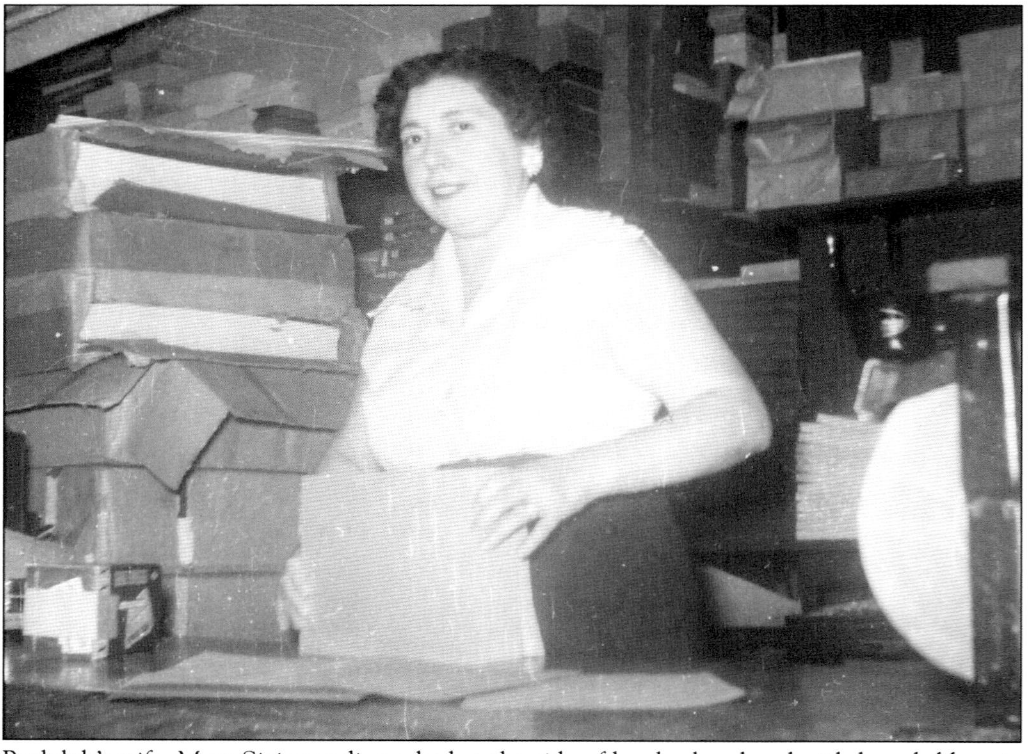

Rudolph's wife, Mary Sigismondi, worked at the side of her husband and with her children in the Bradford Press.

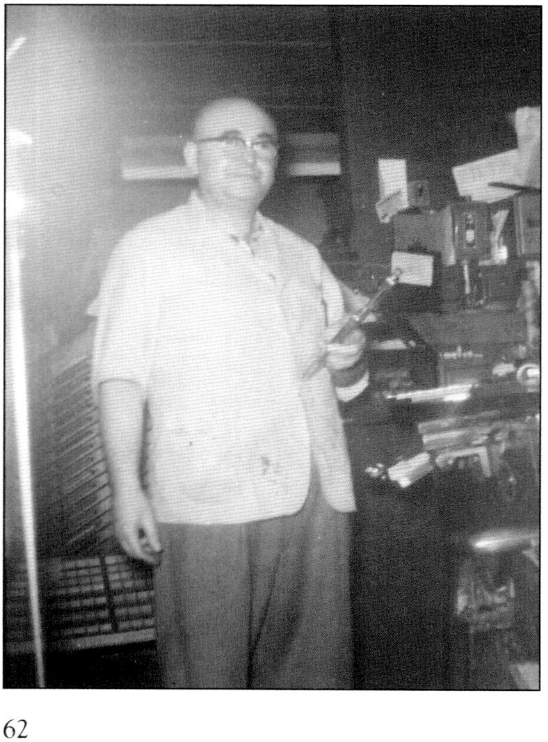

Rudolph Sigismondi is picture here in the Bradford Press in 1957. A very genial man, he was known for generosity and absolute dedication to excellence in printing.

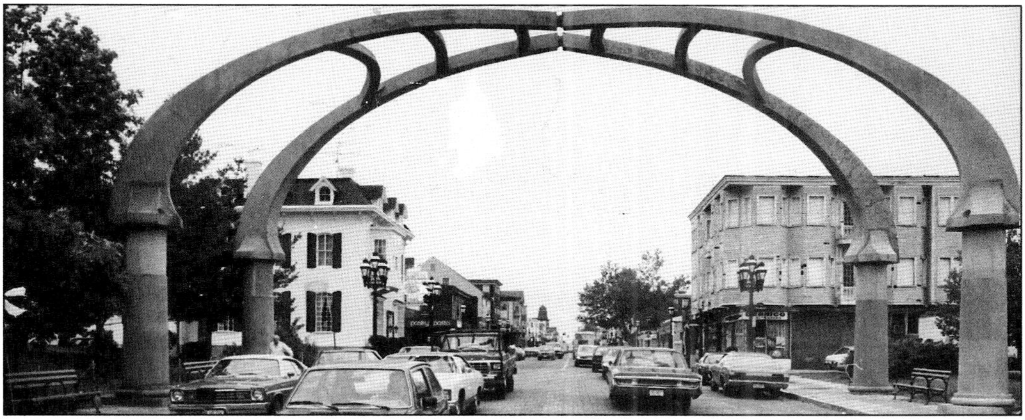

Yesterday, it lacked its "Welcome," in a manner of speaking. This is the great arch before the bronze La Pigna (The Pine) was suspended, the ancient Italian/Roman symbol of hospitality. To the left is the Old Canteen and to the right is a large, former apartment building which today is completely restored and home to several businesses, including a pizza parlor and the *Federal Hill Gazette*. Photo by Ernest A Myette, collection of Joe Fuoco.

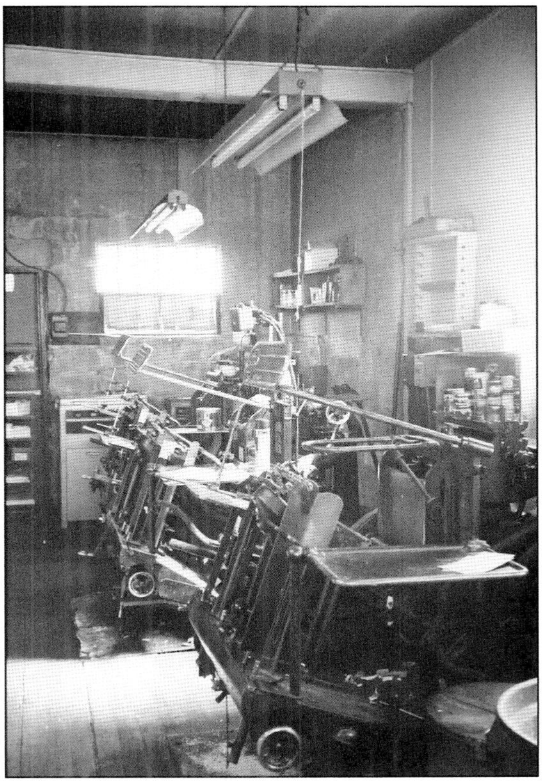

Though a contemporary photo, this picture might have been taken, for its quality of light and rustic tone, in the early 1900s. The Bradford Press, vitally alive today, still looks a lot like it did in the past, and that is the enduring quality of its charm and nostalgia.

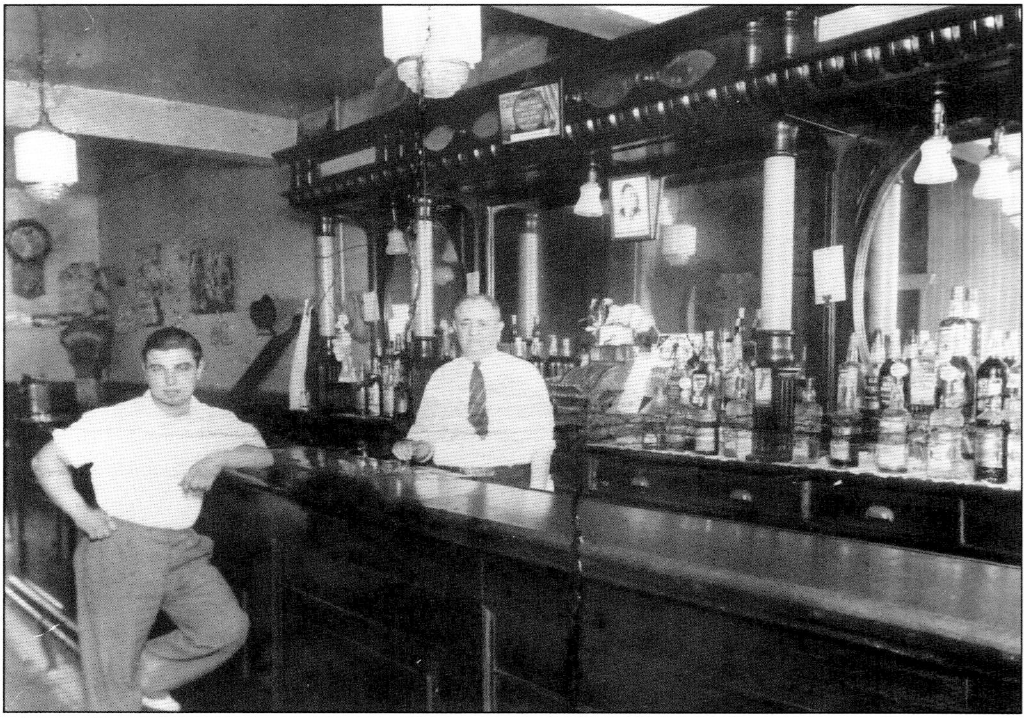

This is the way it was in 1936. The saloon, many years later to become Caffe Verdi and now Lucy's, still retains its magnificent mirror, columns, and molding. Pictured are a saloon keeper, Donato Fantetti, and a patron we know as Mr. D'Amico. Photo courtesy of Lucy's.

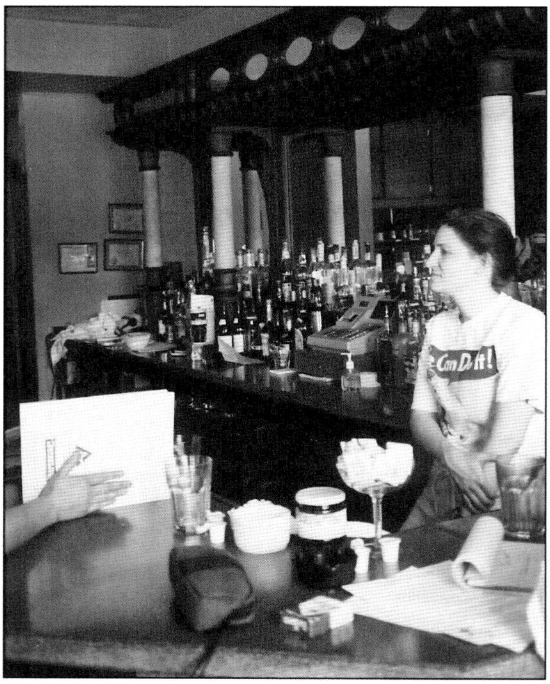

And the way it is now—not very different. Owner Wendy Davis (she is co-owner with Diane Slater) relaxes for a moment against the beautiful wall behind her, the only one of its kind on the Hill and intact as it was in 1936.

Six
Sports Briefs

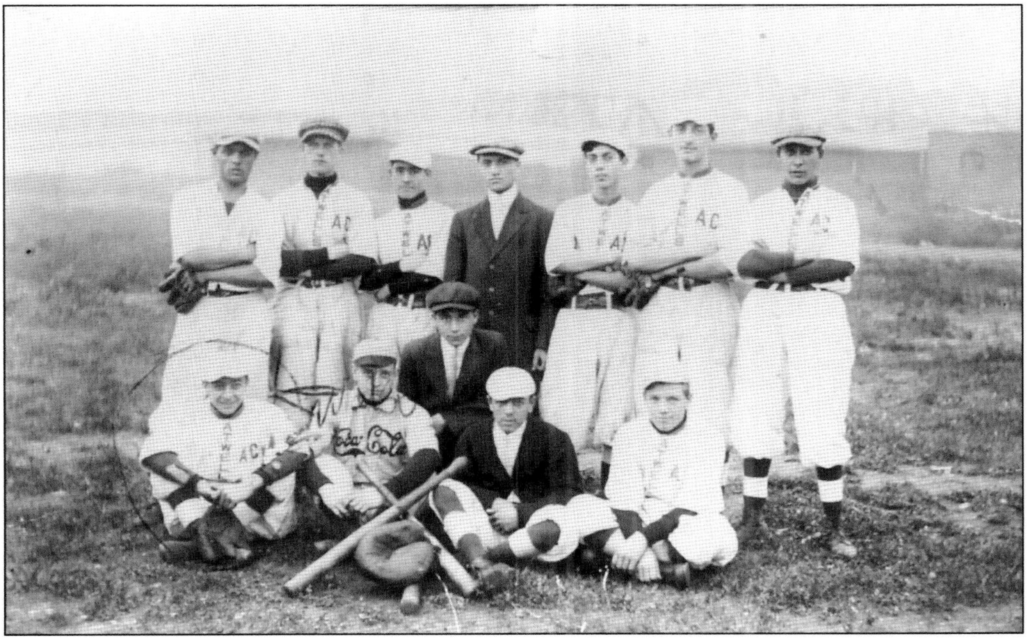

The Atwells Avenue baseball team is pictured here in the teens. This was the original, the very first baseball team on Federal Hill. The gentleman in the circle (front row, far left) is Vincenzo Marino. Photo courtesy of Antonette Marino.

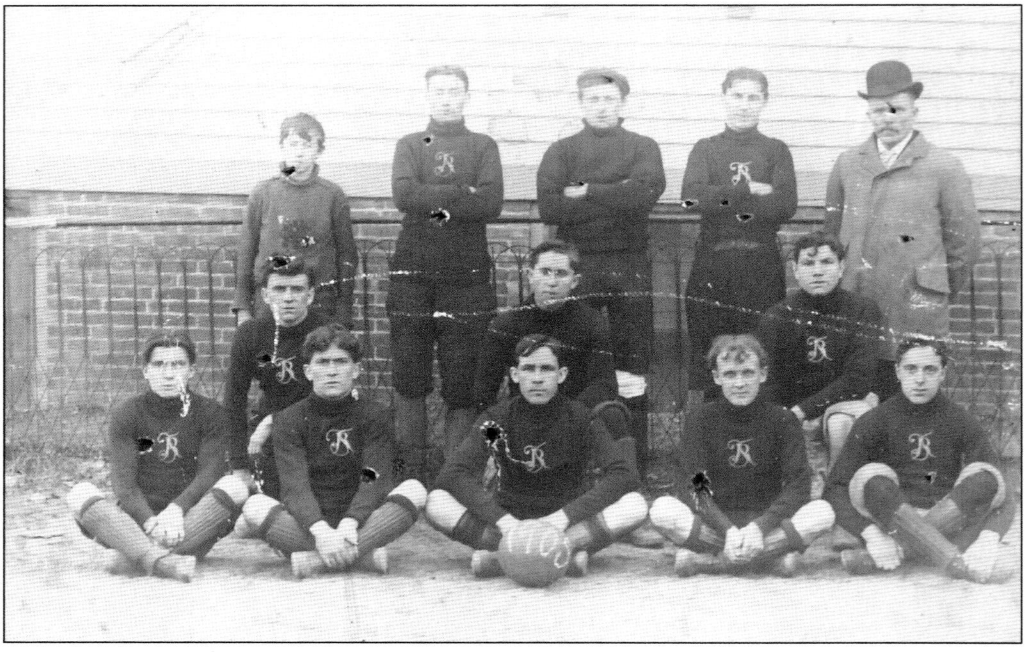

A soccer team is shown here in 1905. The only identifiable person (center row, middle) is the player Giovanni Tella, whose brothers owned Tella's Bar in Federal Hill. Photo collection of Joe Fuoco.

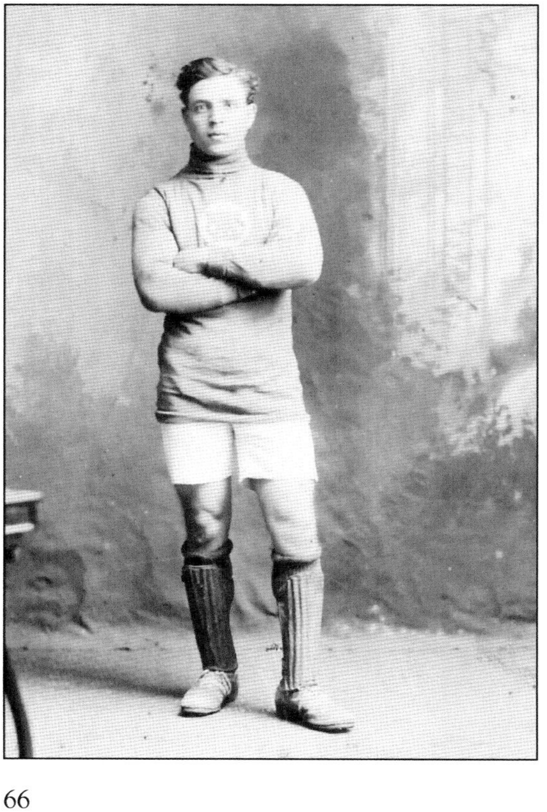

Posing before a backdrop, a soccer player whose name is lost is dressed in the style of the early twentieth century. Photo courtesy of Viola La Chapelle.

Boxer Johnny Curcio of Federal Hill, who later was a masseur at Curcio's Health Center, looks dapper and does not at all sport a cauliflower ear. A dashing young man, he was to put Federal Hill on the pugilist sports map in the 1920s and 1930s. Photo courtesy of Tommy Curcio.

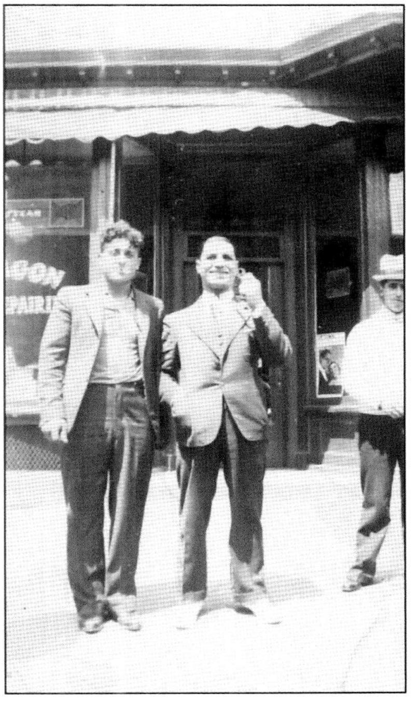

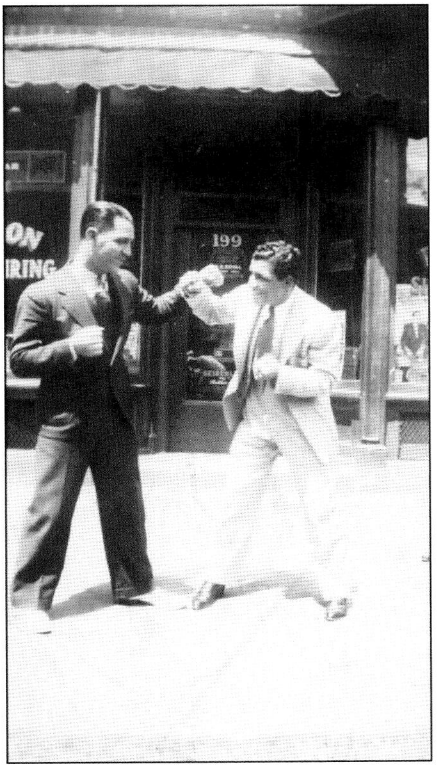

On the left is Johnny Curcio, the champion, and on the right is Johnny Mandell. We assume this is only shadow boxing because they were really good friends. Photo courtesy of Tommy Curcio.

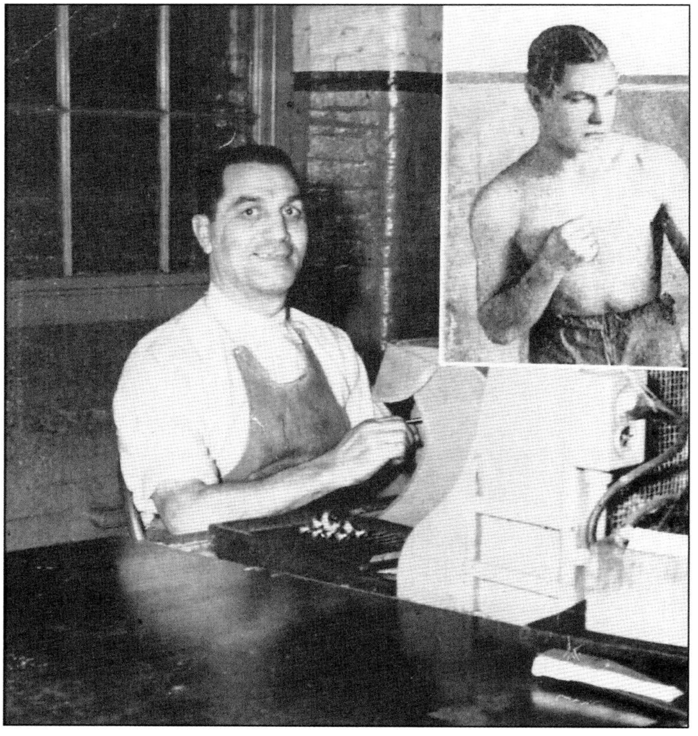

In his later years Johnny worked at Uncas, a jewelry manufacturing firm. Many had forgotten, but he remembered the days of glory when he had fought well and with great dignity. Curcio lived to the age of 83. Photo courtesy of Tommy Curcio.

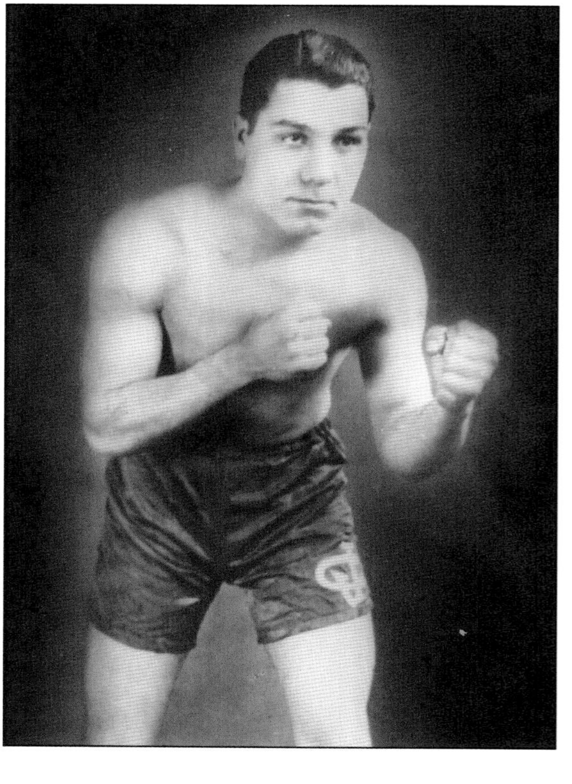

Johnny Curcio's, famed boxer from the Hill, story is something of a saga. A champion with fantastic looks (his first name was really Romeo), Johnny was the Federal Hill middleweight of the late twenties and thirties, and from 1934–1937 he held the New England welterweight and middleweight titles. Photo courtesy of Tommy Curcio.

And again, these are anonymous sportsmen at the turn of the century. Posing before a nondescript backdrop, they seem almost overdressed for sports. Studios on the Hill were forever immortalizing local sports heroes. These were probably two of them. Photo courtesy of Viola La Chapelle.

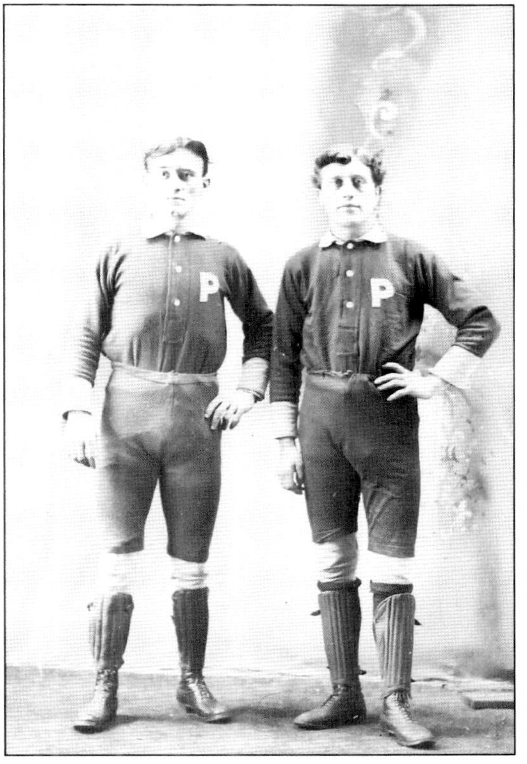

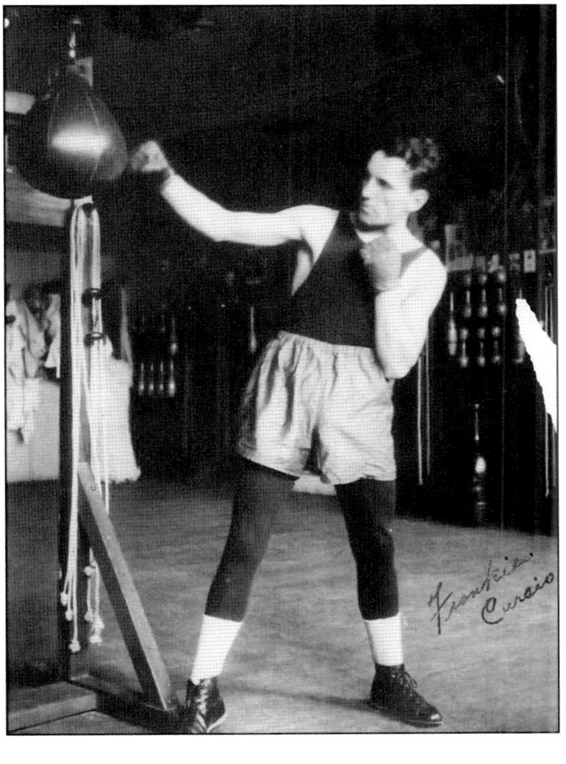

And yes, another Curcio, this one is Frank Curcio, a lightweight who was described in the twenties in the *Italian Review* as a "clean living young man who always keeps himself in good condition." Hailing from Boston, he came to Federal Hill in 1922. Photo courtesy of Tommy Curcio.

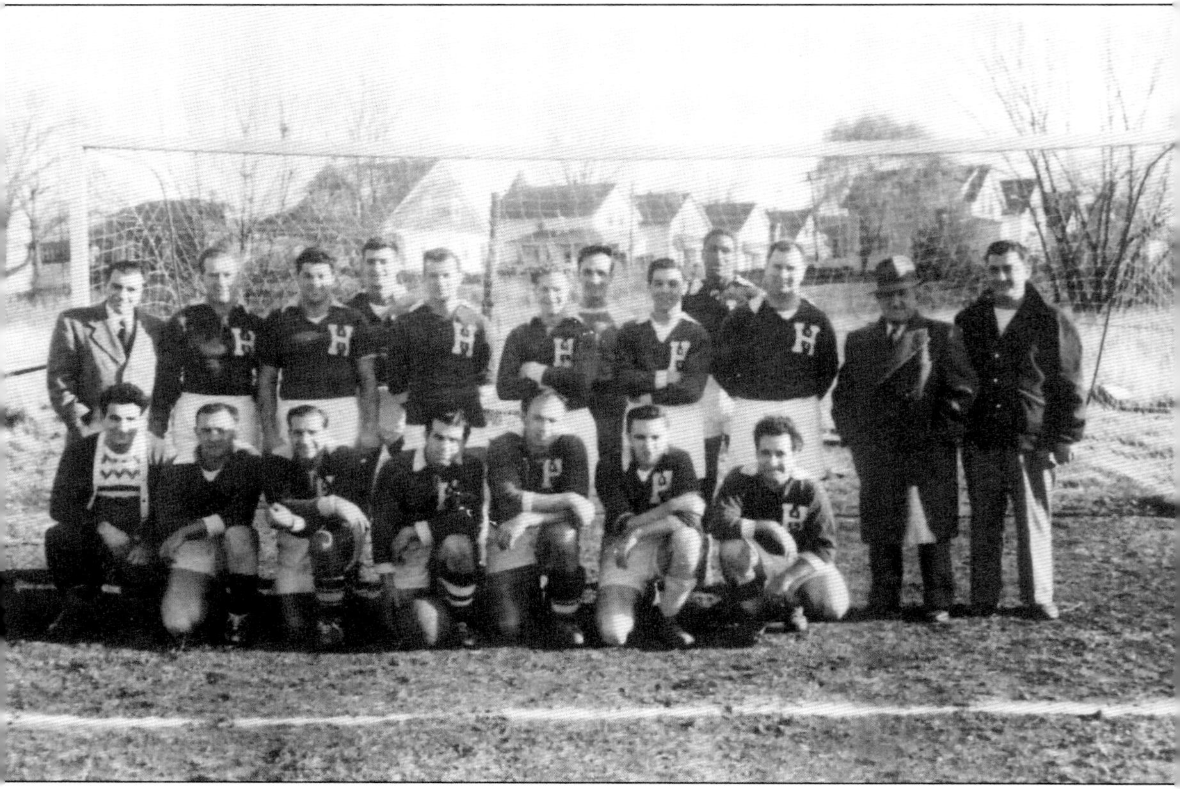

This is a soccer team of the 1940s. Now this team was not just a collection of soccer enthusiasts; for example, among the familiar faces is Frank Marrapese (front row, fourth from the left), one of the most famous soccer players in all of New England, a man who won awards and acclaim. Today, in his seventies, his memories of the good old days of soccer are priceless. Photo courtesy of Frank Marrapese.

Seven

The Boulevard, Etc.

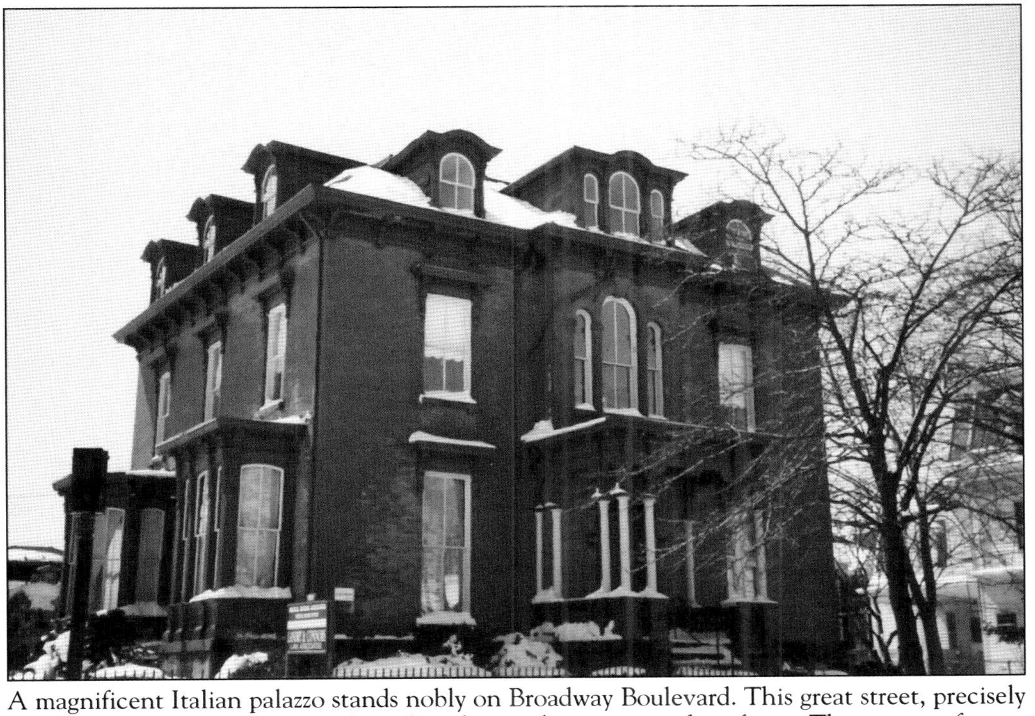

A magnificent Italian palazzo stands nobly on Broadway Boulevard. This great street, precisely one mile long, is the home today of professionals, artists, and students. The names of some of the houses bear witness to their creators, the English. Later, many of these homes became known by their illustrious Italian occupants.

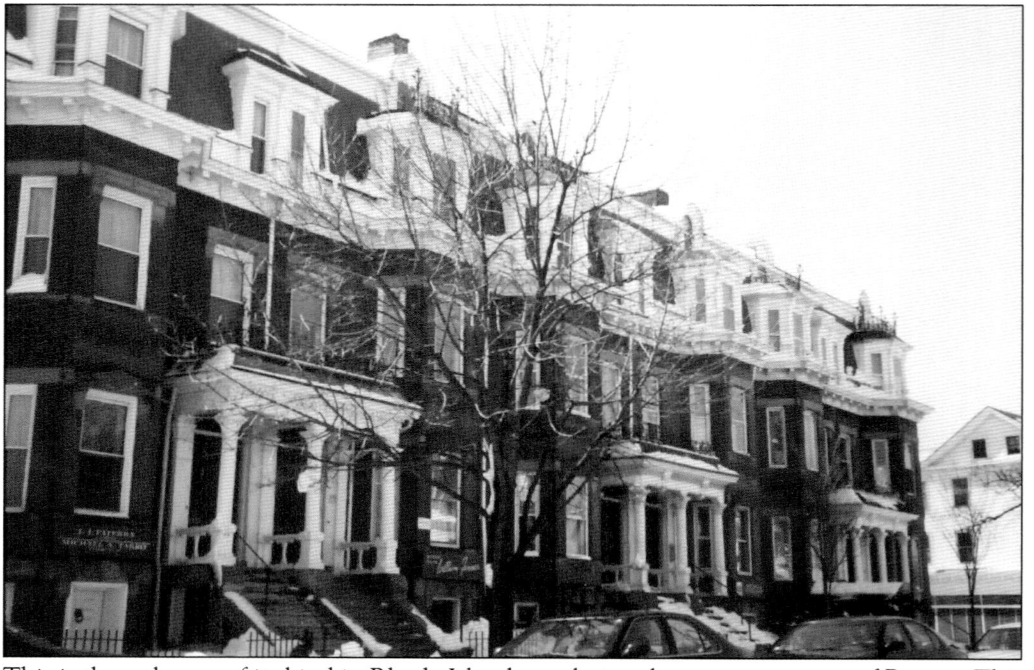

This is the only row of its kind in Rhode Island, emulating the row apartments of Boston. This superbly restored trio of connected apartments on Broadway is occupied by lawyers, interior designers, etc.

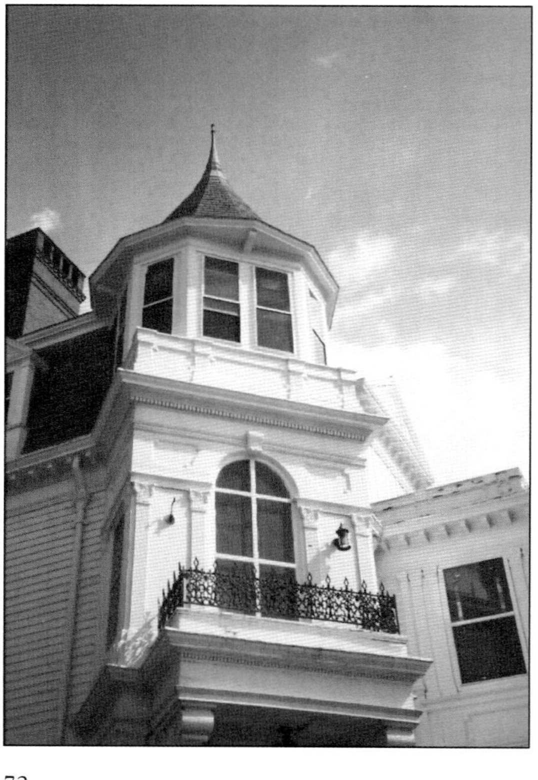

This is an example of architecture that is unequaled anywhere in Rhode Island, except for Newport. This superb, stately corner of a great house boasts a fenced veranda and a series of gables. Notice the size of the chimney.

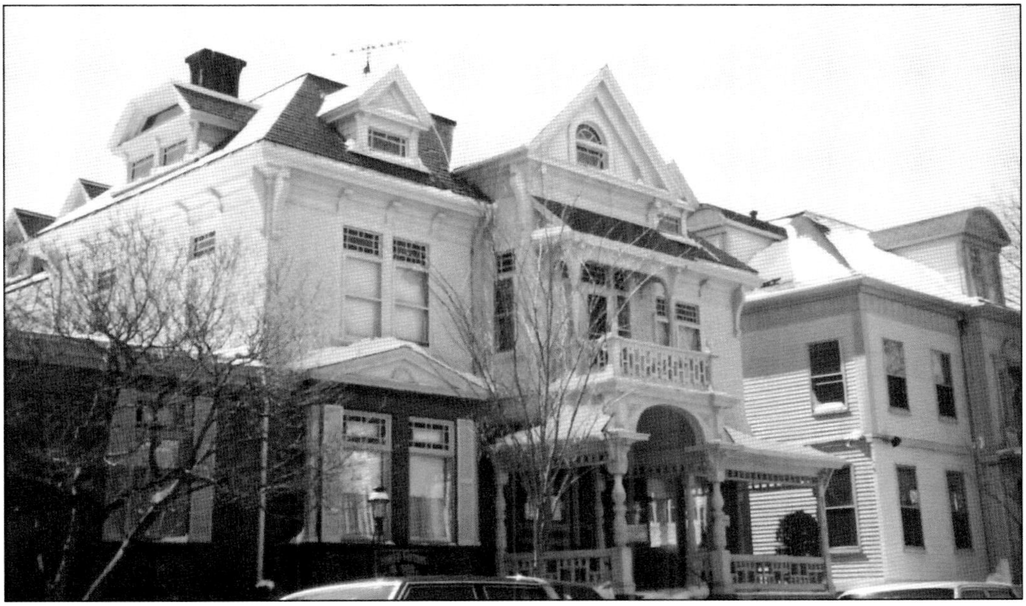

These are great houses that have become funeral homes. Their elegance restored and their interiors breathtaking, these two beautiful mansions are funeral homes which were established many years ago and maintained by several generations of descendants. The Thomas Gattone Funeral Home has been here for decades.

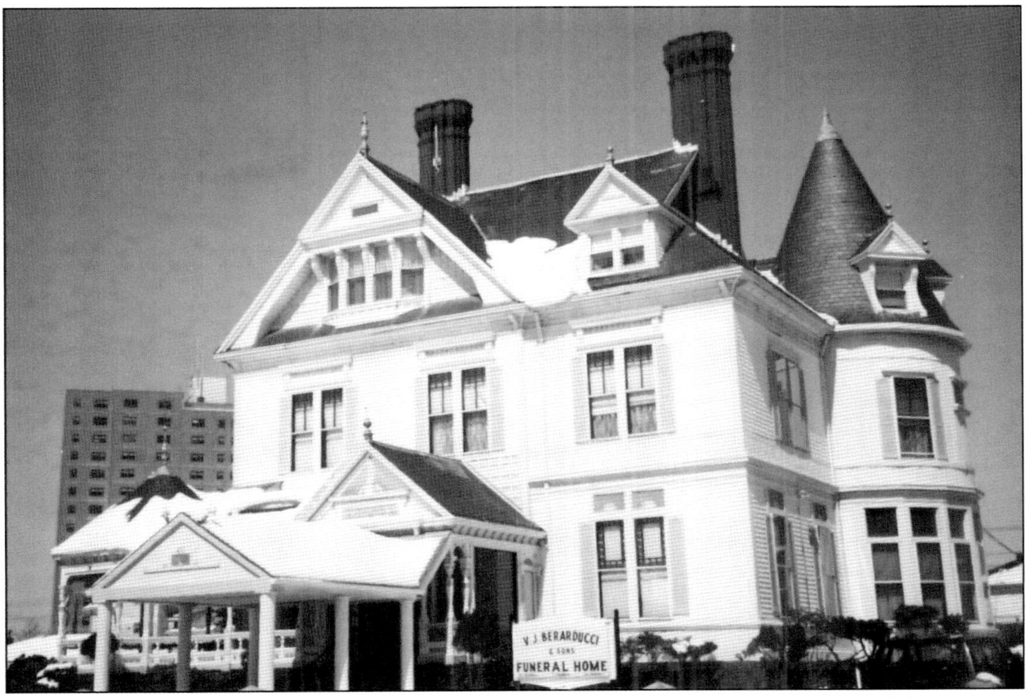

The sprawling, formidable V.J. Berarducci Funeral Home, unquestionably one of the greatest homes on the Boulevard, possesses an interior perfectly Old World in elegance. It was chosen by movie director Michael Corrente for a very important appearance in his film *Federal Hill*.

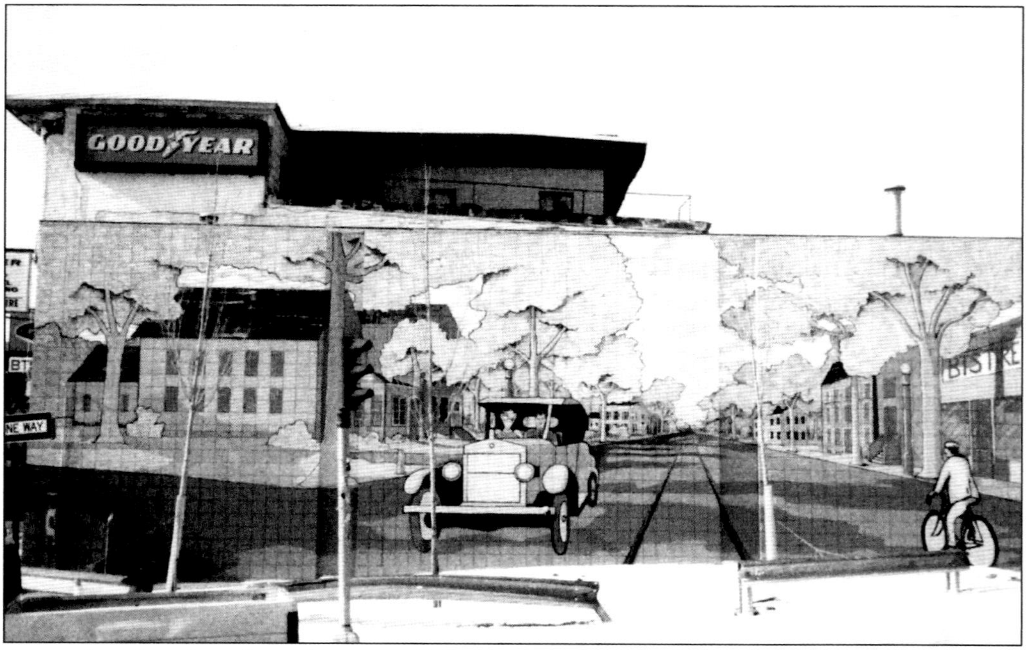

A mural on Broadway faces downtown Providence. Real signs seem to be part of the perspective painting. In the past few years, the Hill has blossomed with murals. Several more are included in this book.

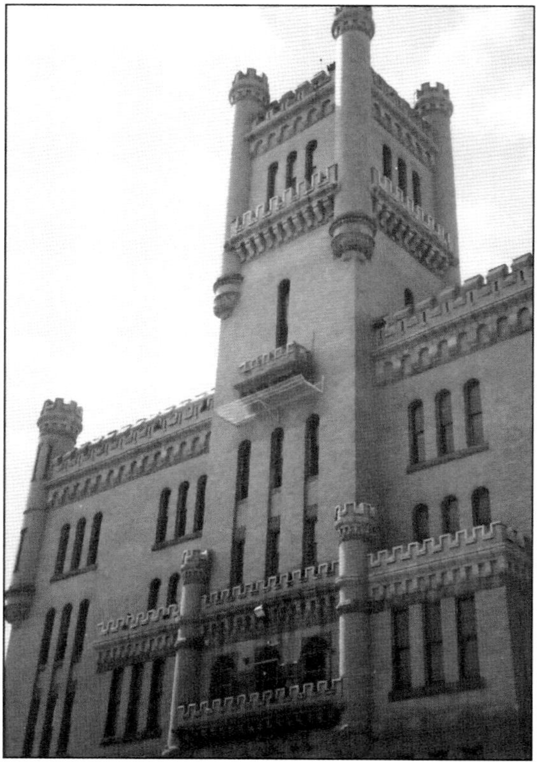

Although not sitting among the mansions of Broadway, but clearly seen from Broadway and its parallel Westminster Street, no photographic record of the Hill would be complete without the Armory, a sprawling, massive structure. "The Castle," as it has always been called, has served as a sentry protecting the neighborhood. Today, saved by concerned people, it may become a sound stage for movie productions.

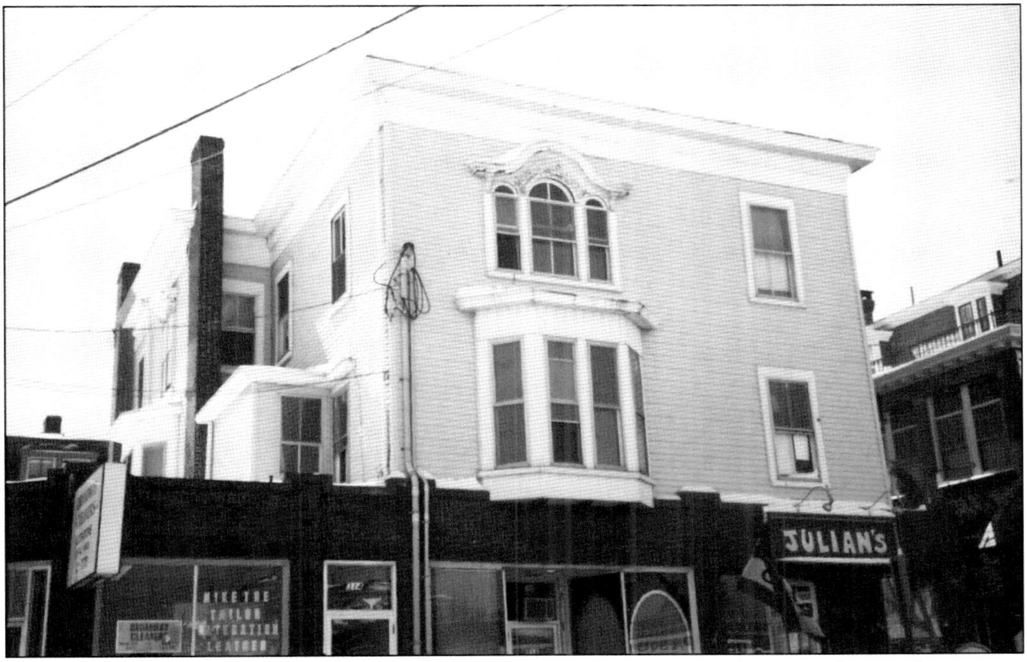

Sitting like the glorious topping of an unlikely cake, this mansion long ago lost its bottom to business. Today there is a tailor shop, a small market, and a restaurant called Julian's supporting the house.

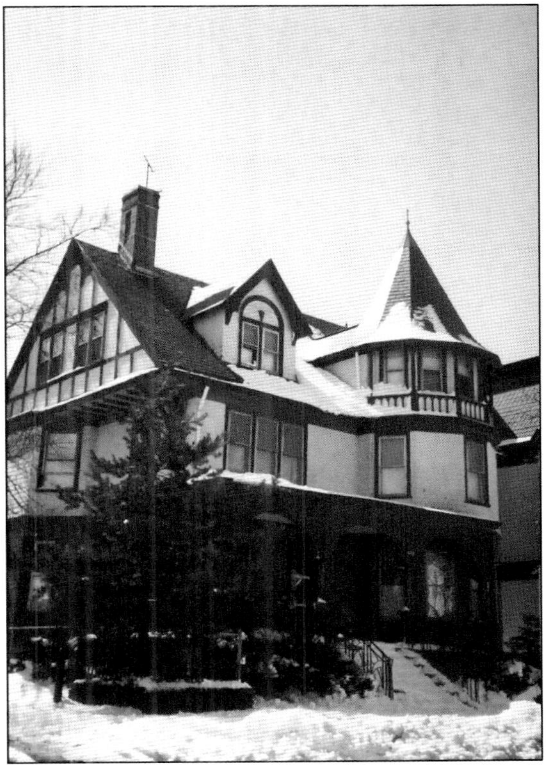

Like a house out of a fairy tale, this English-styled manor house with its beautifully appointed tower illustrates the way architectural orders have been blended successfully.

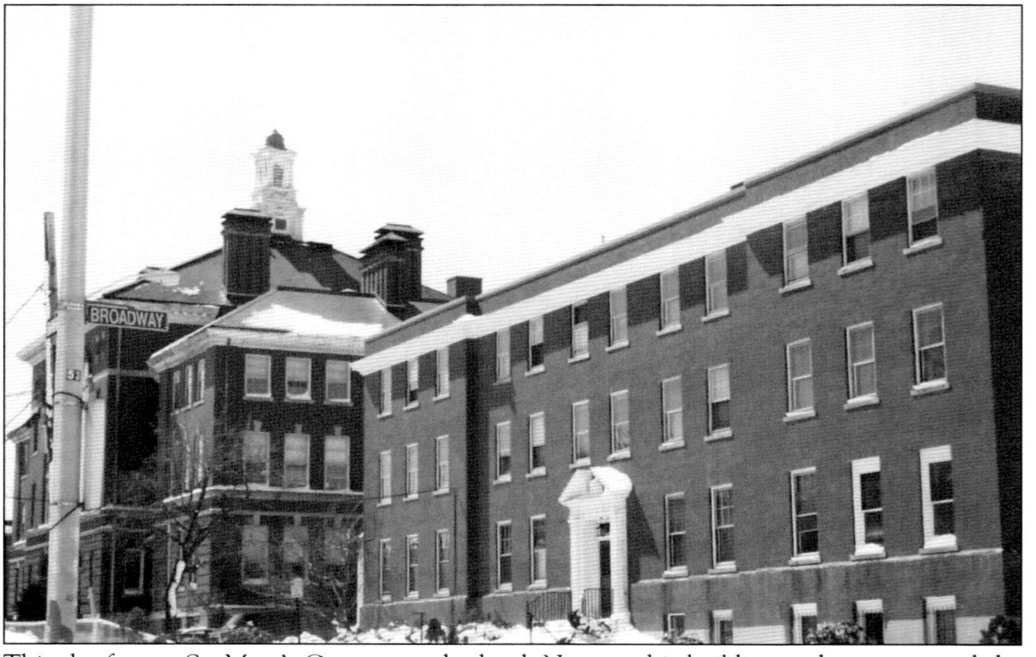

This the former St. Mary's Convent and school. Next to this building is the rectory and the great Gothic-styled, towered church of St Mary.

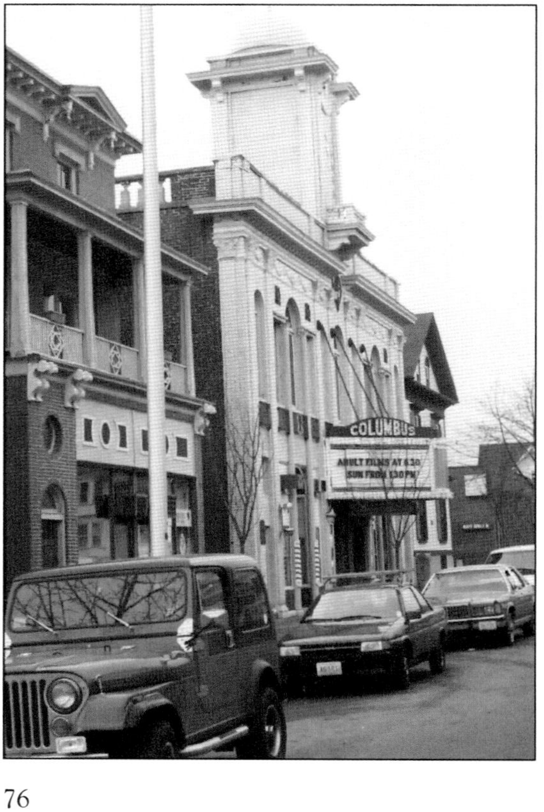

An Italian jewel, that's what this is. The interior of the Columbus Theatre is one of the most beautiful theaters found anywhere, for it is red and white, and elegant. Unfortunately, the Columbus Theatre, once the home to opera, Italian films, and later the great Japanese and Swedish films of the 1950s and 1960s, is now a Broadway house showing pornographic films—but that may change.

Eight

Memorable Views, People, Places, and Things

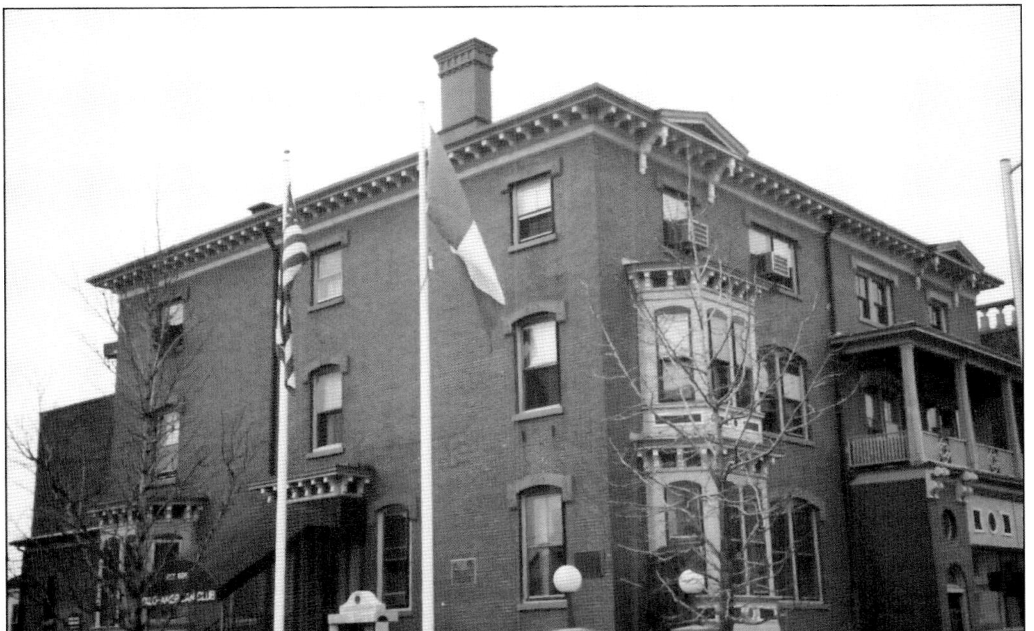

On Broadway, this is the Italo-American Club, a beautiful building with an Old World interior and known for some great food. A bastion of pride for keeping an ethos alive, it recently dedicated a beautiful monument to its deceased members. It invariably flies both the American and Italian flags. Photo collection of Joe Fuoco

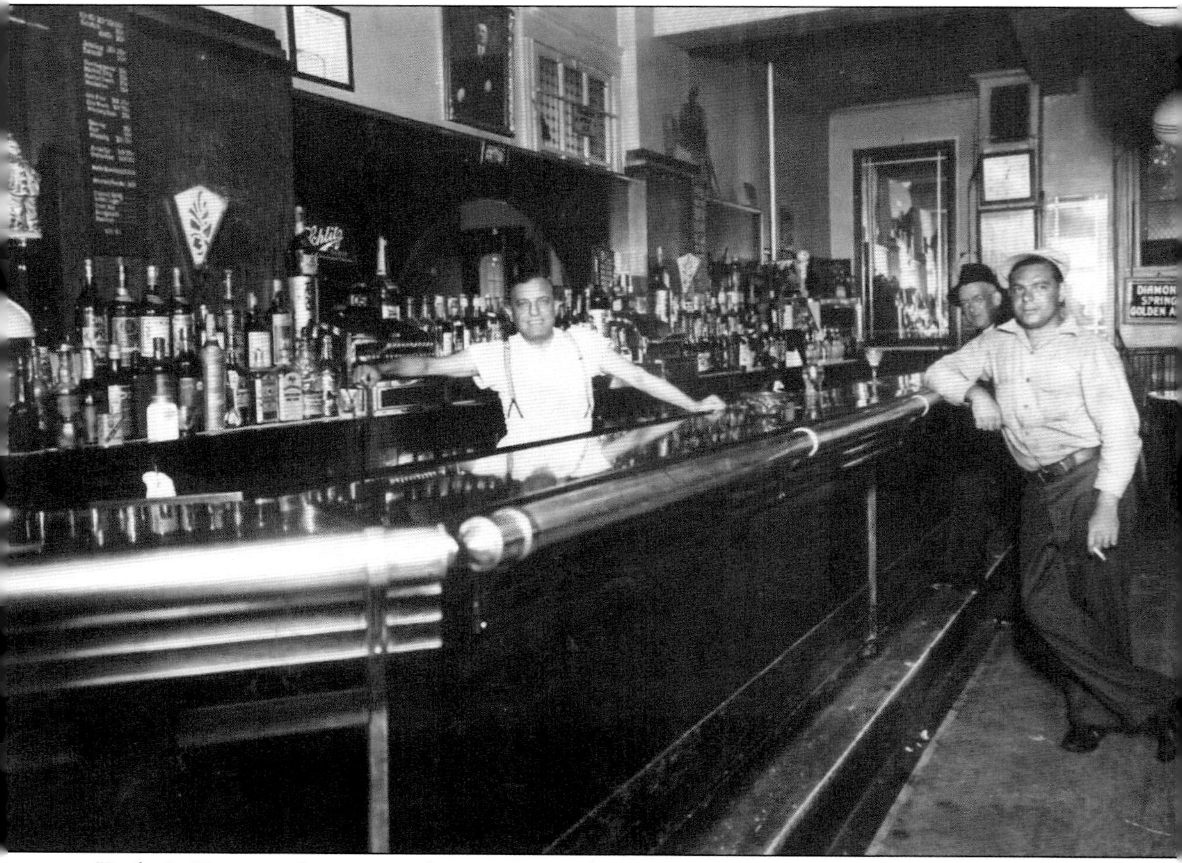

Taylor's Tap is a gleaming, reflecting bar with a copper railing, which you don't find around anymore but as relics of the past. Notice the sign to the left listing the prices of drinks. There was virtually nothing over 70¢!

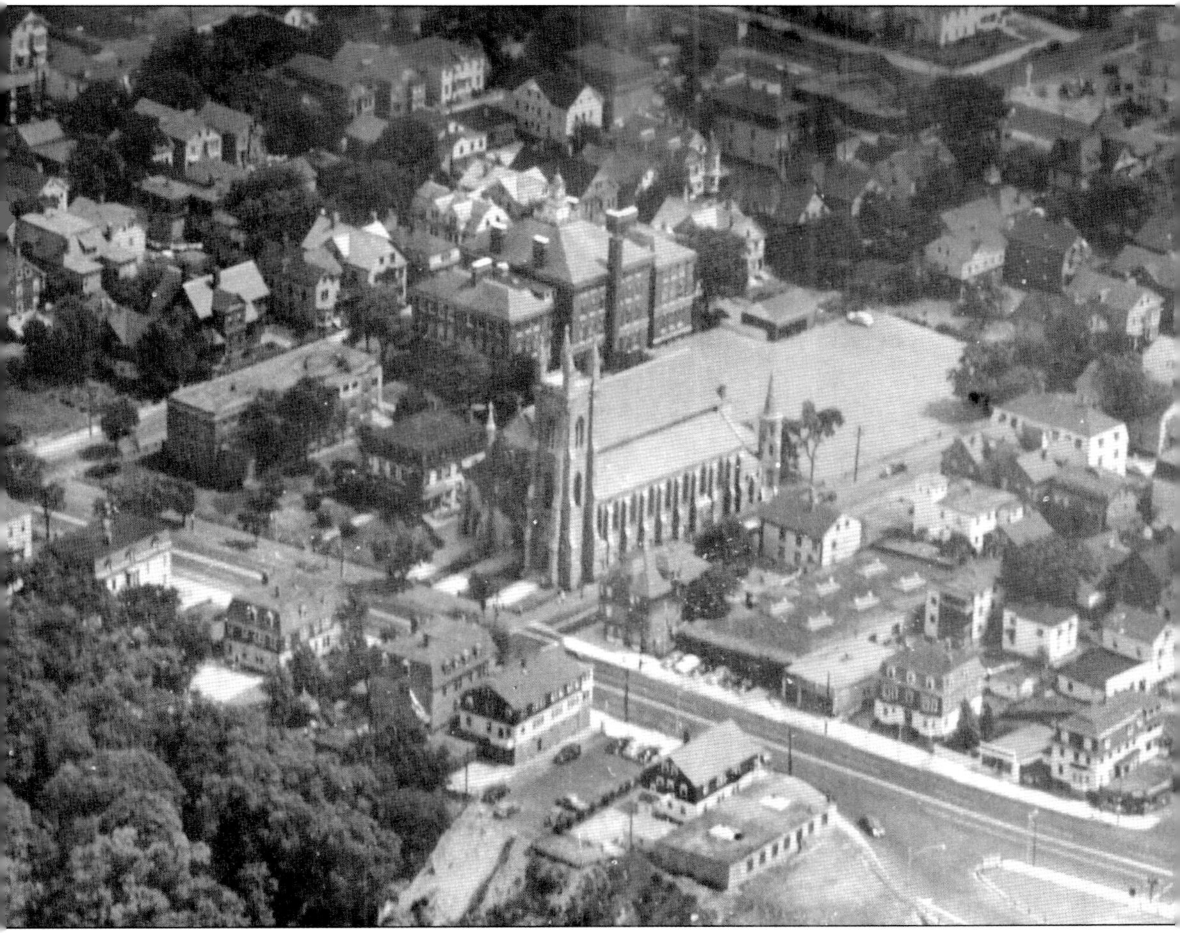

This is an aerial view of some of the area shown in this chapter. St. Mary's Church dominates the scene. Many of the mansions are visible on both sides of Broadway. This is but one small view of a mile-long boulevard. Photo courtesy of St. Mary's Church.

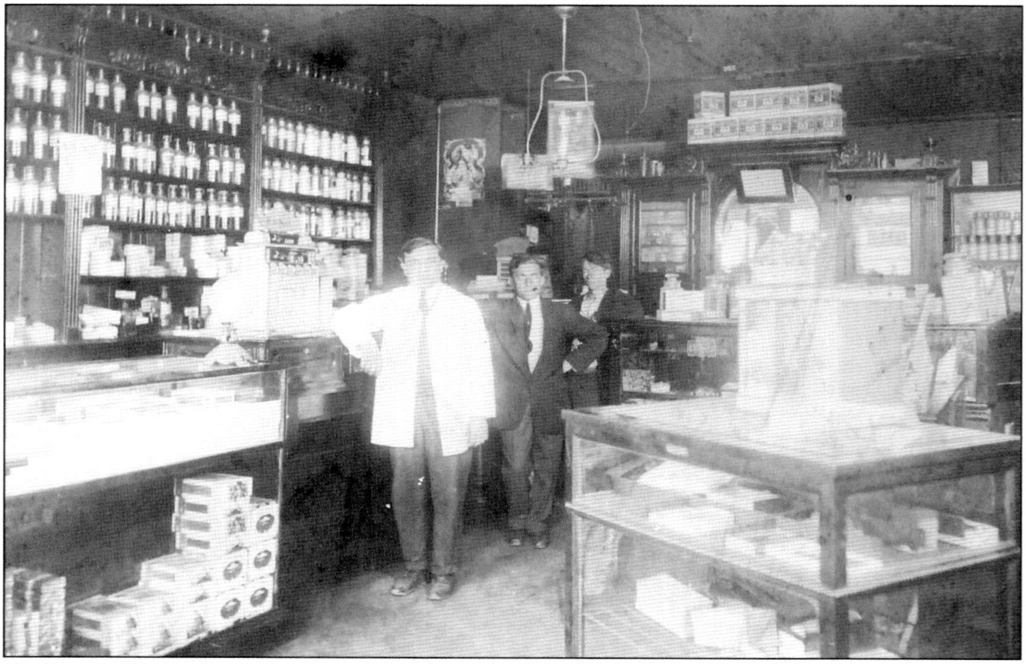

A photograph, dating from the turn of the century, is of the store owned by the Tella's. Tommy Tella is dressed like a druggist, but he wasn't. This busy place sold cigars and what appears to be tonics of some kind on the shelves. Notice the gas light suspended from the ceiling. Photo courtesy of Viola La Chapelle.

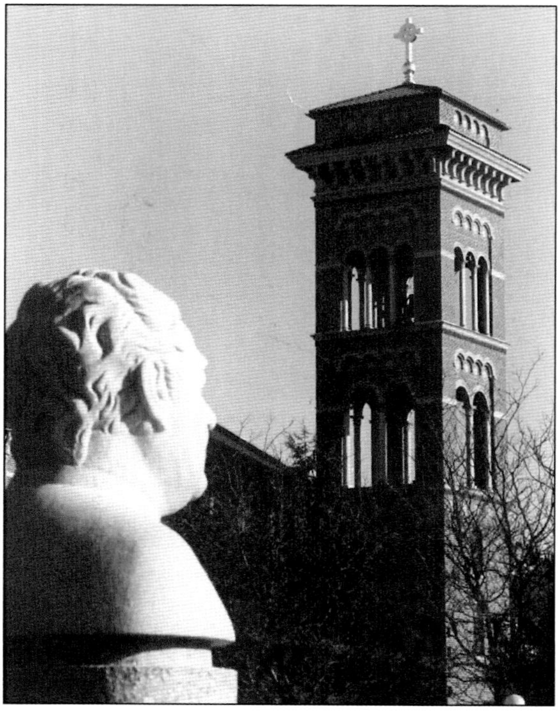

Monsignor Galliano Cavallaro looks to his beloved church, Our Lady of Mt. Carmel. A colorful, sometimes controversial figure, Monsignor Cavallaro spoke his mind and defended his friends even when it was not popular, and he was so revered on the Hill that a stone bust was created in his honor at a busy intersection. Photo collection of Joe Fuoco.

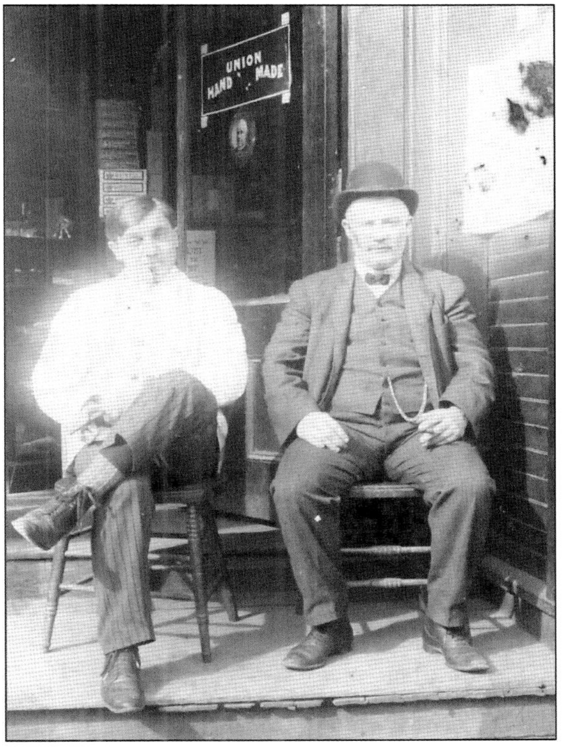

This is the way it was. Union handmade cigars were sold here. Again, this is Pasco Tella, sitting on a warm afternoon in front of his store. We do not know the man to his right, but one might suspect that the gold chain is a treasure. Photo courtesy of Viola La Chapelle.

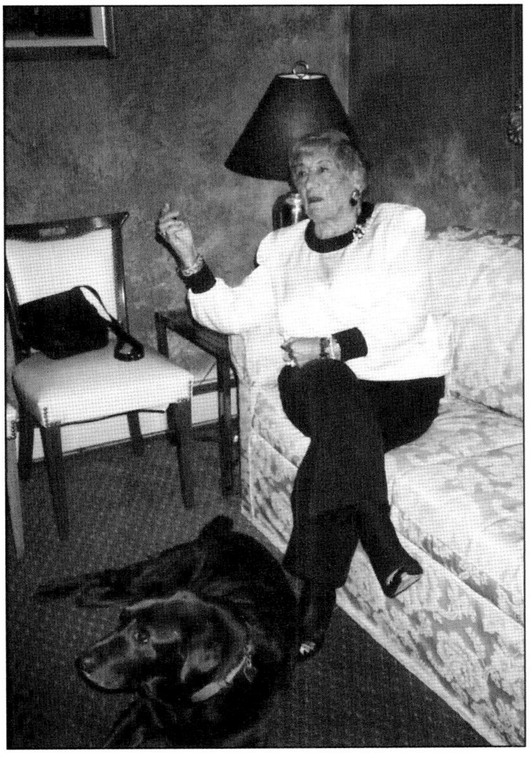

The Doyen of Federal Hill and the matriarch of Camille's Roman Garden Restaurant, Camille sits in her plush and elegant restaurant with her beloved, ever-present labrador Apollo. Camille Parolisi is the "Grand Dame of the Avenue."

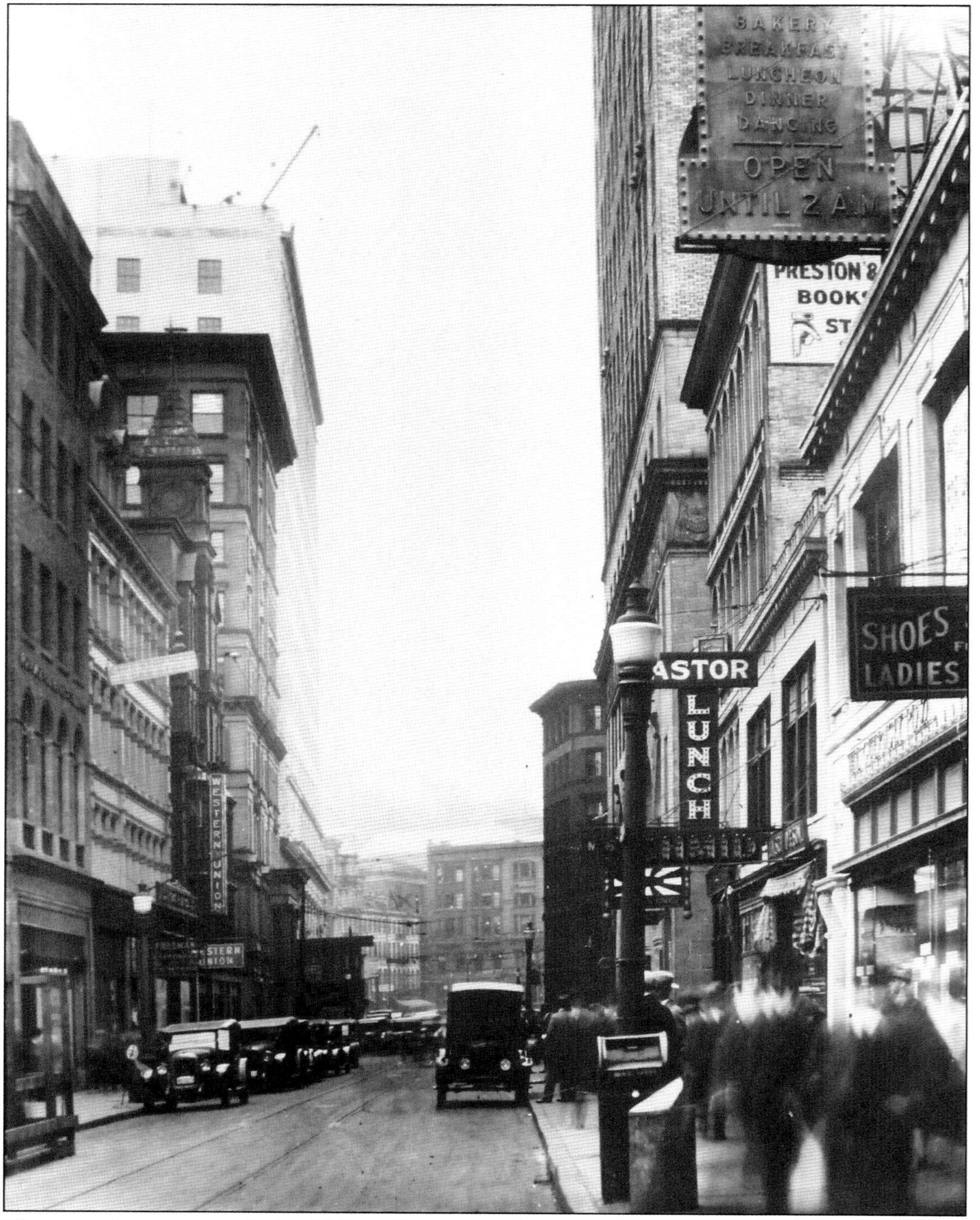

The very lower part of the Hill really flattened out to downtown Providence, and what many consider parts of the "City" were once included in the Hill. This photo from the early 1930s shows one of the busiest spots. The feel of the era is captured in the old cars, wedged together buildings, and in the far distance, the hazy diffused historic architecture of the river area. Many of the buildings are still here, although the businesses are long gone. Photo collection of Joe Fuoco.

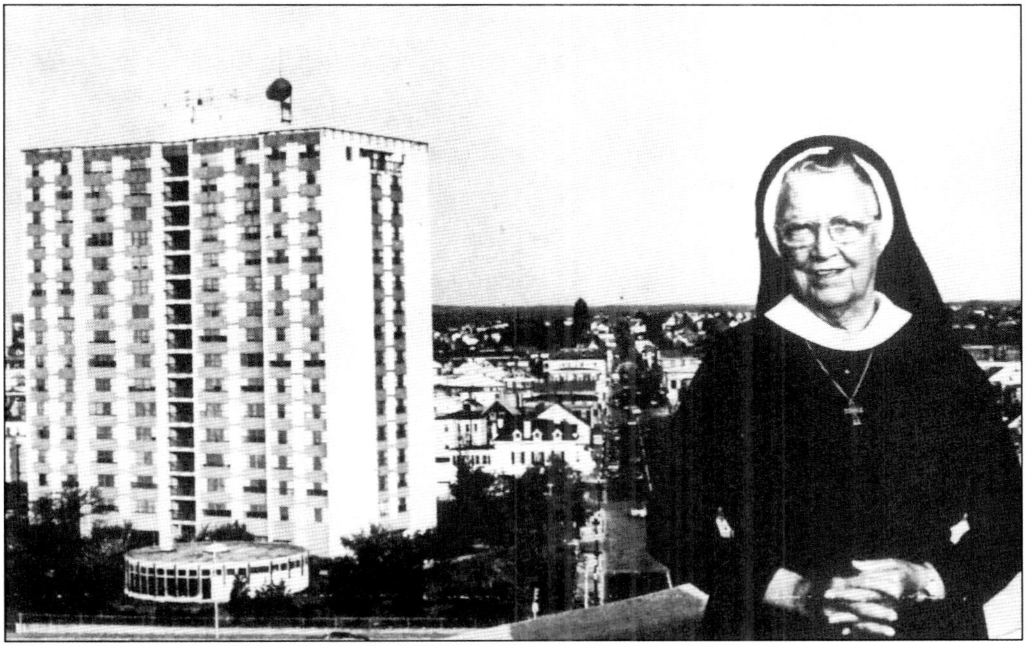

This is a wonderful shot of a beloved nun and her namesake. Sister May Domenica Woodcock, R.S.M. was one of the most beloved sisters on Federal Hill. Her tireless work for the aged and the disabled was noted by the high rise behind her, the Sister Domenica Manor, which was a home to residents of all ethnic peoples on the Hill. Photo courtesy of the Holy Ghost Church.

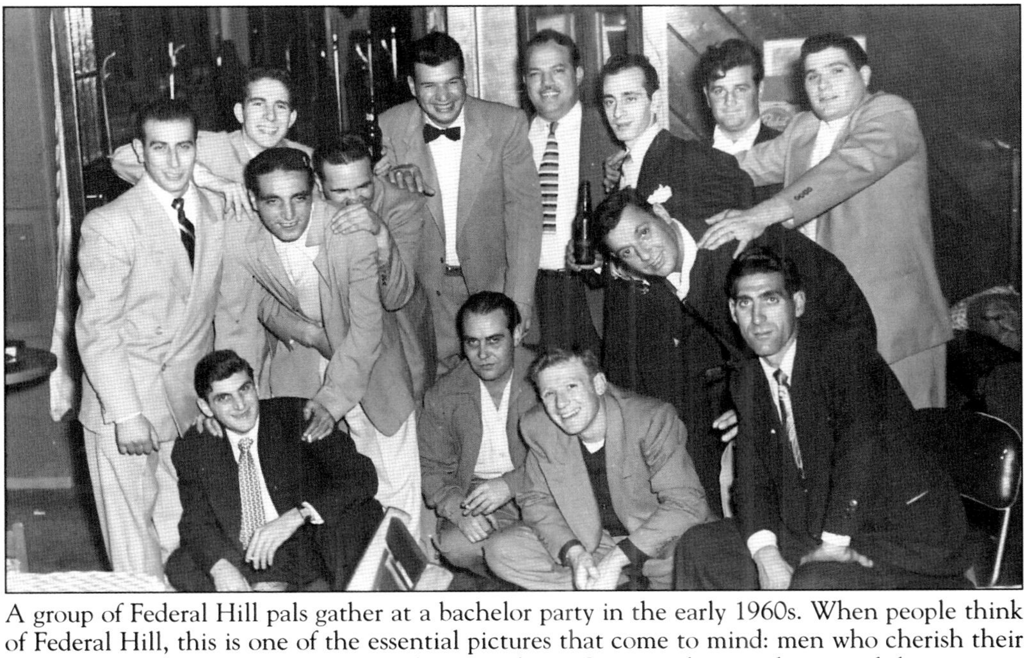

A group of Federal Hill pals gather at a bachelor party in the early 1960s. When people think of Federal Hill, this is one of the essential pictures that come to mind: men who cherish their friendships and the honor that existed among them. One wonders just how much knotty pine was really in the Knotty Pine Room to the rear. Photo courtesy of Frank Marrapese.

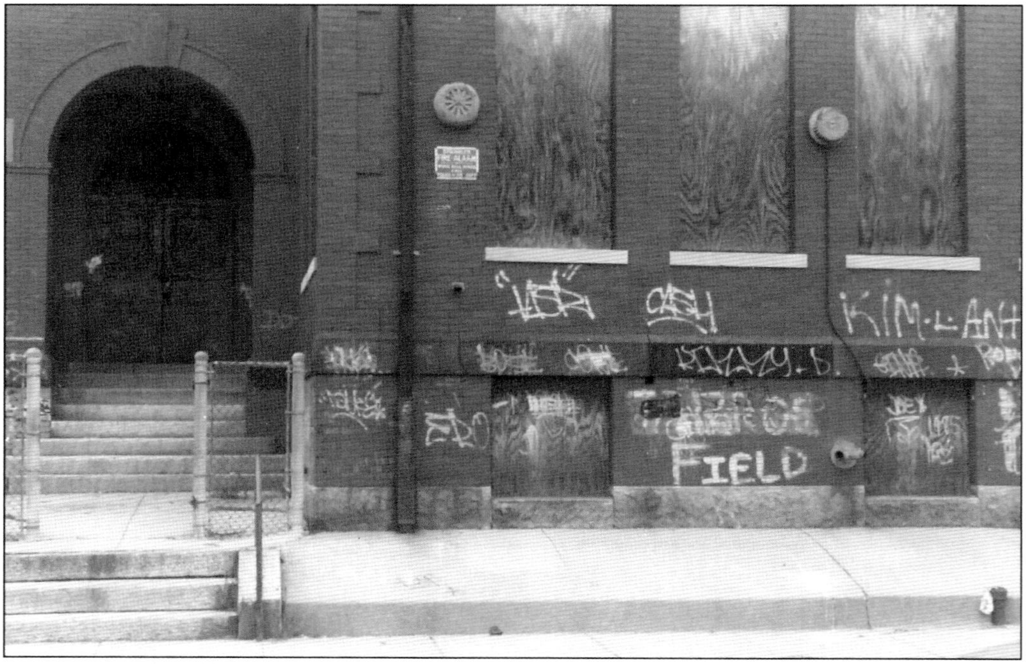

A memory of graffiti, this marked wall of a school no longer exists to tell this story. The school, a beloved vacant building that had been on the Hill for decades, was the victim of an incendiary.

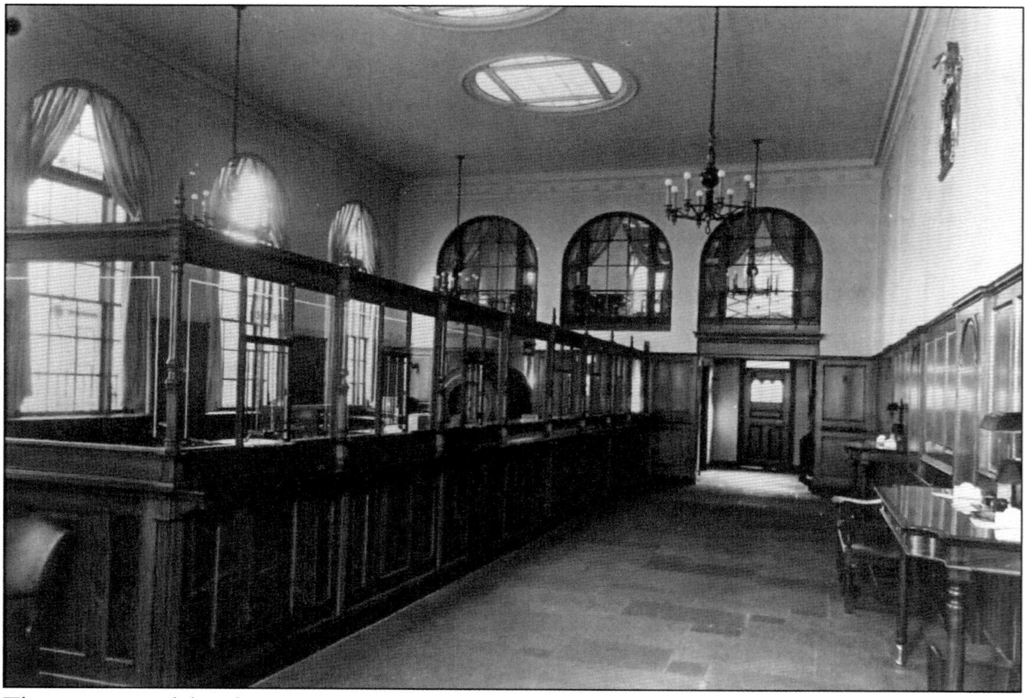

This is a view of the elegant interior of the old Hospital Trust Bank, now converted into a much needed library in one of the less affluent sections of the old Hill. Photo collection of Joe Fuoco.

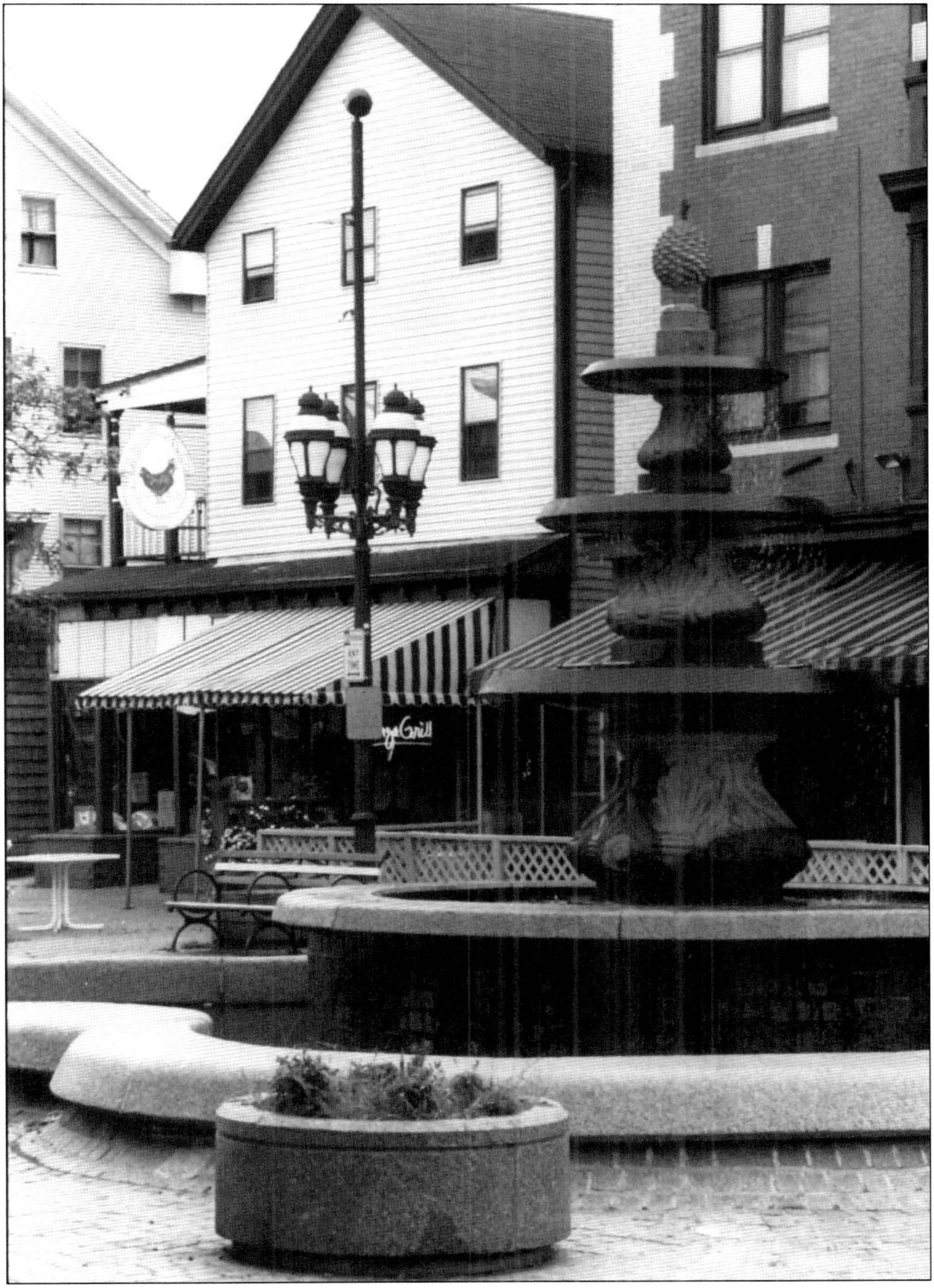

This is the great Plaza a few years ago—not much has changed. The Plaza Grill is still there, and the red rooster (Rhode Island's mascot, by the way) still sits above Antonelli's poultry shop. Photo collection of Joe Fuoco.

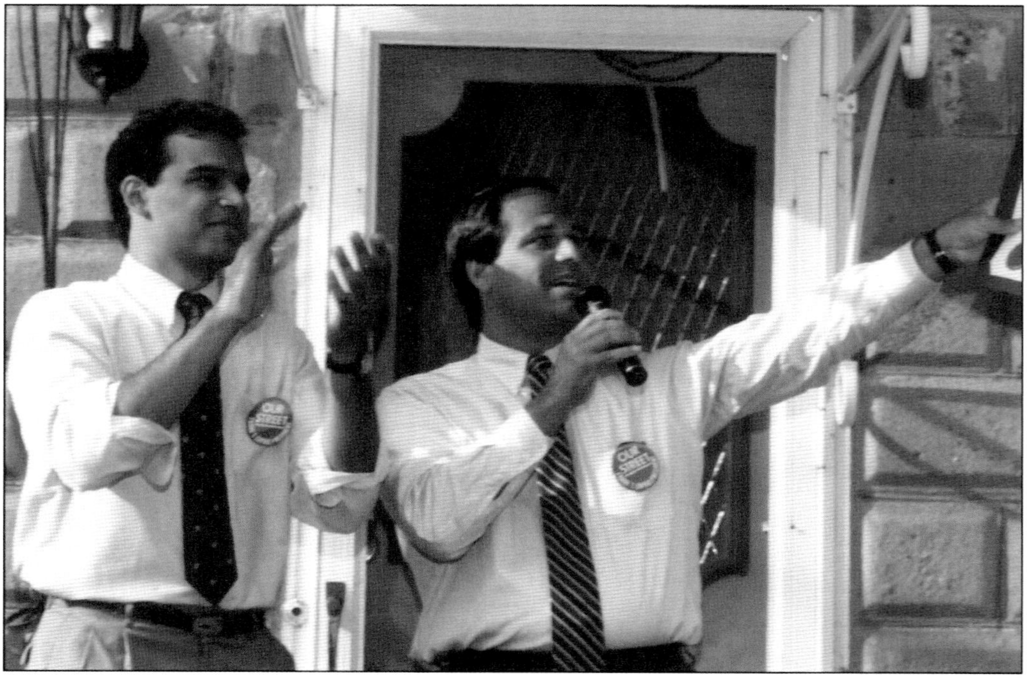

The Hill has traditionally been a hotbed of politics. Here are two politicians, Rep. Frank Caprio and former Mayor Joseph R. Paolino stumping, or campaigning, on the Hill. It usually works. Photo collection of Joe Fuoco.

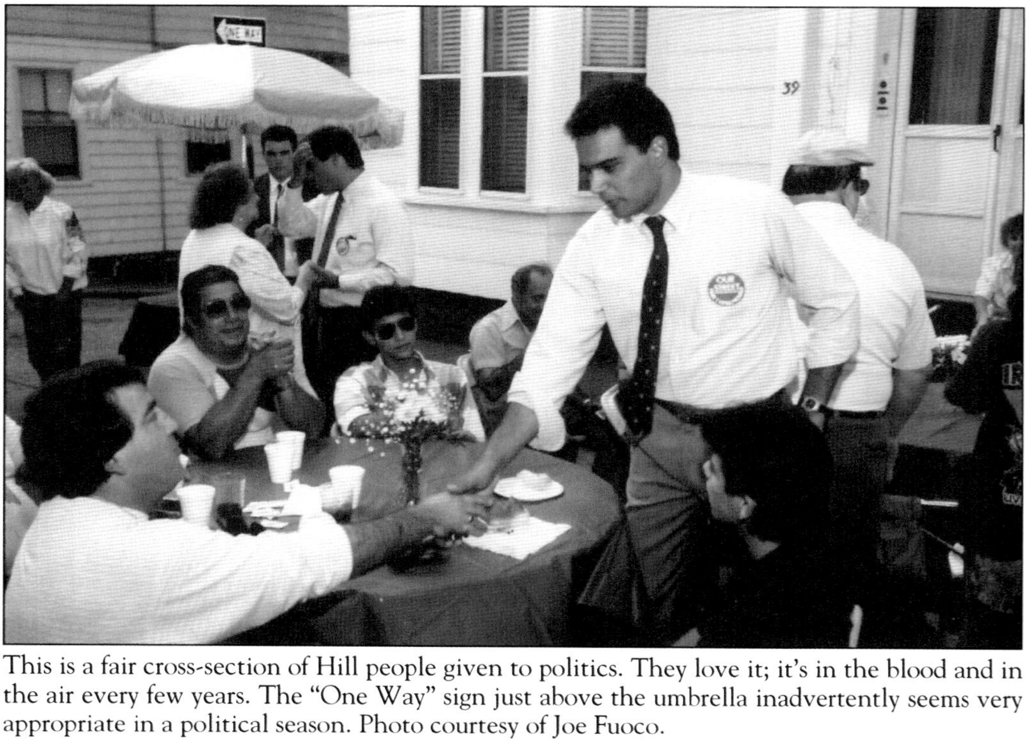

This is a fair cross-section of Hill people given to politics. They love it; it's in the blood and in the air every few years. The "One Way" sign just above the umbrella inadvertently seems very appropriate in a political season. Photo courtesy of Joe Fuoco.

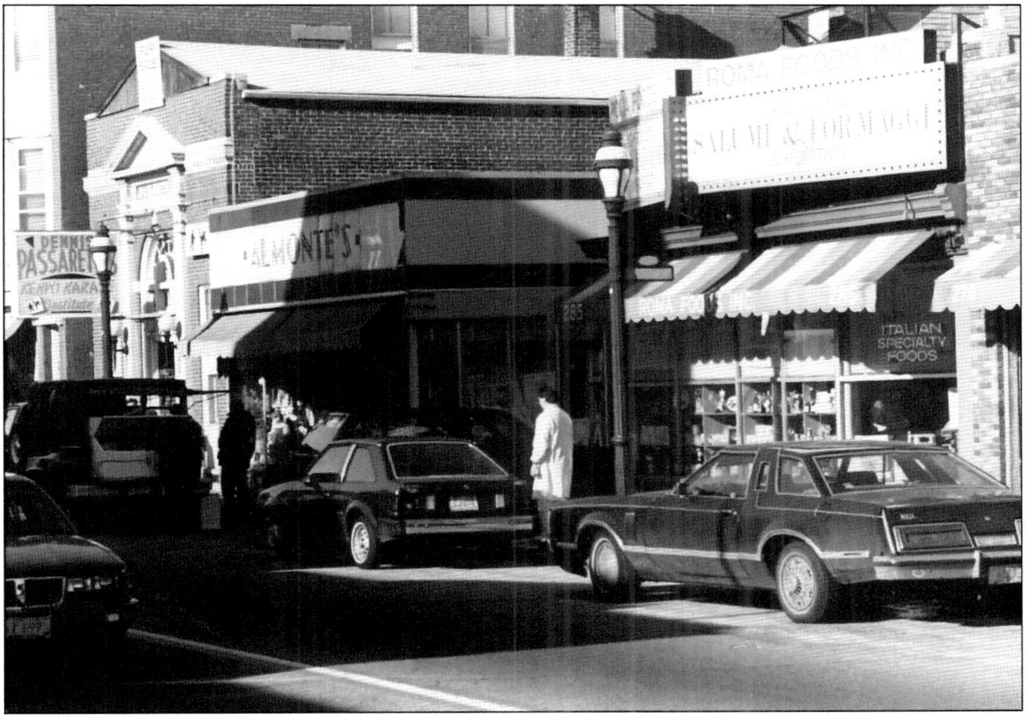

The Hill, old or new, is always a crowded, bustling place. Roma Foods is no longer at this location, but across the street, bigger and better is Almonte's, an eternal staple of the community, for Mr. Almonte, in his nineties, is still on the job every day. Photo collection of Joe Fuoco.

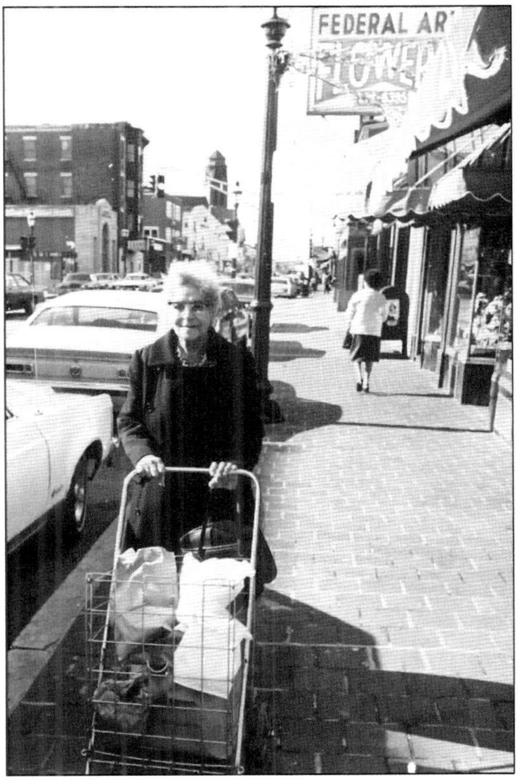

This is a view of the Hill a number of years ago. Notice the bell tower in the distance. The tower belonged to St. John's Church and was demolished after a bitter protest by its parishioners. Photo collection of Joe Fuoco.

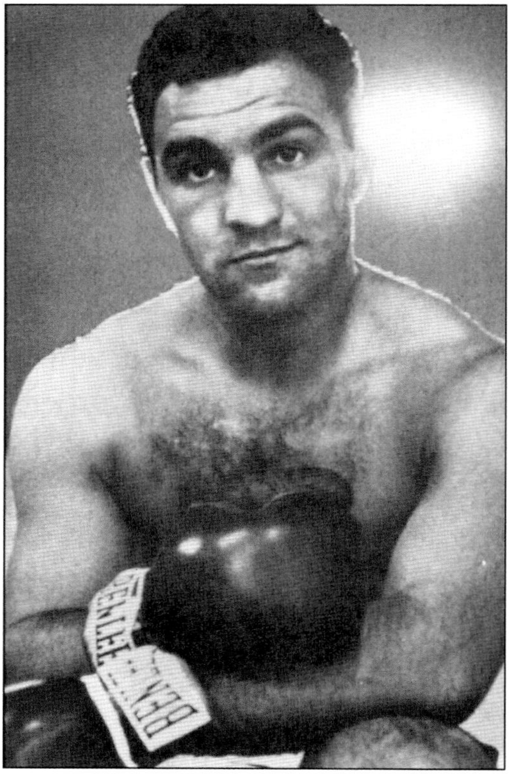

Even sports heroes and legends came to the Hill, especially to the Aurora Club on Broadway. Here is Rocky Marciano in the 1950s. He was a frequent visitor to the Hill.

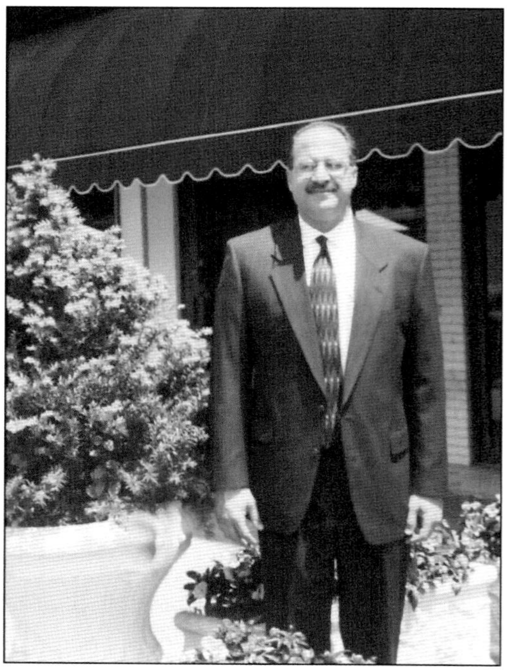

A very familiar person on Federal Hill, born there, raised there, and working there in his law firm on famed Broadway, is 13th Ward Councilman John Lombardi. He is standing here on beautiful De Pasquale Square not far from the magnificent fountain. John is at the very forefront of the great restoration and renaissance on the Hill. He speaks of himself as "married to the Hill."

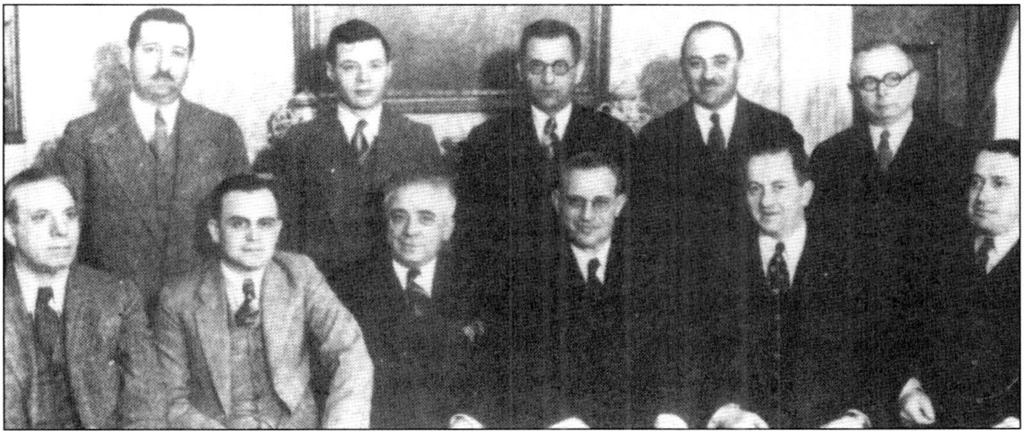

This is an august assembly of the members of the Aurora Club, an Italian-American club on the Hill. This historic photo is of the Aurora Club's first officers and board of directors (1932).

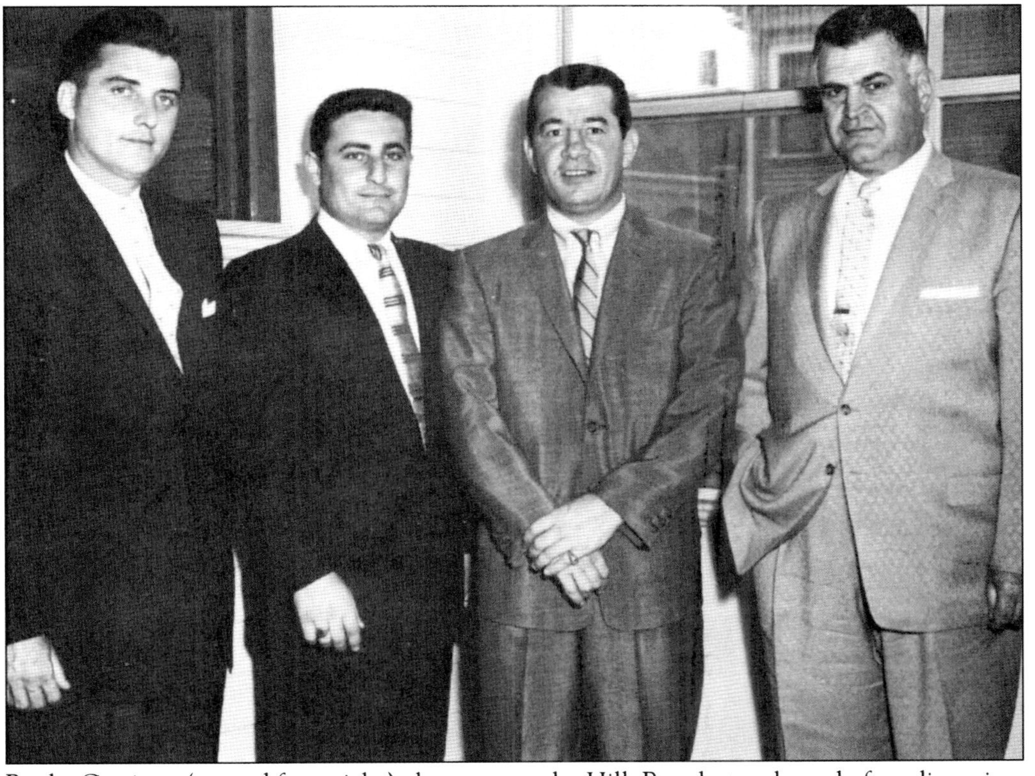

Rocky Graziano (second from right) also came to the Hill. Rough, tough, and often disarming, this former boxer was something of a gentleman at the Aurora Club.

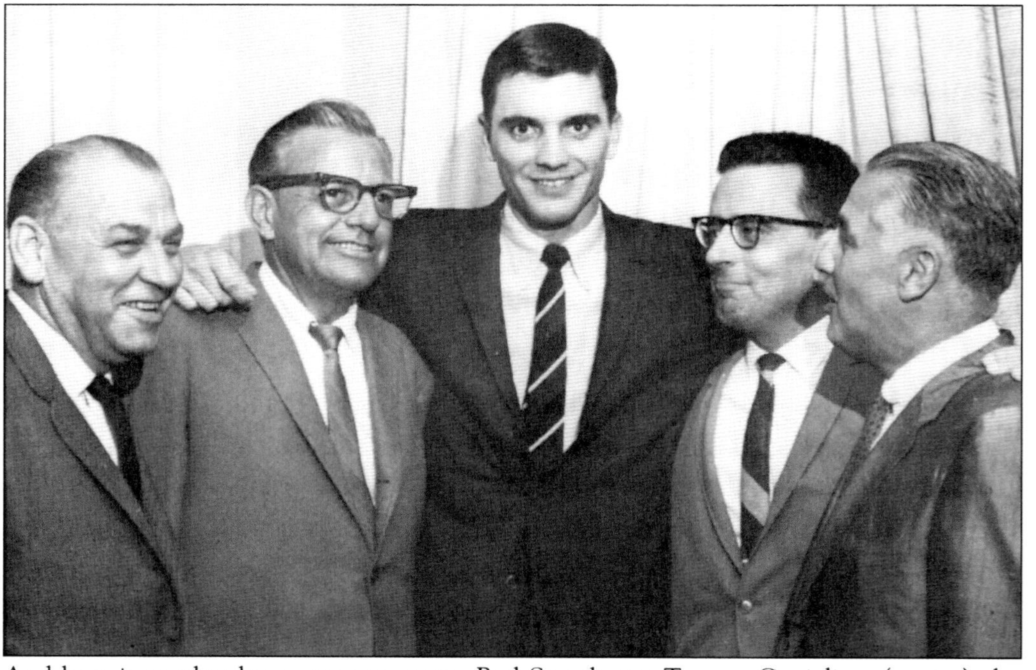

And here is another hero, gone too soon. Red Sox slugger Tommy Conigliaro (center) also visited the Aurora Club. With him are former governors, mayors, and prominent businessmen.

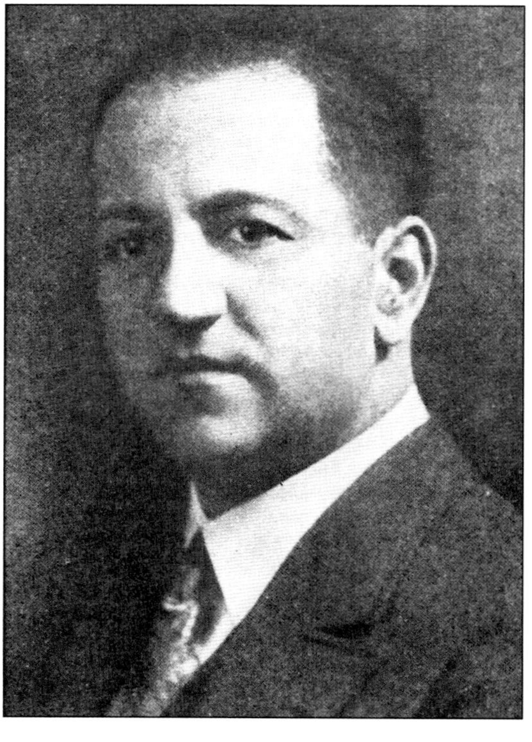

This is a dramatic portrait of "Mr. Aurora" Vincent Sorrentino, who rose from a jeweler's apprentice to the president of the Uncas Manufacturing Company. He defined the successful Italian American, for he was a self-made success and did not forget his origins.

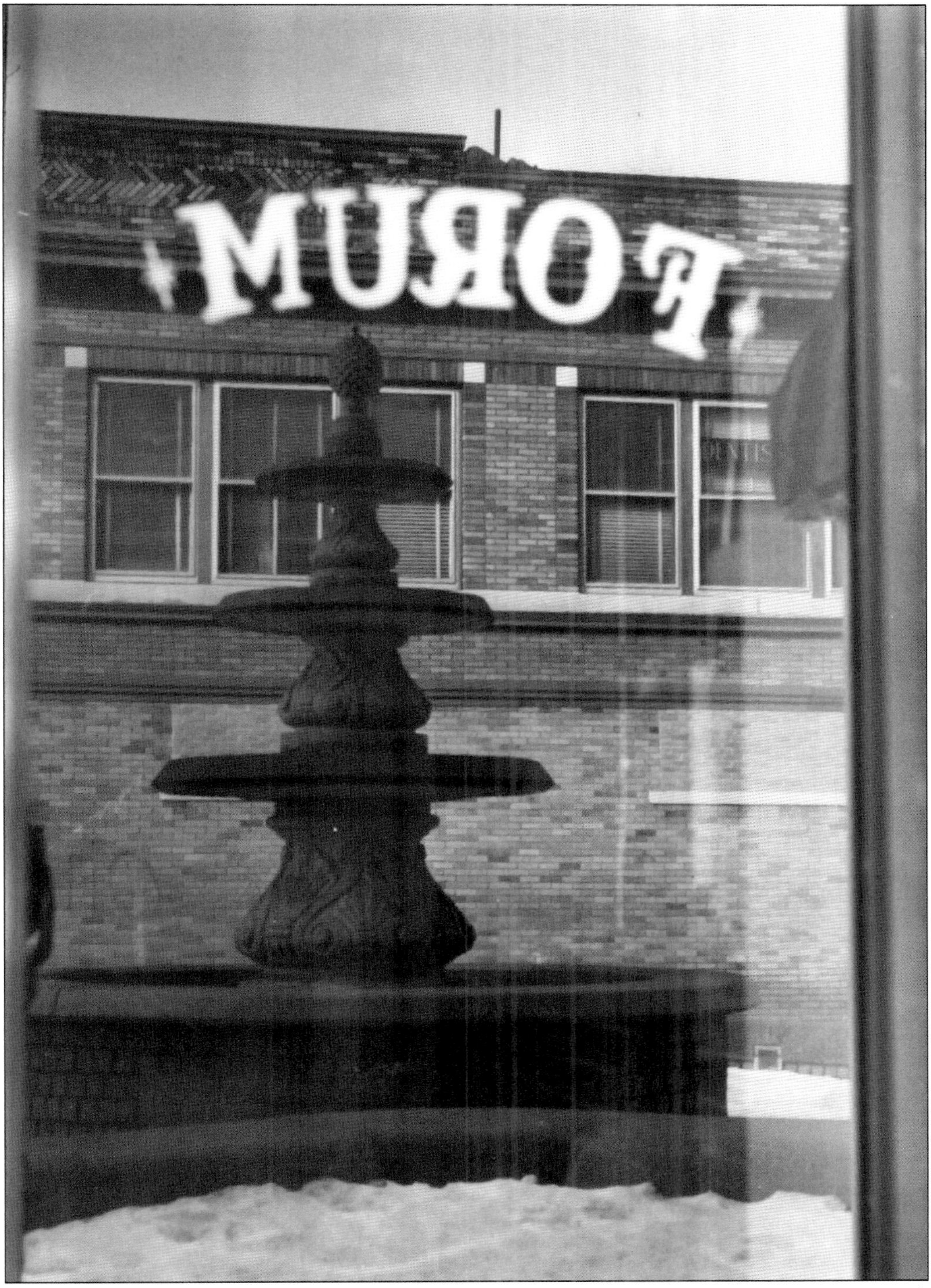

The Forum is no more, but it occupied one of the beautiful buildings on the plaza. A superb restaurant, the Forum reflected the glory of ancient Rome. This shot is from within the Forum looking out to the plaza. Photo collection of Joe Fuoco.

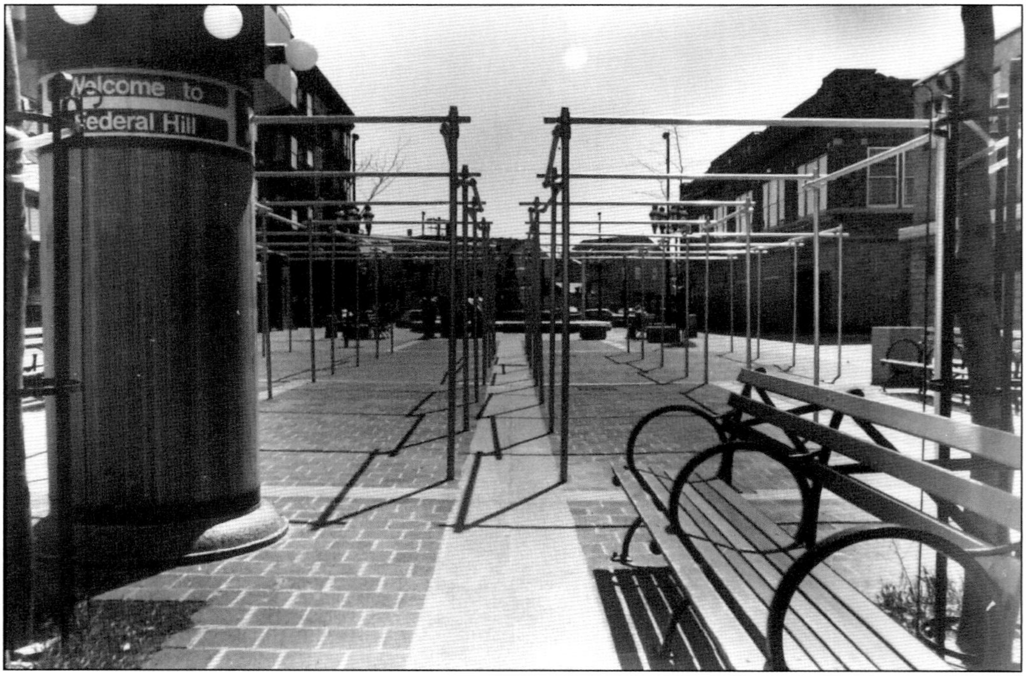

This is the way the great plaza looked before it became open. This view is looking toward Atwells Avenue. The fountain is in the distance but is obscured by the network of metal poles. Today, concerts are given in the plaza. Photo collection of Joe Fuoco.

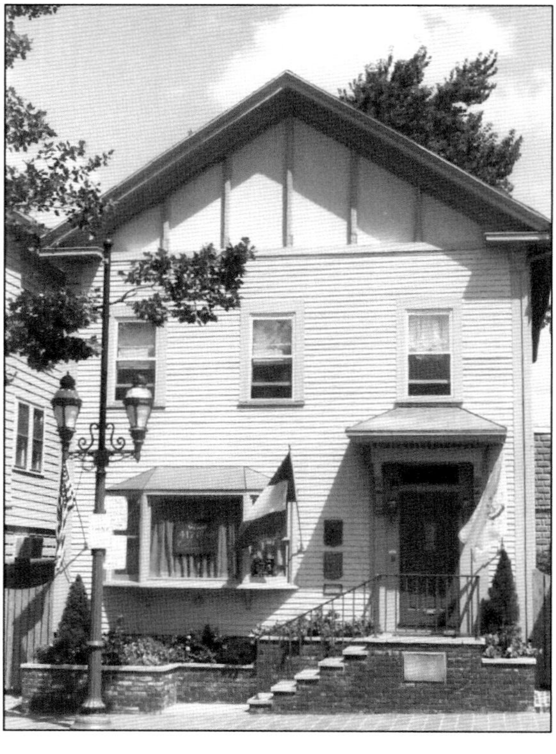

Art is on the Hill—well, it was. This beautiful building was home to an art gallery until several years as ago. Today, the Hill, moving more and more into the arts, is considering establishing a gallery on Atwells Avenue. Photo collection of Joe Fuoco.

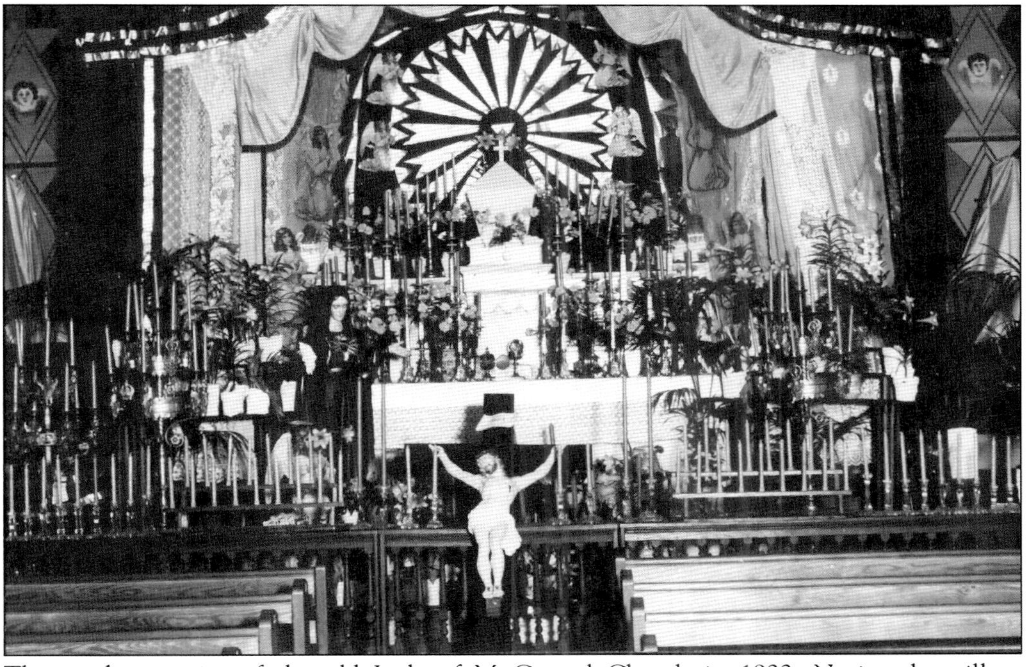

This is the interior of the old Lady of Mt.Carmel Church in 1922. Notice the village preoccupation with baroque decoration, a reflection of the ways of the immigrants. The decorations are for Easter week. The old church at the corner of Brayton and Spruce Streets was later used as the rectory and for parish activities once the new church was built. Photo courtesy of Frank Melucci.

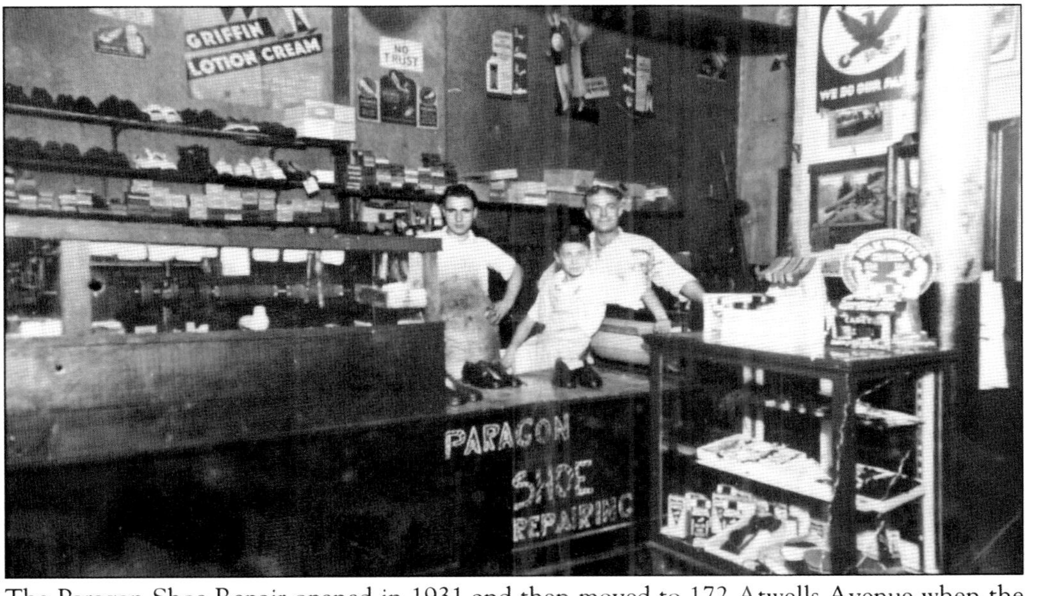

The Paragon Shoe Repair opened in 1931 and then moved to 172 Atwells Avenue when the building burned. Pictured are Angelo Melucci, owner (right rear); ten-year-old Frank Melucci (center); and Frank Carcieri (left rear). Angelo remained at 172, a building owned by the Caldarone's, until his death at the age of 84 in 1979. Photo courtesy of Frank Melucci.

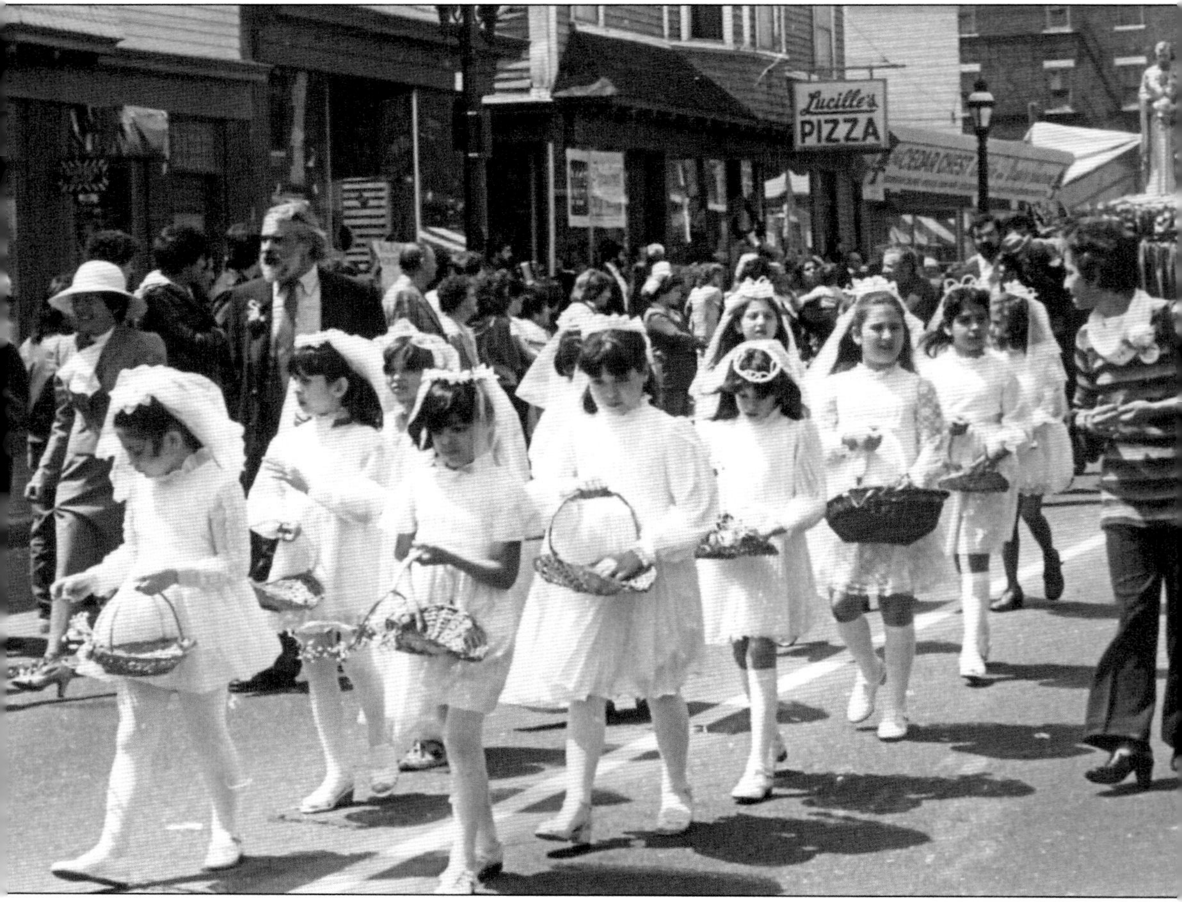

So long as there is a Federal Hill, there will be processions. They are a part of the tradition, even the lore of the Hill. This procession from the 1970s shows girls in communion dress dropping flowers in the street. The statue of St. Joseph, for whom one of the biggest feasts on the Hill is celebrated, follows. Photo collection of Joe Fuoco.

Nine

Up the Avenue Today

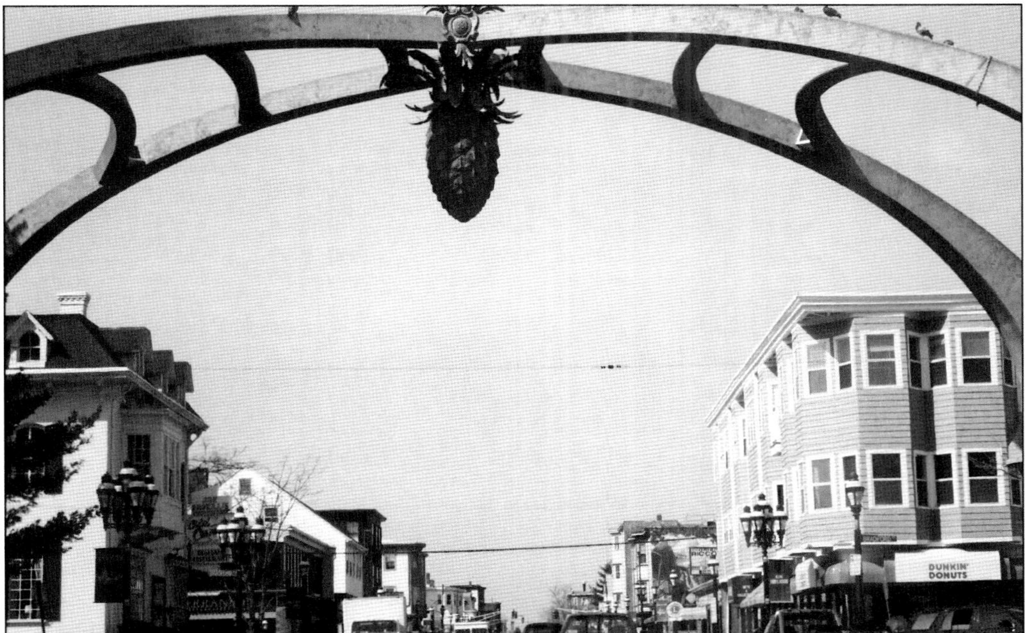

This is the greeting, the welcome, looking up Atwells Avenue today. The skyline has changed. Remember the bell tower of St. John's? It is no longer there. The building to the right has been completely restored, and already renovations, like siding, painting, reinforcing, etc., can be detected.

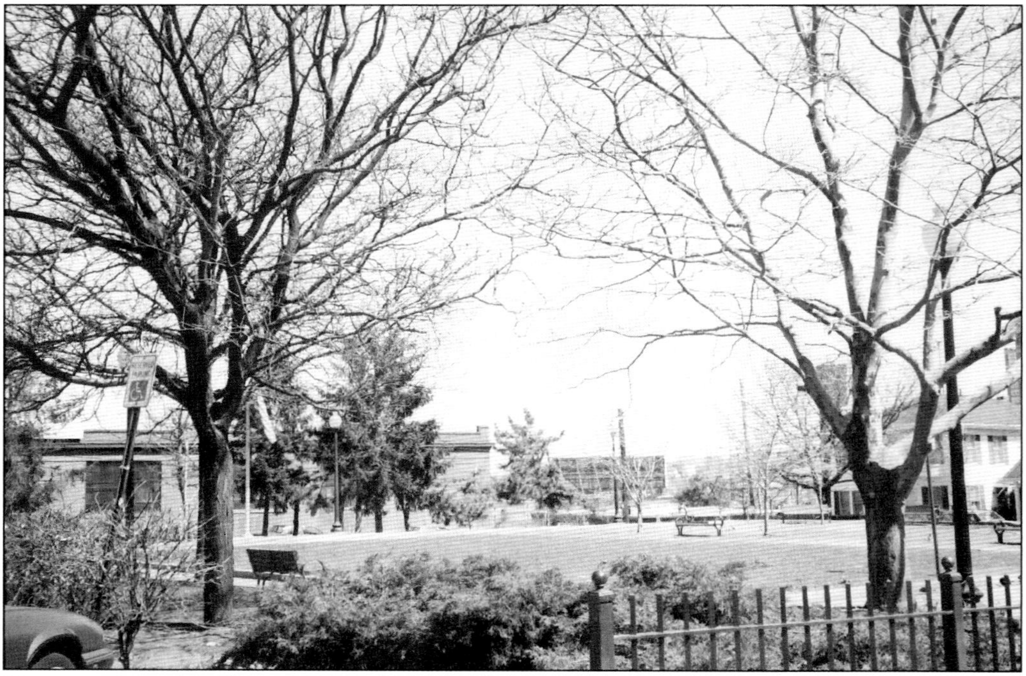

Here on summer nights, the people of the high-rise apartments across the street and others come to sit, to play music, to eat, and to talk in this park just under the arch.

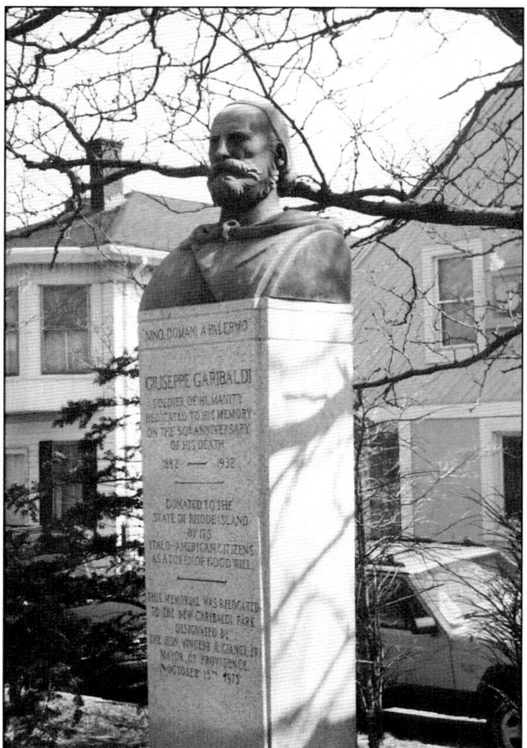

A monument to Italian patriot Giuseppe Garibaldi in the park is almost forgotten. Few seem to know it is there standing at the edge. Yet, this monument's bronze head of the Italian Unifier, dedicated in 1932, faces Atwells Avenue.

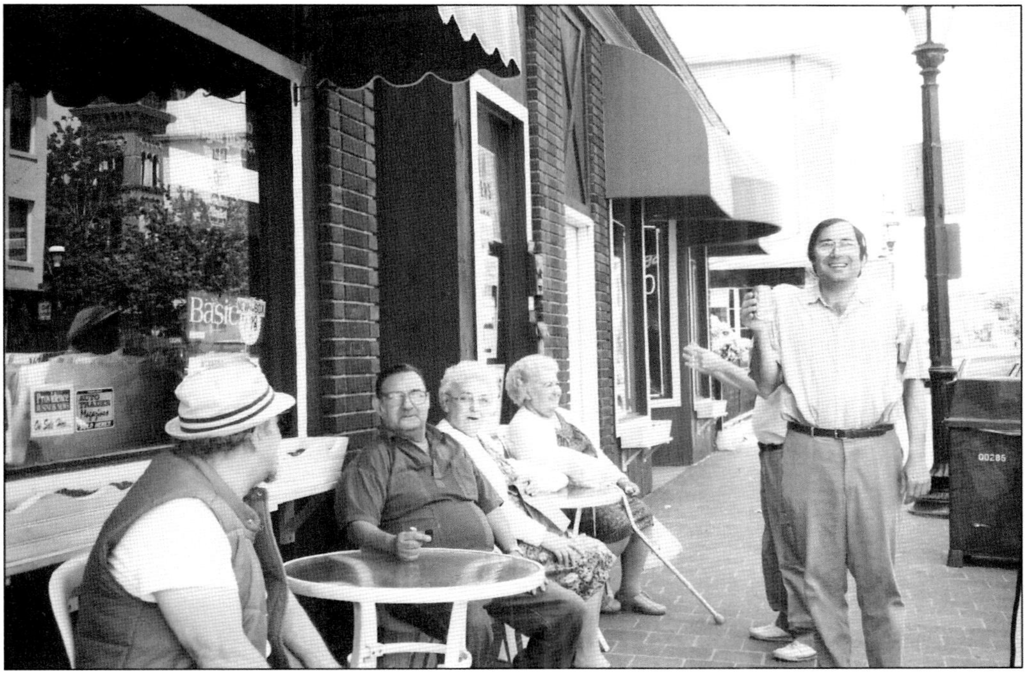

People of the Hill sit daily at the tables along Atwells Avenue here in front of Bradford Variety. Facing us is a smiling Tommy Dwyer, a Hill-ite from day one: born here, educated here, still here, and loving it here.

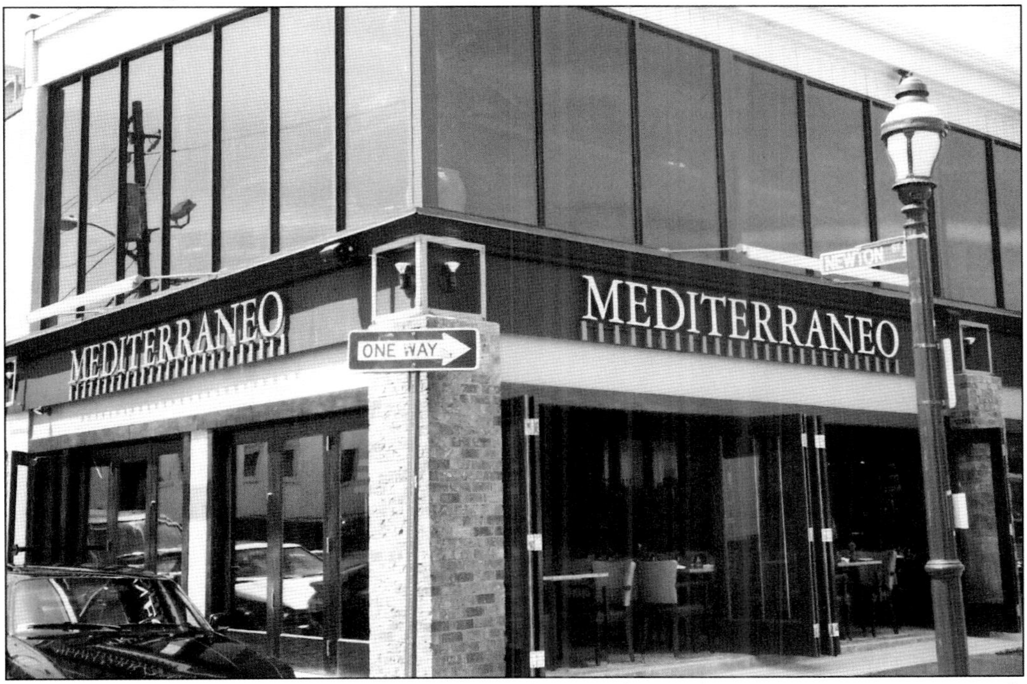

An open-air restaurant in the style of European bistros, the Mediterraneo is as young as a colt and appeals especially to the young, for the Hill is getting younger and younger.

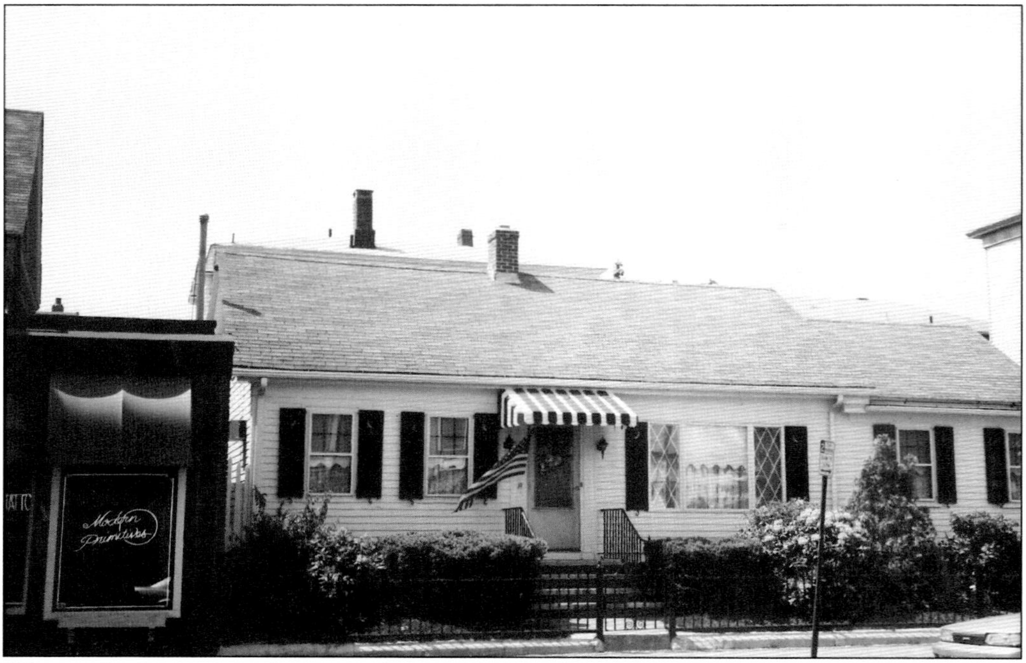

What is this house doing here? Looking unlikely and even incongruous, this lovely home which has been here for many years sits between a florist shop and a tattoo parlor. Across the street is also a famous restaurant. Somehow, it fits in with the area.

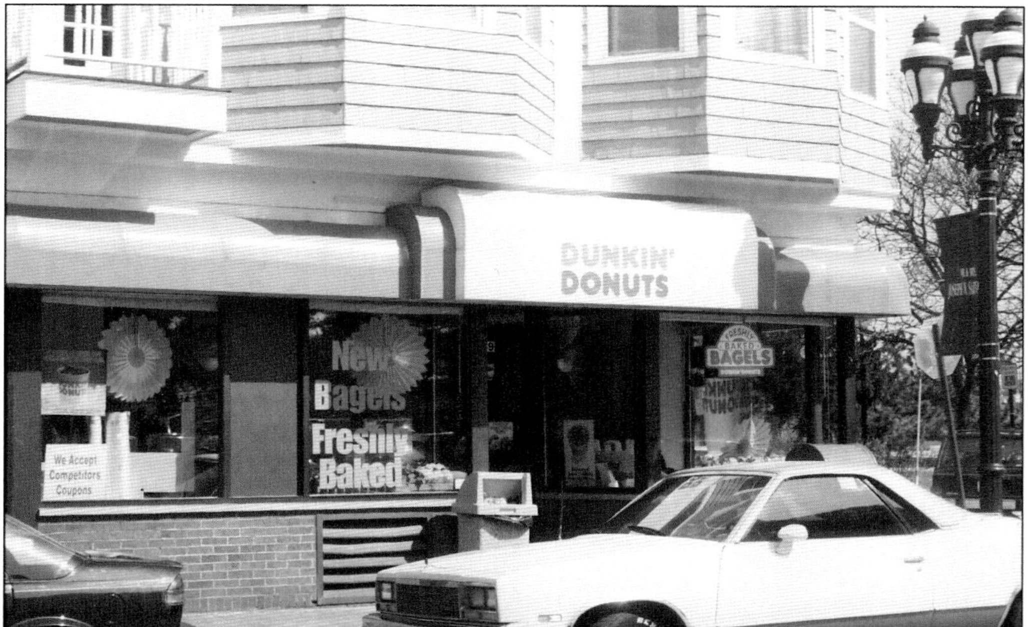

Did anybody ever think that Dunkin' Donuts would come to Italian Federal Hill? Well, it has come, and it is a welcome sight among coffee and bagel lovers. The Hill is in flux, changing all the time.

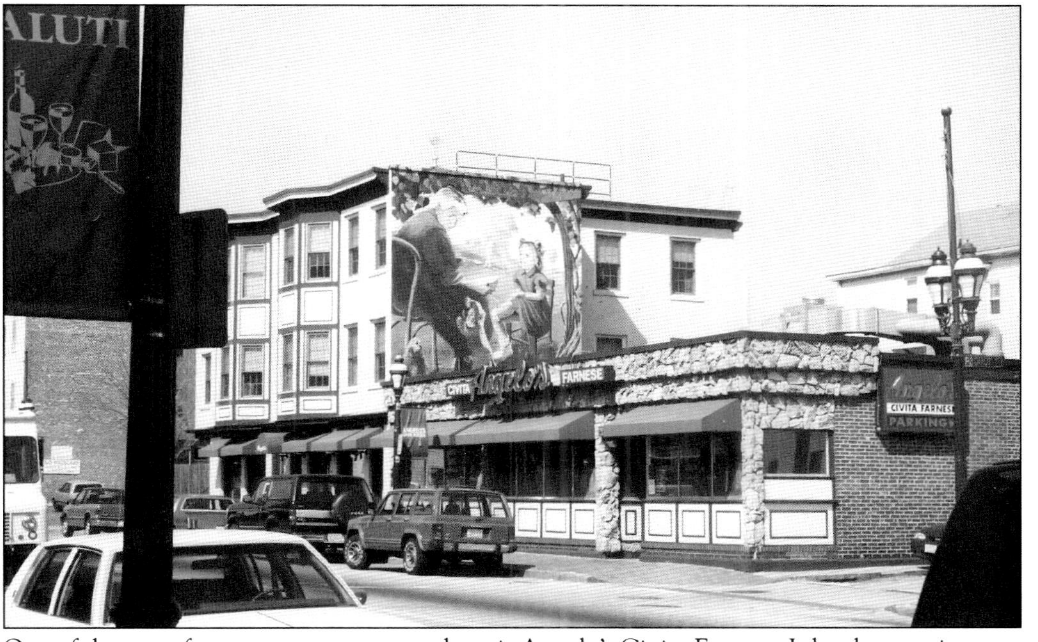

One of the most famous restaurants anywhere is Angelo's Civita Farnese. It has been written up in the most prestigious magazines in America. So taken by the place was film director Michael Corrente that he filmed critical scenes inside and out. Notice the superb mural on the wall of a loving grandmother and her granddaughter.

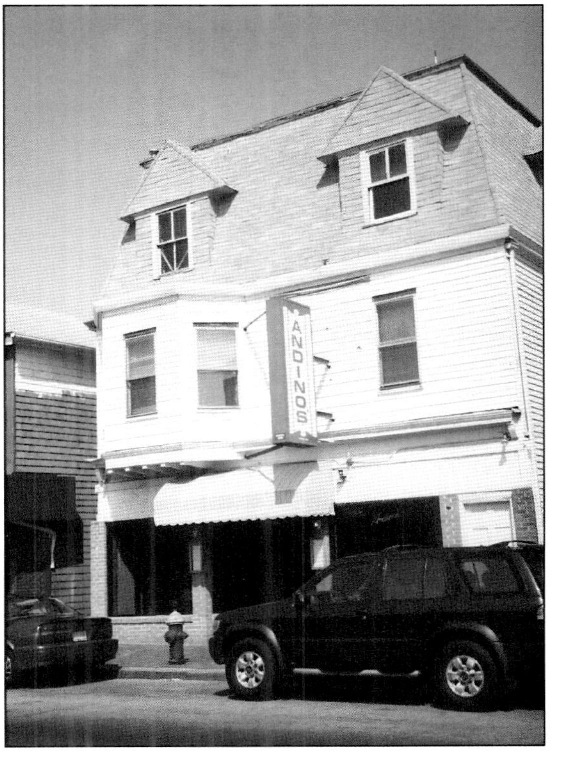

The Hill is home to over forty restaurants, and the list continues to grow. Here Andino's, a warm, neighborly restaurant, is separated by only a few feet from Cassarino's, a restaurant with a lovely upstairs dining area and fine view of the avenue.

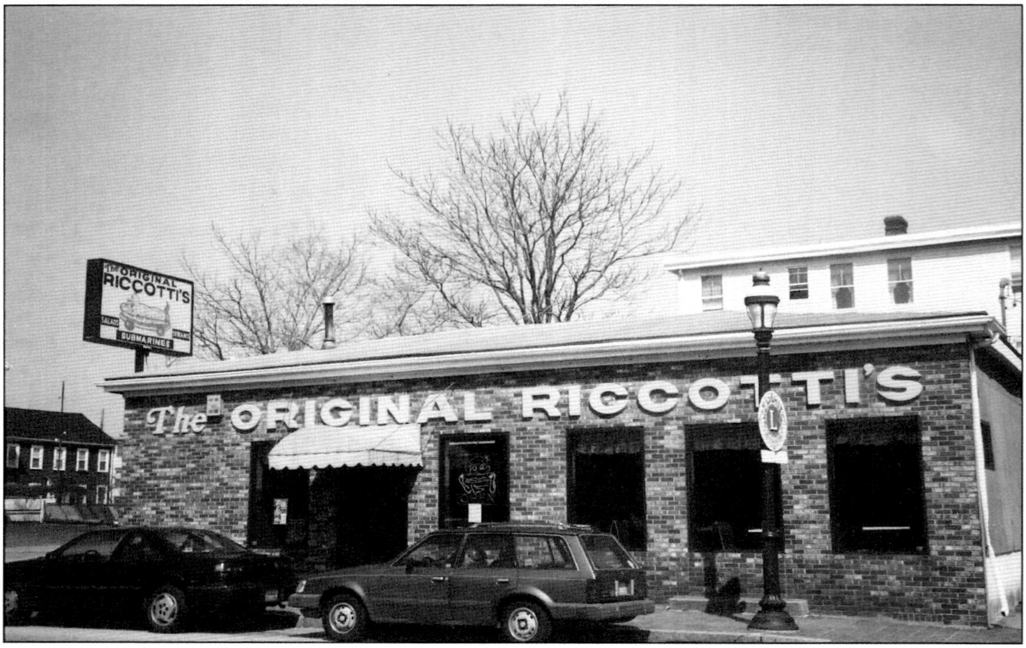

Yes, even the Hill has condescended to fast food here and there. Ricotti's sits next to famed Angelo's and across the street from the very famous Old Canteen and the new Mediterraneo. There is room for every taste!

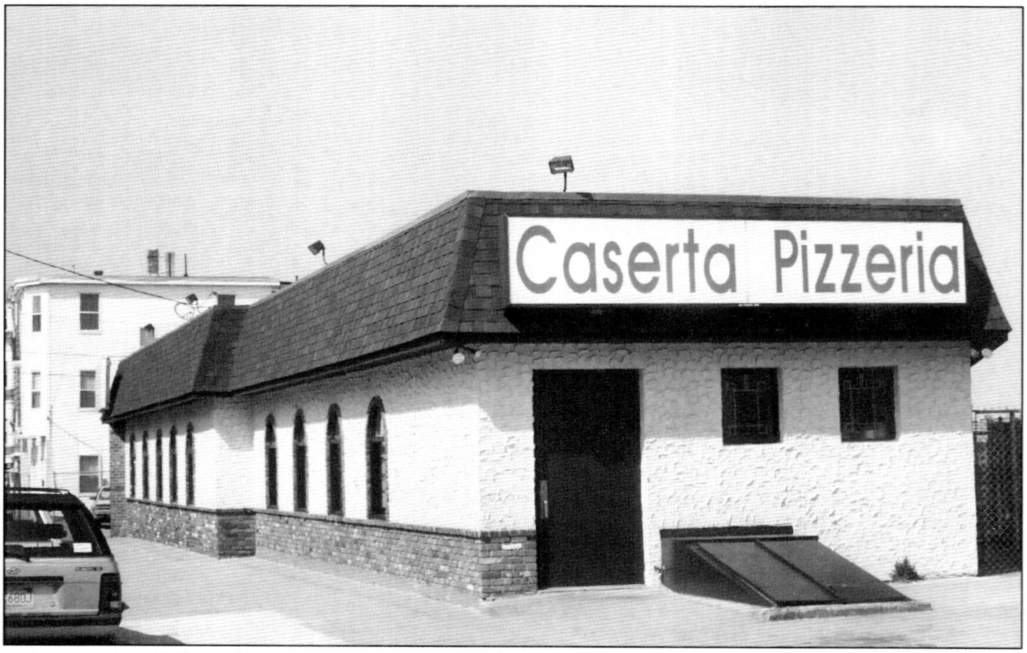

What is the Hill without pizza? It is unthinkable. Federal Hill boasts a Ronzio's, a Sicilia's Pizzeria, and the most famous of all, Caserta Pizzeria. Not to have tried Caserta's is a sin, and not to have eaten pizza on the Hill, whether it be of the gourmet style on the plaza or the basic kind anywhere else, is a mortal sin.

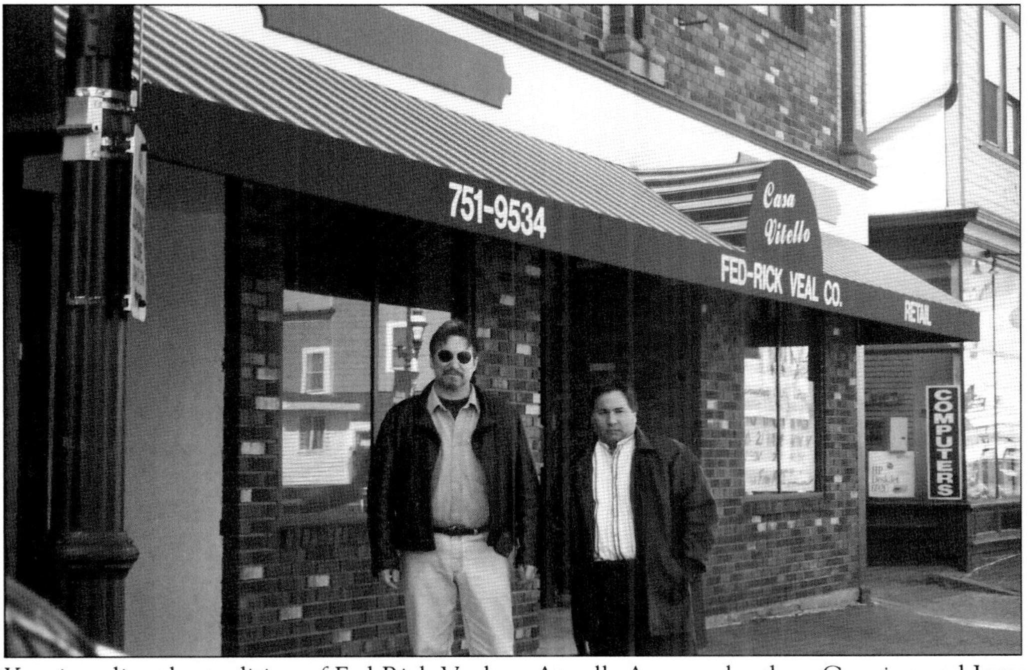

Keeping alive the tradition of Fed-Rick Veal on Atwells Avenue, brothers Carmine and Jerry Balzano have expanded their business. They have served veal to everybody, even the Olympic teams in Atlanta. Their business is a family tradition going back to their father.

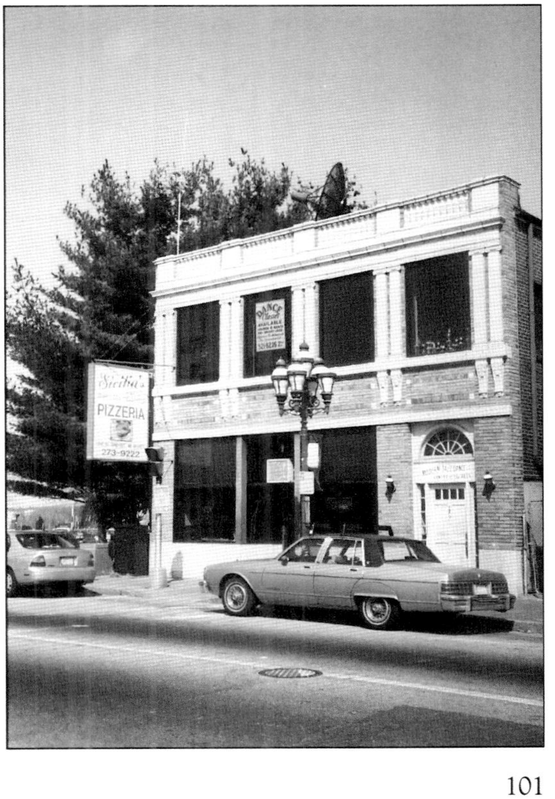

A pizzeria is on the first floor and a ballet studio on the second. This is the way it is today on Federal Hill.

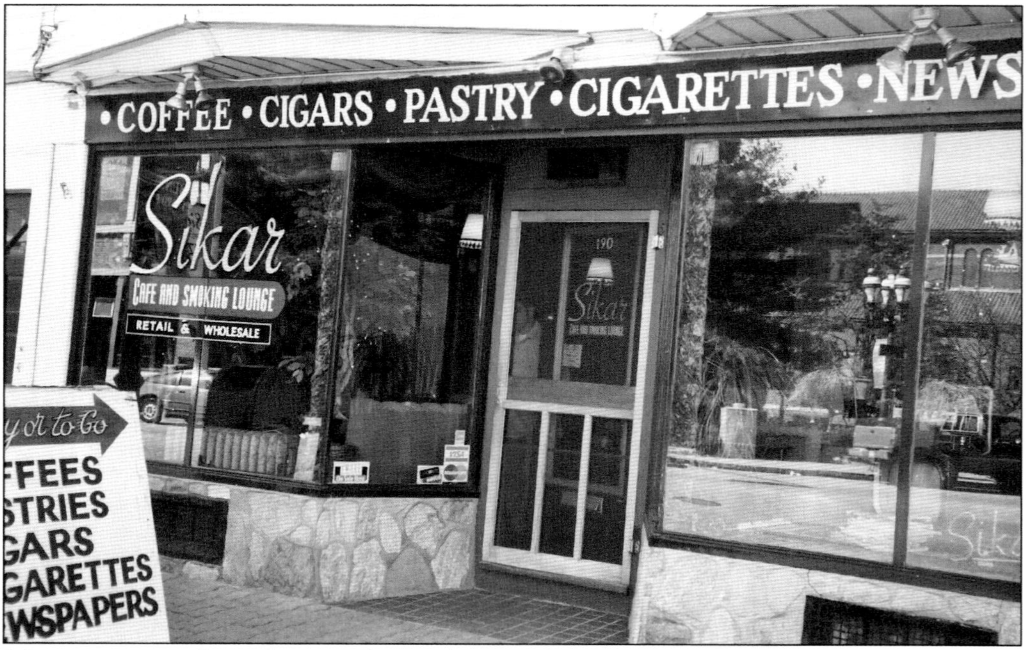

Sikar is—yes, on the Hill—a smoking palace, a salon for smokers who may sit, if they wish, in the windows above the street and relax as they watch the action on the avenue.

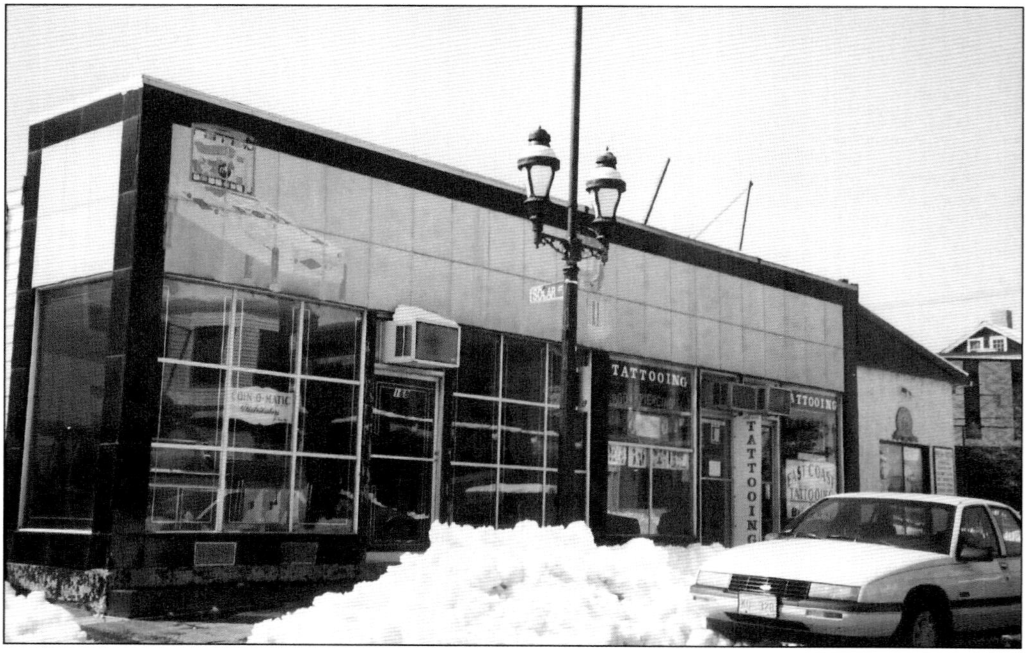

Famed and infamous, the Coin-O-Matic next to a tattoo parlor (there are three on the Hill) enjoys its own dark history, for according to the FBI, this was the headquarters of Raymond L.S. Patriarca, reputed late crime boss of legendary status. Whatever it may have been, it has a certain allure the visitor to the Hill cannot ignore.

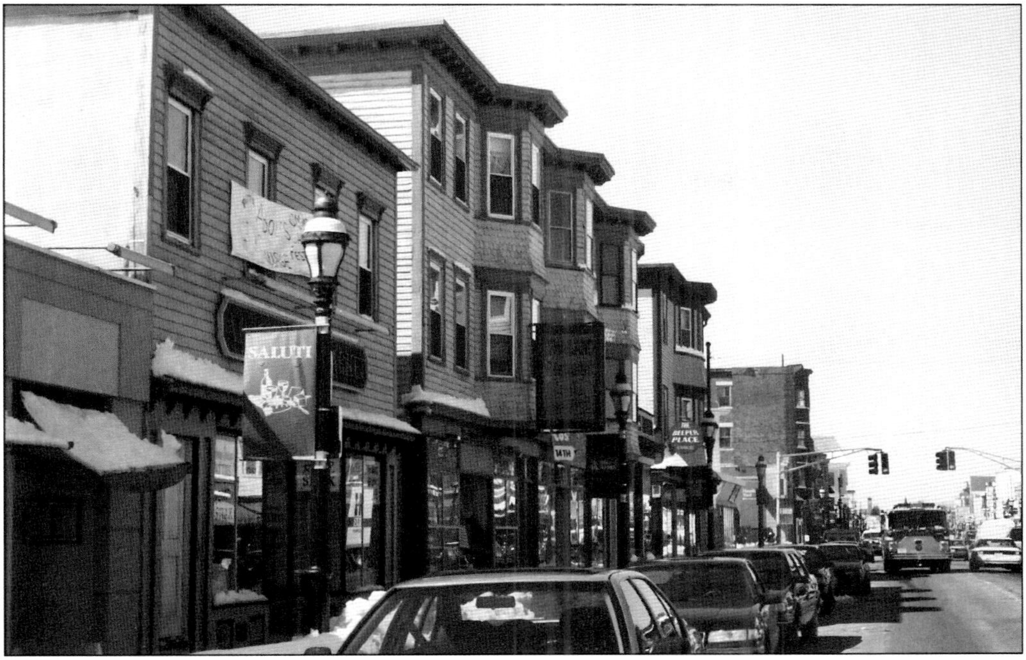

This is a view looking up Atwells toward the barely visible bell tower of the Holy Ghost Church in the distance. From this angle, the Hill looks very much as it has for over sixty years.

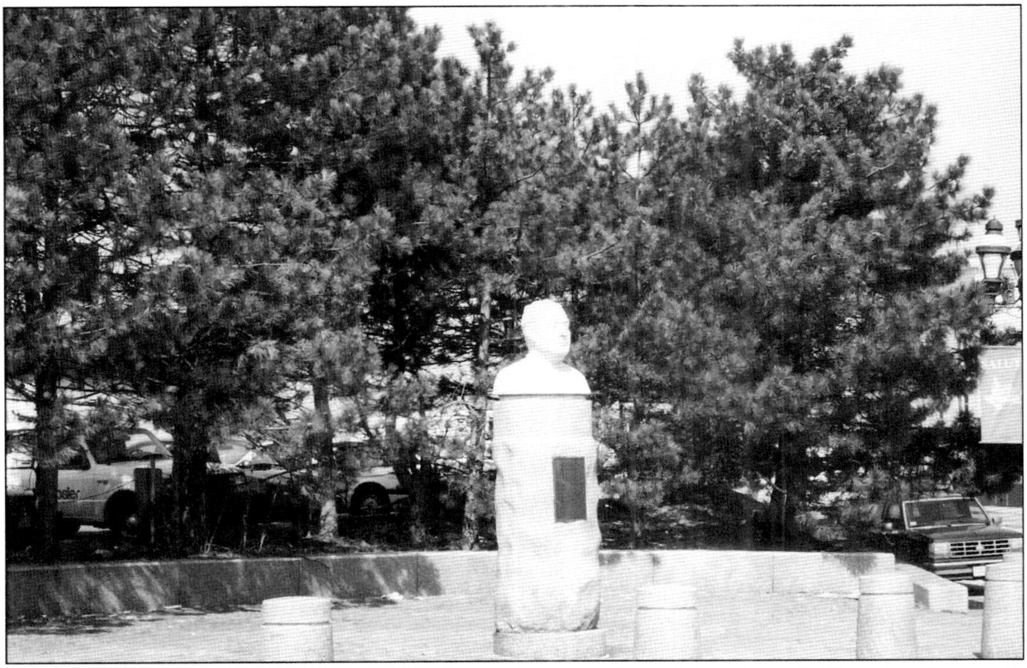

Monsignor Galliano Cavallaro was a pastor of Our Lady of Mt. Carmel Church who made such an impact on the Hill that this monument was dedicated to him in a small park.

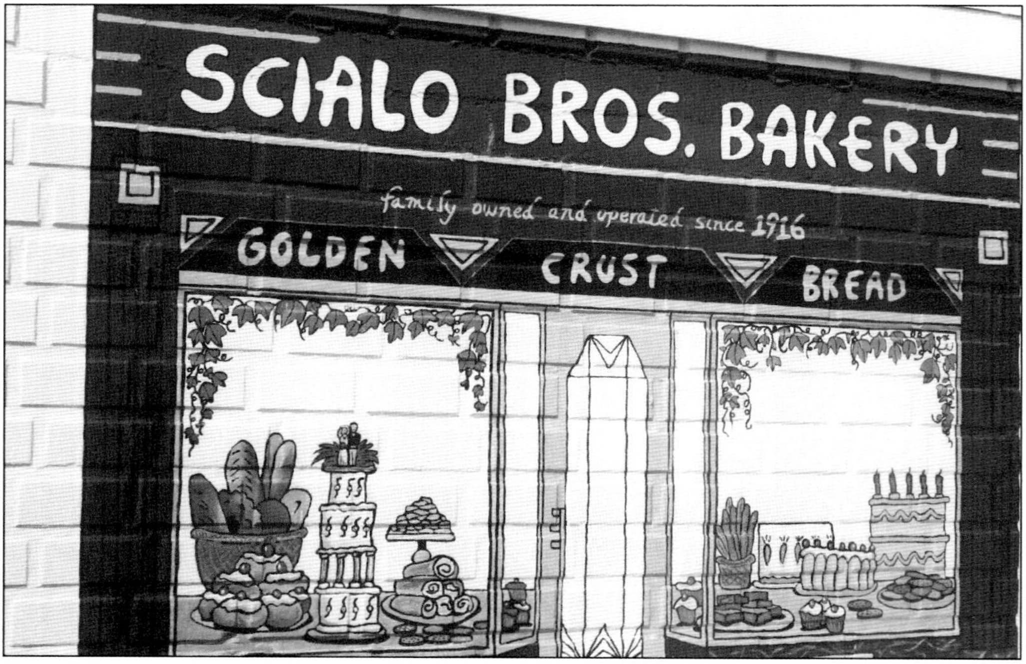

One of the most famous bakeries in Rhode Island, Scialo's goes back generations to its founder. What you are looking at is a mural painted on cinder blocks, a duplicate of the real main entrance around the corner.

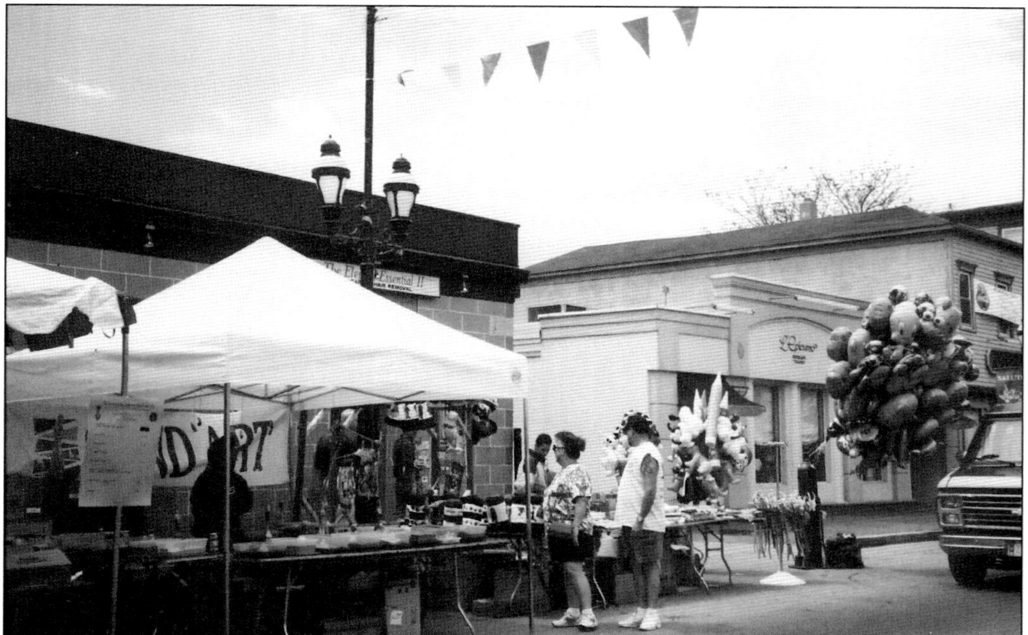
Feasts and festivals fill the streets several times a year. This is a street fair photographed on Memorial Day.

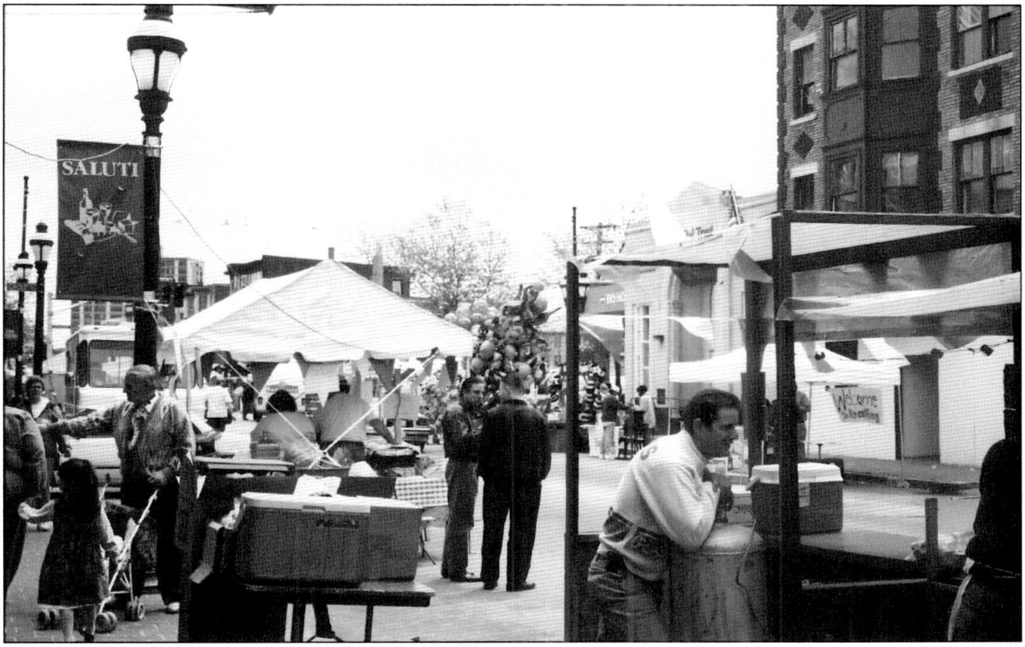

Food, conversation, doughboys, pizza, sausage and peppers, veal, pasta of all kinds, and a myriad of foods associated with Italians create an aroma in the streets for four days and nights. Federal Hill has become famous for its festivals.

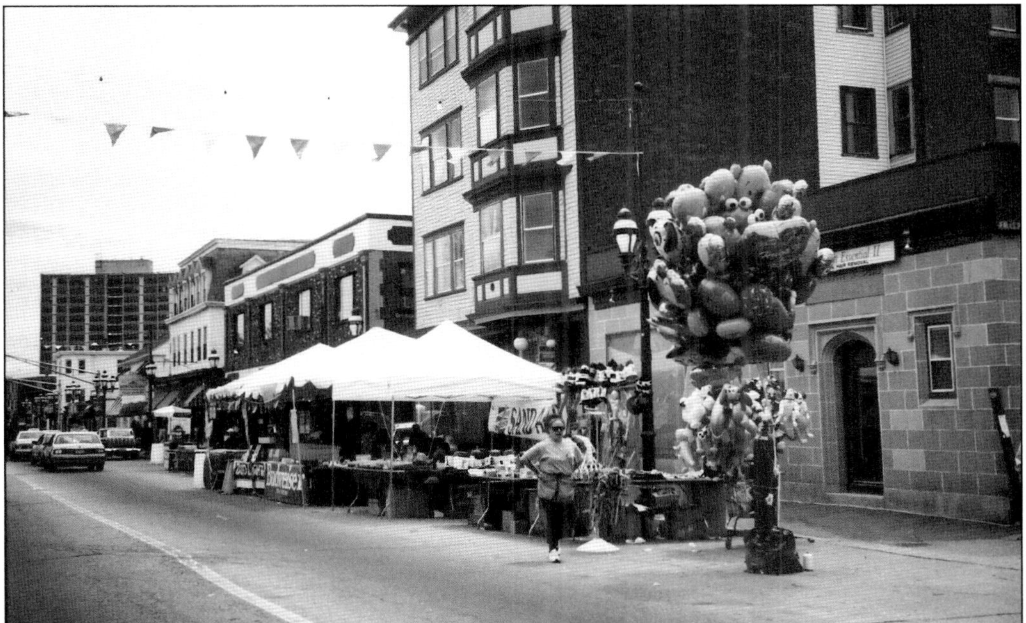

Everything is available, from sandals to African sculptures and from jewelry to balloons. Crafts and works of a variety of people from different cultures have added to the richness of the Hill.

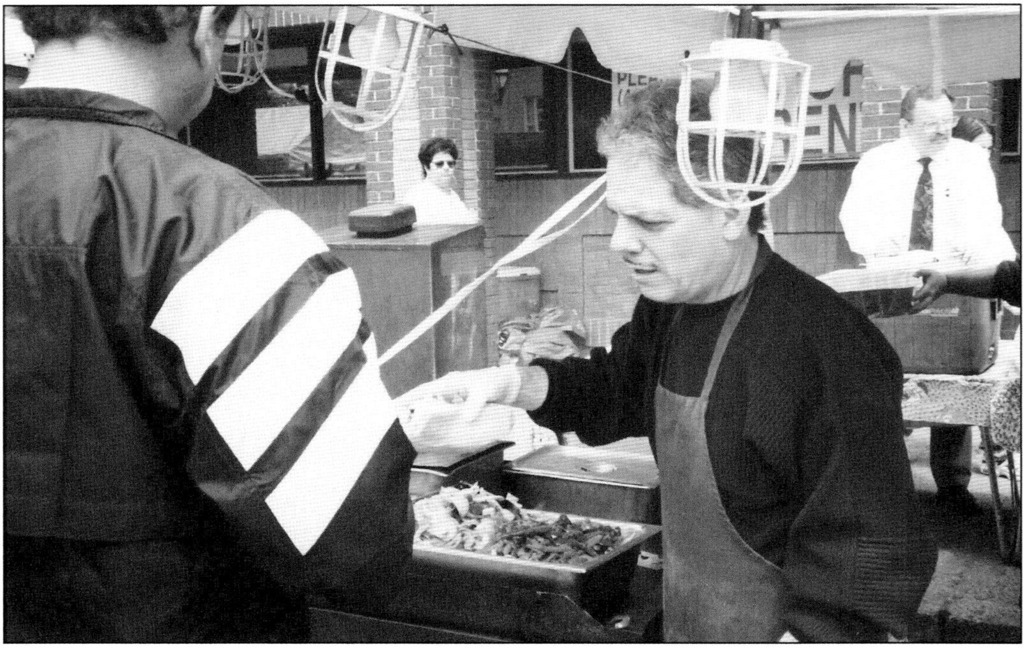

This vendor has cooked sausage and peppers, with great ringlets of onions, in the open, and his food is delicious.

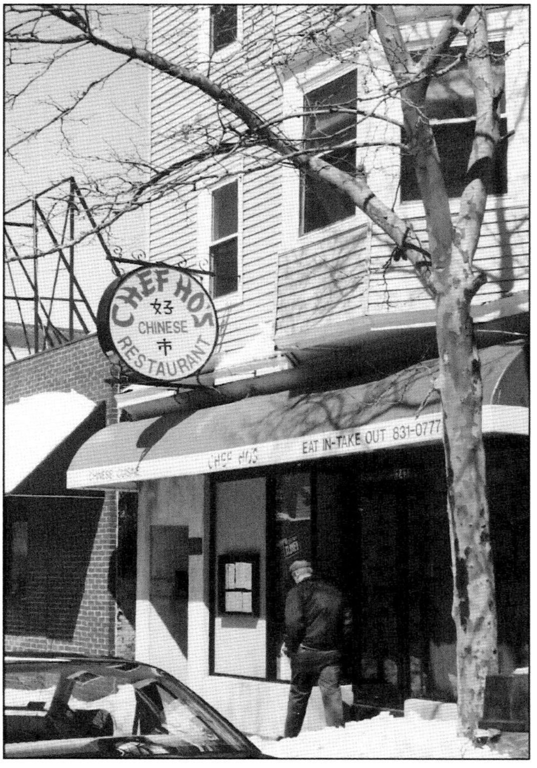

Chinese food invaded the Hill some years ago, and it has stayed. Who doesn't like Chinese food? The cuisines of a number of ethnic peoples are represented on the Hill. As a result, Federal Hill has become a mecca for people who must love to eat and eat well.

This is an unusual and beautiful view of the plaza and the fountain looking out to Atwells Avenue. This same place was once covered with metal poles; now clear, it serves as a true al fresco dining experience, as it should.

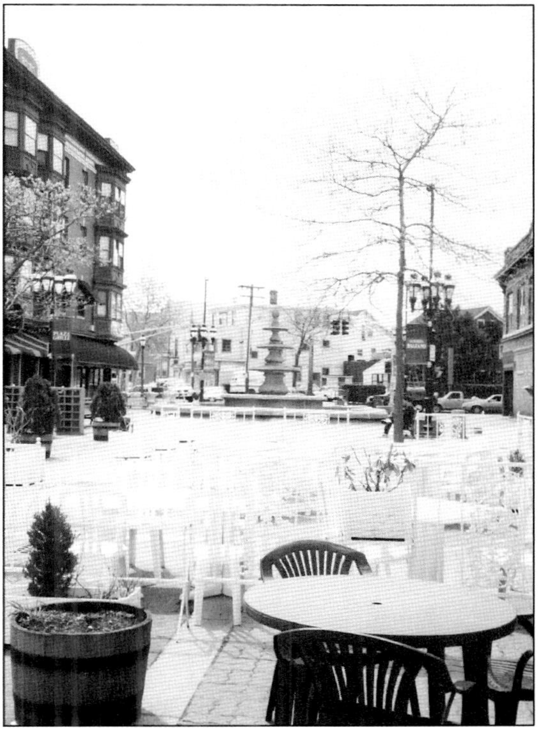

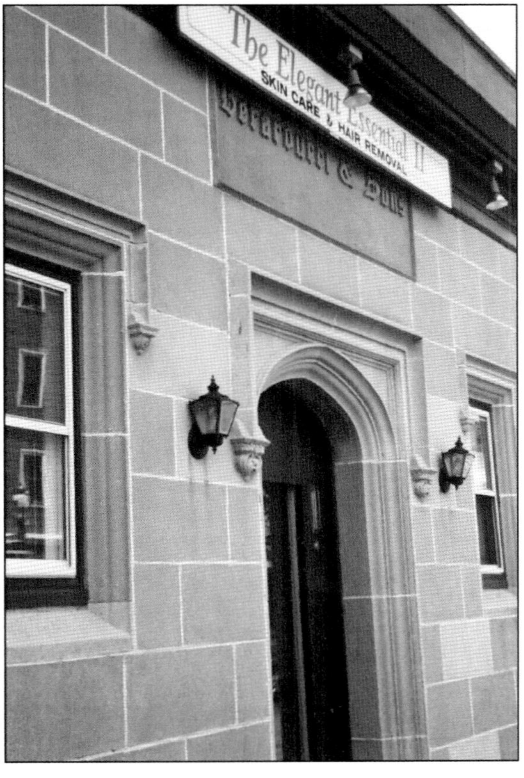

Underneath the sign advertising skin care and hair removal, notice the Gothic letters that spell out Berarducci & Sons. This was a funeral home, looking properly gothic and ecclesiastical. The new home, in a magnificent mansion on Broadway, opened in 1946.

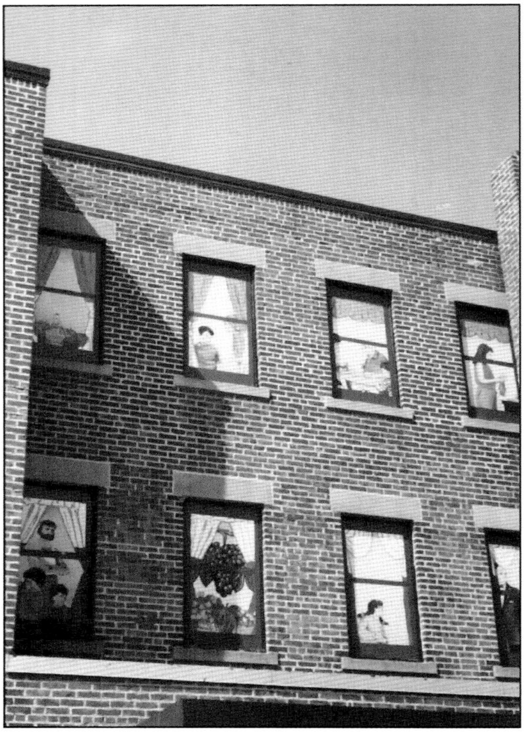

These are not people looking out, but painted faces in the painted windows of Gasbarro's Liquors. The Hill is ablaze, literally, with murals everywhere one looks.

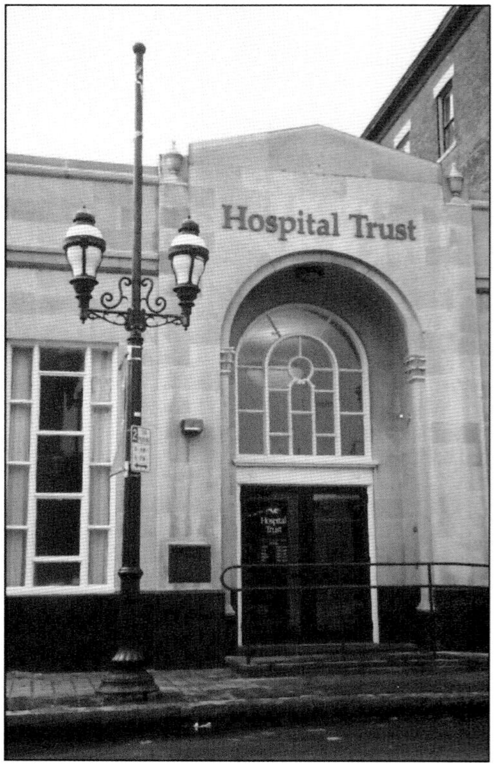

The Hospital Trust Bank, recently remodeled, but so aware of its unique architecture, has kept its outside virtually intact.

This view is looking up Atwells toward the overpass in the distance. Atwells Avenue is just under one mile. Again, on the wall of Gasbarro's is a mural painted by a Rhode Island School of Design artist depicting a mythical Italian town atop a hill.

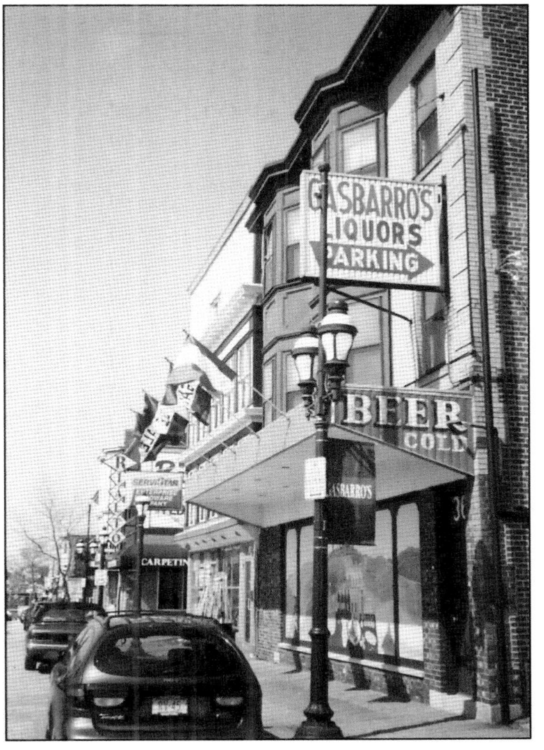

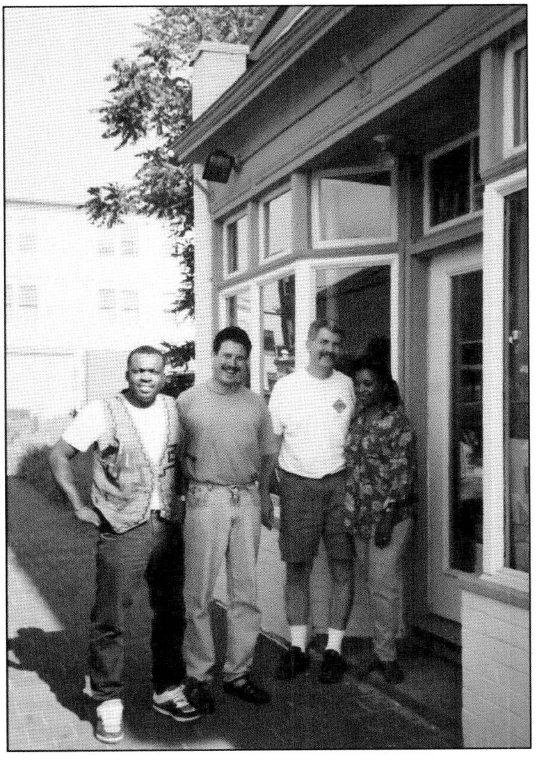

An absolutely new look on the avenue is Montego Bay, a Caribbean restaurant offering spicy foods from the Islands. Pictured are, from left to right: Raymond Baker, executive chef; Dan La Combe, manager; and owners Douglas and Denese Carpenter. This new, beautiful restaurant joins established watering holes and famed dining rooms of the Hill, bringing new life to the far end of Federal Hill.

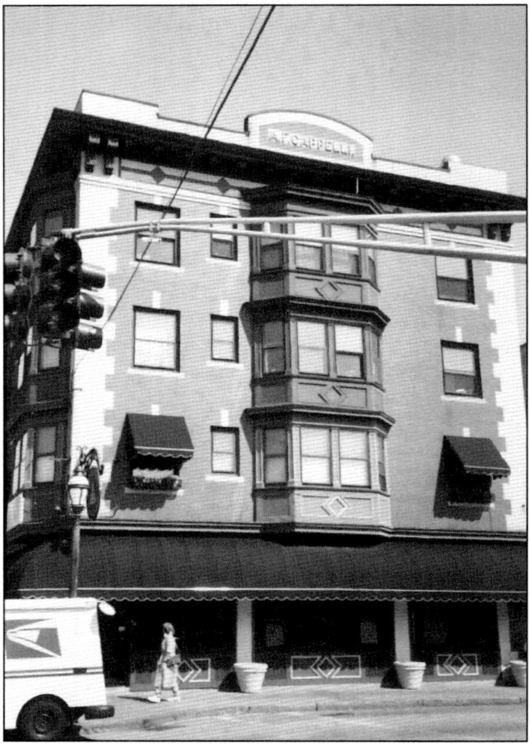

Venda Ravioli is where the world, it seems, comes to buy virgin olive oil, scrumptious breads, and ravioli of every variety imaginable. This building was also the headquarters of Michael Corrente's film company while filming Federal Hill.

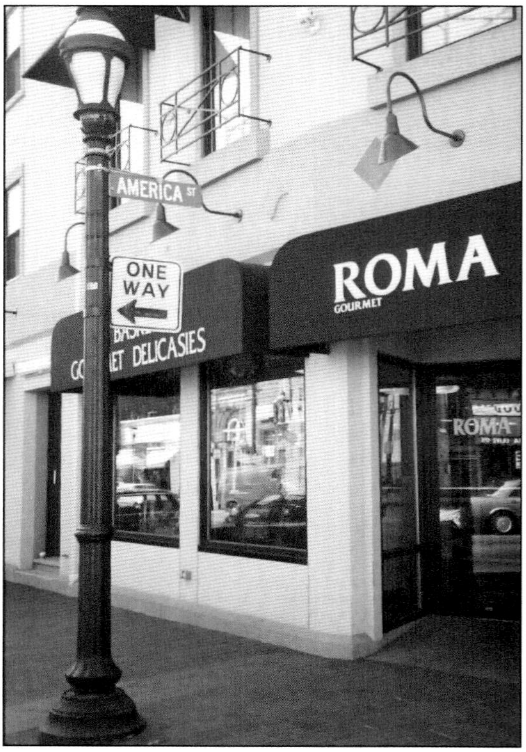

Roma Food's new home is sparkling, flooded with light, and filled with foods and delicacies and imported miracles of Italian cuisine. Located once across the street, this is a double- or triple-size version. Roma is known everywhere.

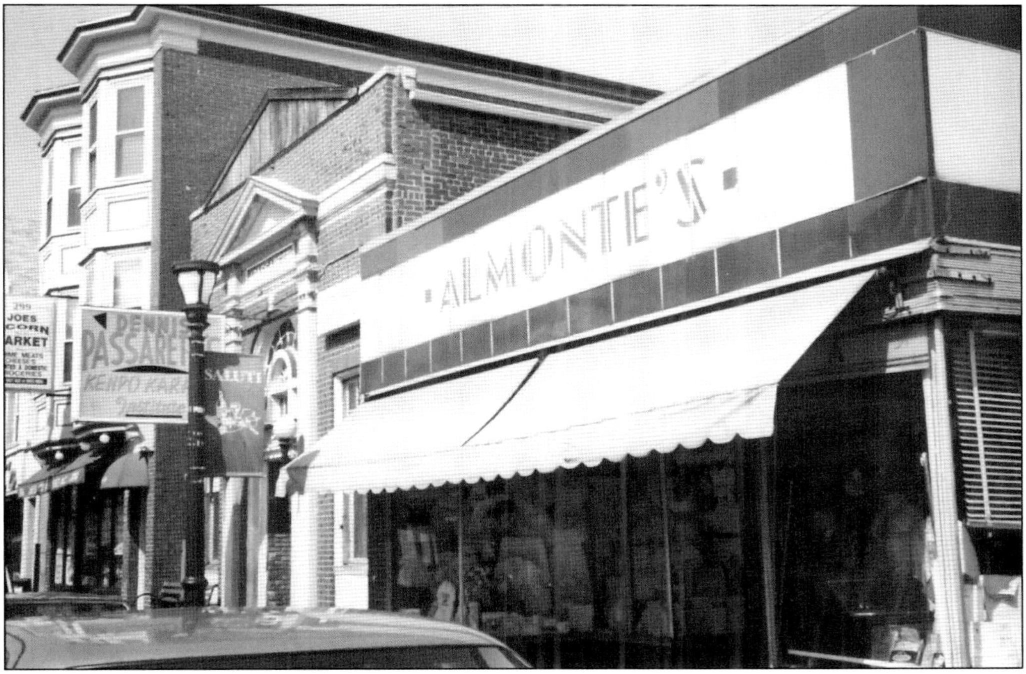

This is one of the oldest intact clothing stores on the Hill. A family store, it has neighborhood ambience—simple, no frills, and always reliable.

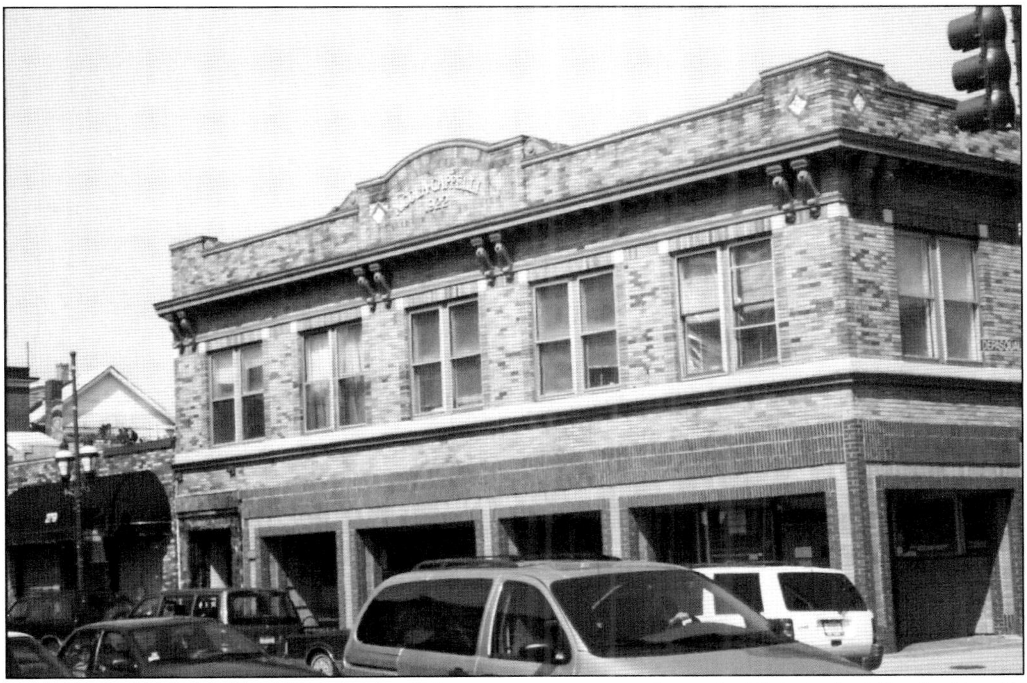

Beautifully preserved buildings such as this remain intact and sturdy. This is the Nicola Capelli building erected in 1922; its superb cornices echo Italian architecture.

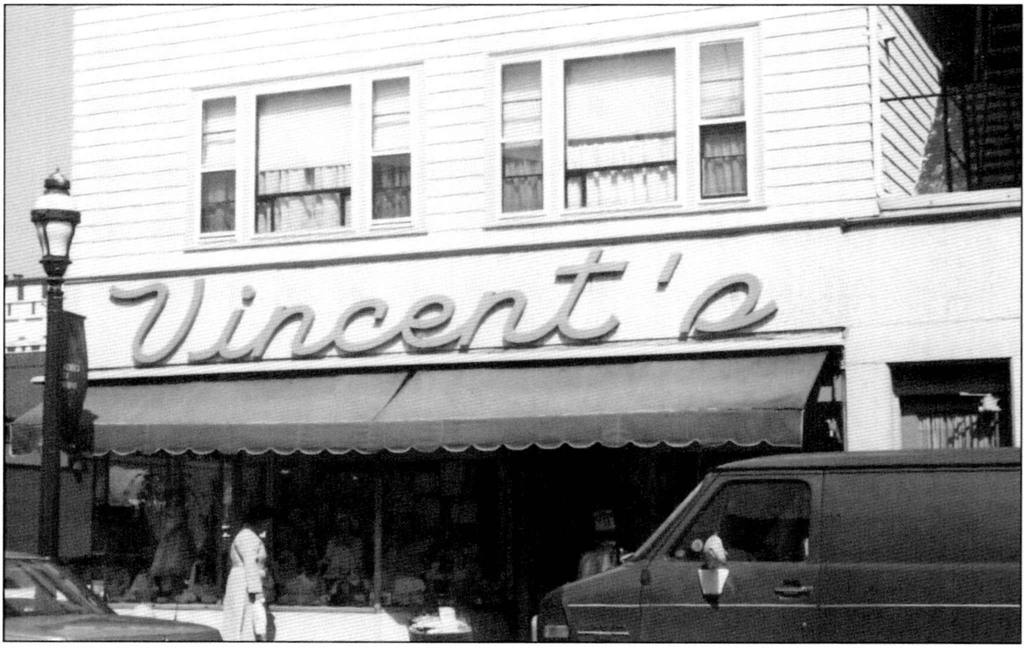

Another enduring business, Vincent's has been open on the Hill for decades. Catering to women's and girls' clothing, it is still the place where communion dresses, baptismal gowns, frocks, etc. are sold.

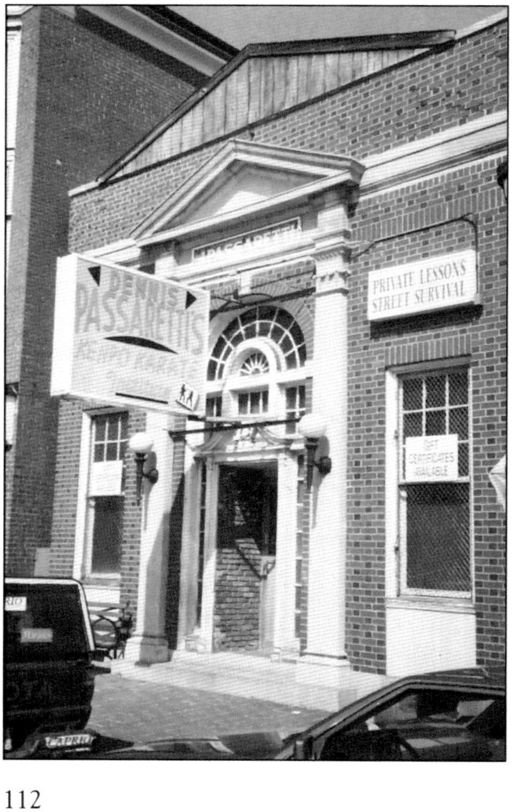

In this superb, temple-like building, one can learn the art of karate, Kempo style. And although the sign says, "street survival private lessons are given," it can't be Atwells Avenue that is being talked about, for it is today one of the safest streets anywhere, at any hour.

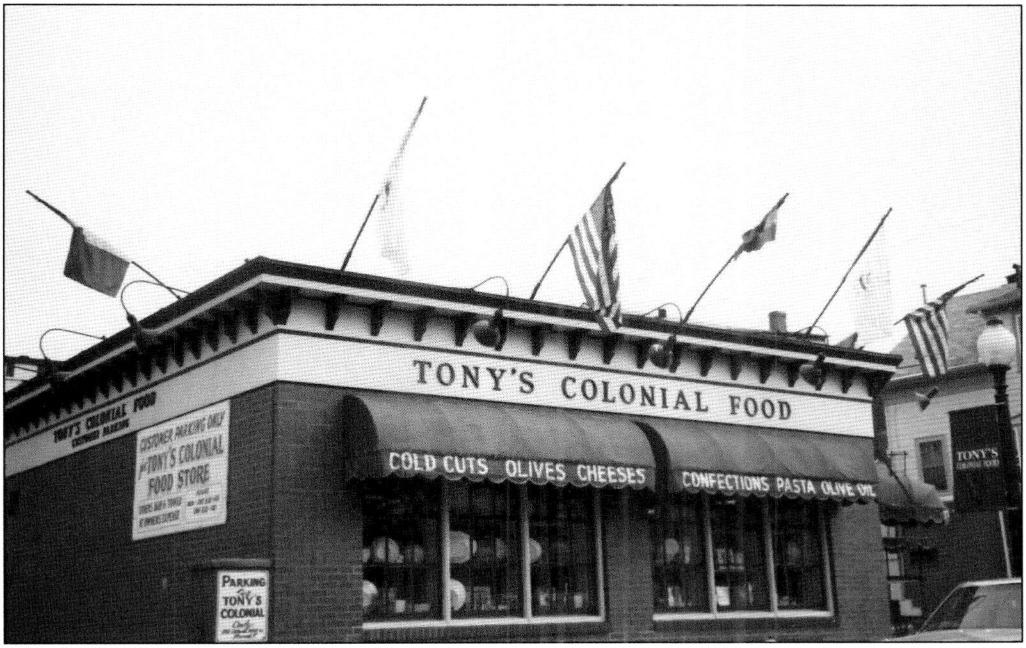

A living legend, Tony's Colonial is pictured here with its characteristic flags always unfurled. This is an exquisite market and gift store offering everything you need and more.

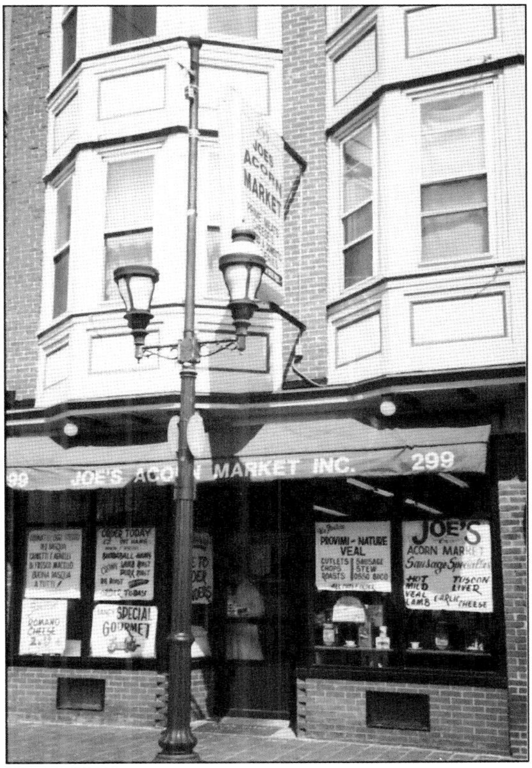

Joe's Acorn Market is the legend of them all, barring none. Here Joe Di Giuglio, now in his late nineties, worked until recently; his son is keeping the tradition alive. A remarkable market, it has withstood adversity, death, and illness and is still there enduring.

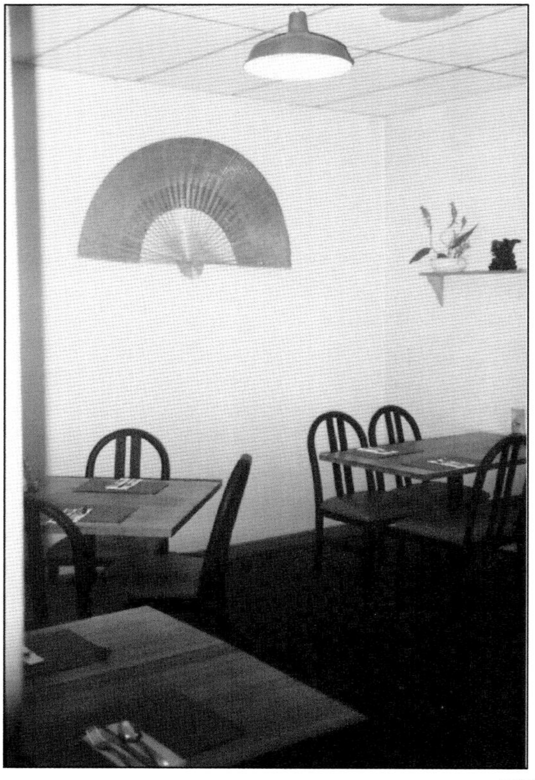

A sparse and simple ambience, the single wall fan and the bareness of the eating area is evocative of an Oriental discipline one would never have imagined would come to the Hill—but it is here.

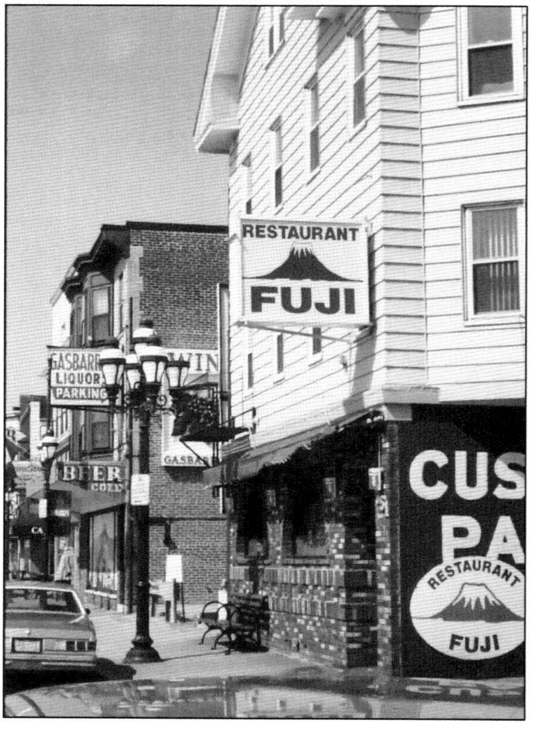

The Restaurant Fuji is the first and only Japanese restaurant on the Hill. More and more, the influx of new and different cuisines is proof of the viability of the Hill, of its renaissance. People believe in this area.

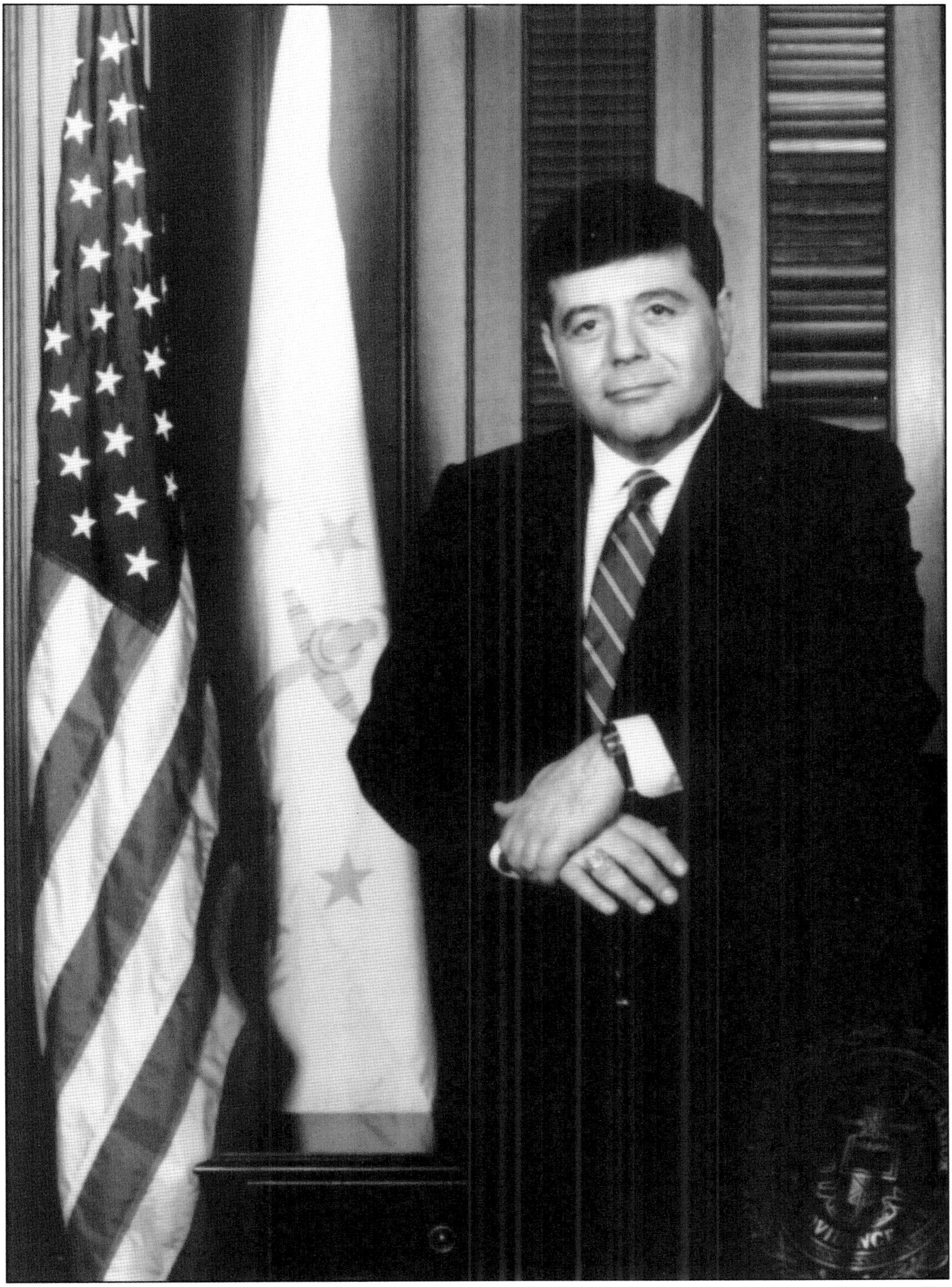

The man who believes in the Hill, Mayor Vincent A. Cianci Jr. has devoted his efforts to the renaissance on Federal Hill. He is there, everywhere, even at the "opening of an envelope," as he likes to say. Politics aside, his presence on the Hill is indelible, and his achievements have helped to bring a renewal to Federal Hill.

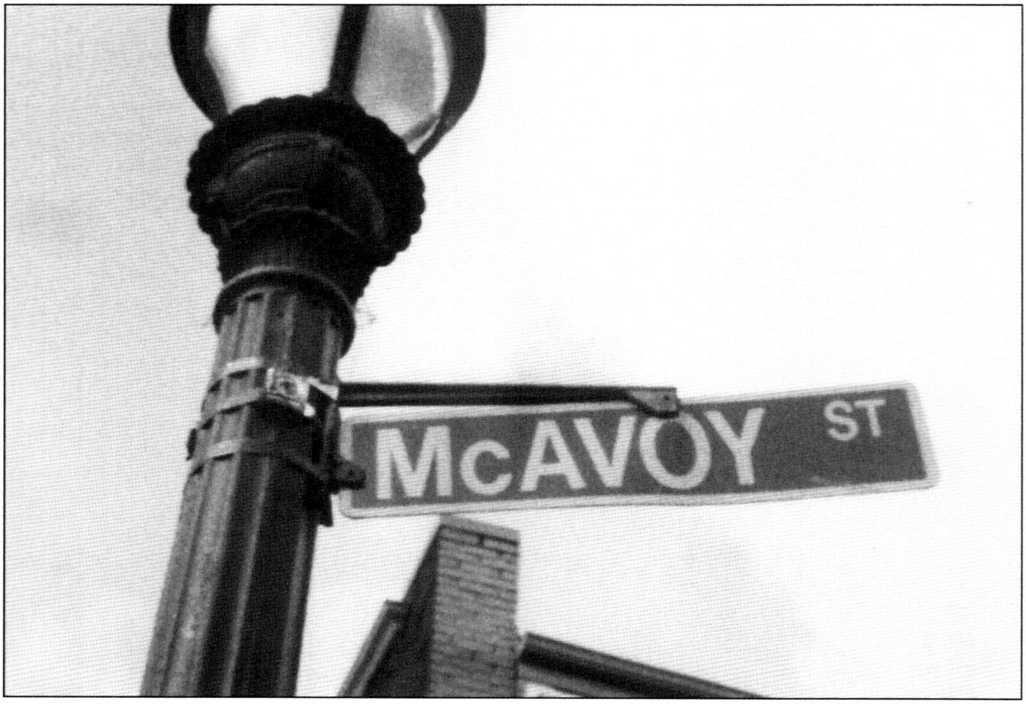

Signs like these on Atwells Avenue tell of a time when the Irish influence was strong. Irish immigrants who settled before the great immigration of the Italians endured much, suffered much, and still maintained their undiminished faith in God.

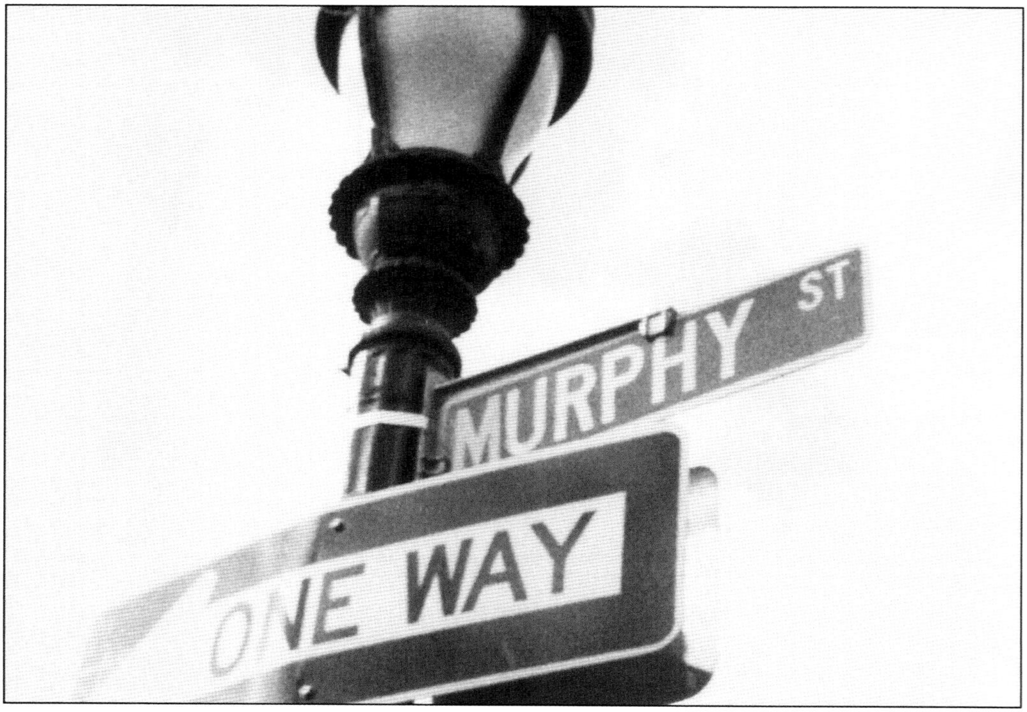

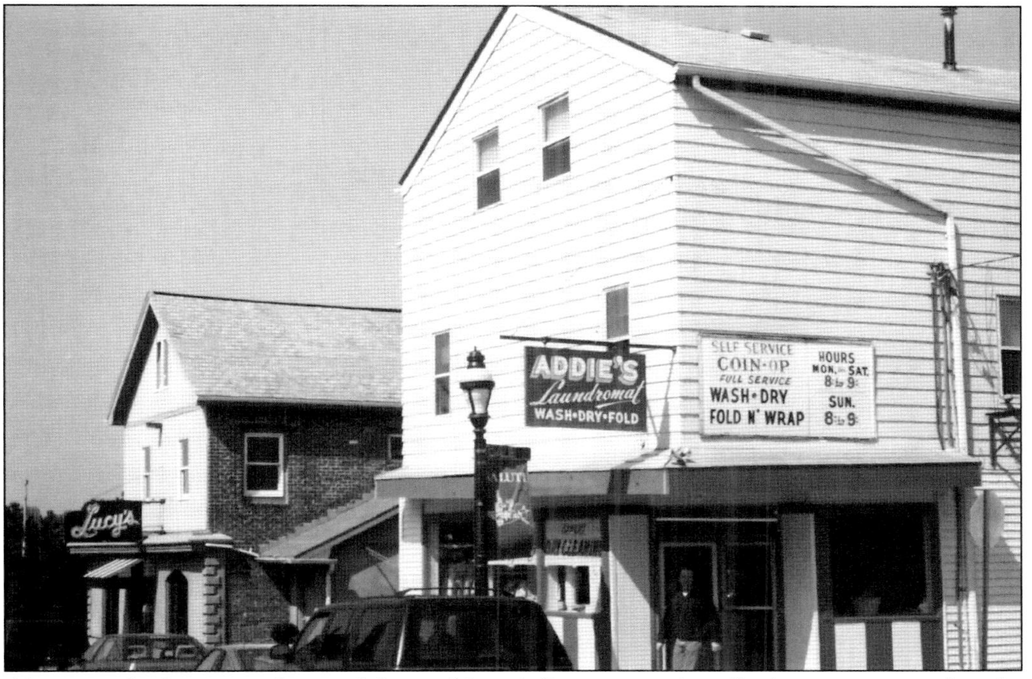

Almost at the bottom, a few yards beyond Lucy's Restaurant, Atwells Avenue, as it is thought of in Federal Hill terms, ends. It does go on physically, but for our purposes, it is no longer the "Avenue" of Federal Hill.

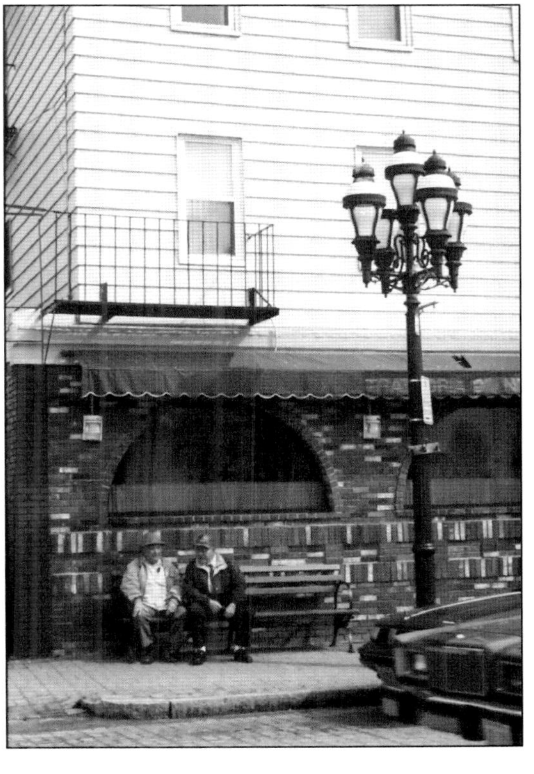

Two elderly gentlemen pass the time of day before the arches of Restaurant Fuji. Years ago, it would have been unlikely. Today, it is all a part of the coming together of the Hill. Federal Hill is the melting, or better, the forging pot for people who come here to work, to be part of this unique society.

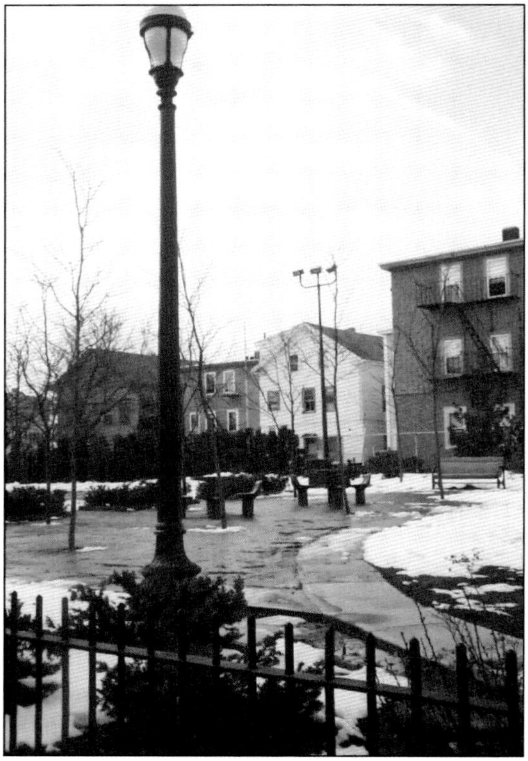

This is a park where a great church once stood. Razed by edict, St. John's Park commemorates where the magnificent St. John's Church once rose. Considered unnecessary, unsafe, and largely unattended, it was demolished a few years ago.

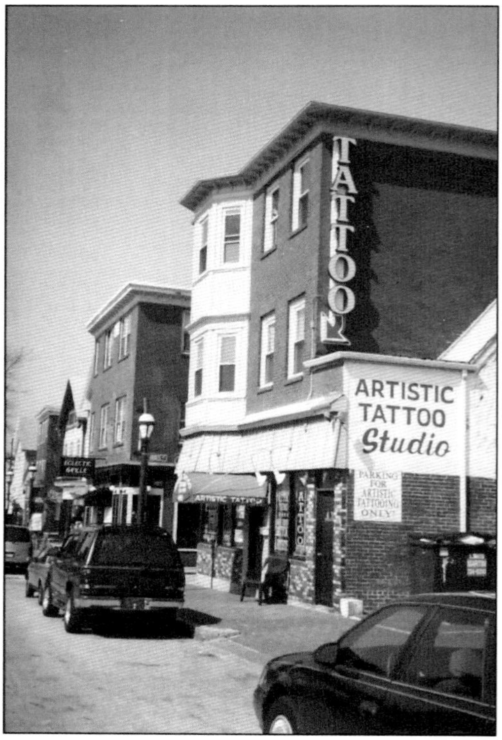

Moving along Atwells Avenue as it slopes to the overpass of a highway, one can see that the Eclectic Grille is a new, warm, and unique restaurant, another of the growing number of restaurants on the Hill.

The ornate street lamps, designed some years ago, flank both sides of the avenue. These lamps with five bulbs are more baroque in style; they are not duplicated anywhere in the state.

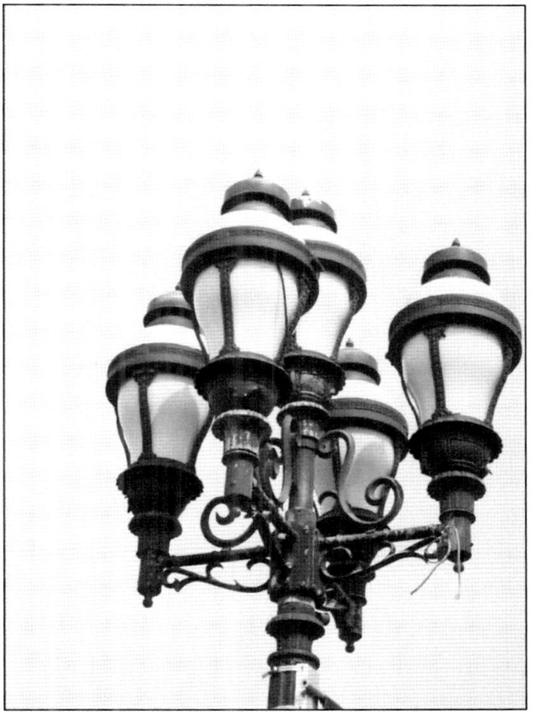

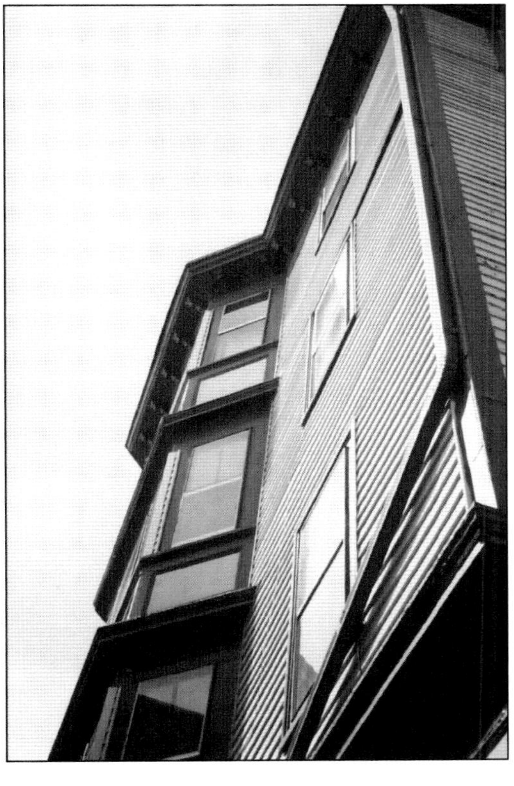

The beauty of symmetry, Atwells Avenue is a treasury of balance and dramatic design. Some of the buildings have bowed to contemporary requisites, like aluminum siding. Others, such as this one, have combined aluminum siding with the original wood siding.

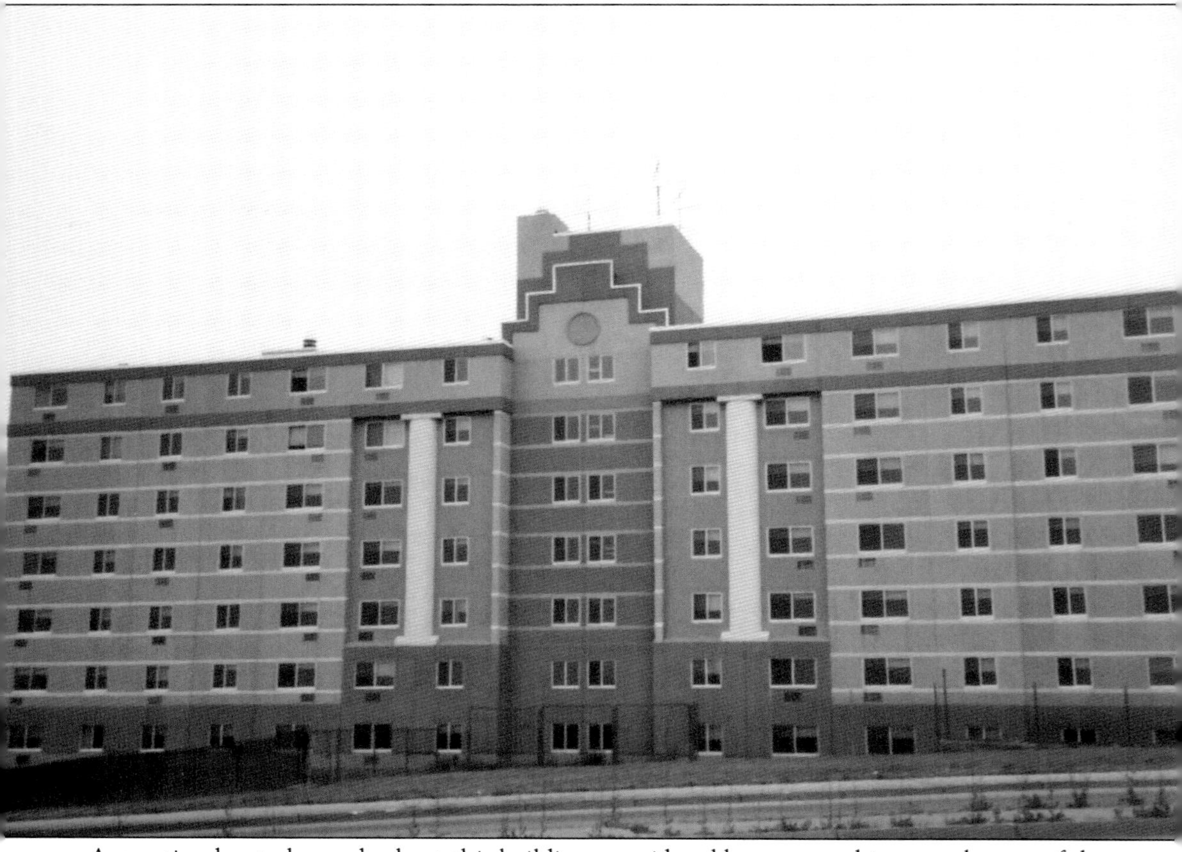

A mention has to be made about this building, considered by many architects to be one of the ugliest buildings ever built. Looking as if it did not know what it wanted to be, a confusion of faux Greek and Aztec and contemporary antiseptic influences, this building, originally built as an apartment house close to a highway, is an ungainly sight as one approaches the Hill from the highway. But it is not on Atwells Avenue and is just off enough to be dismissed.

Ten

The Young and New Hill

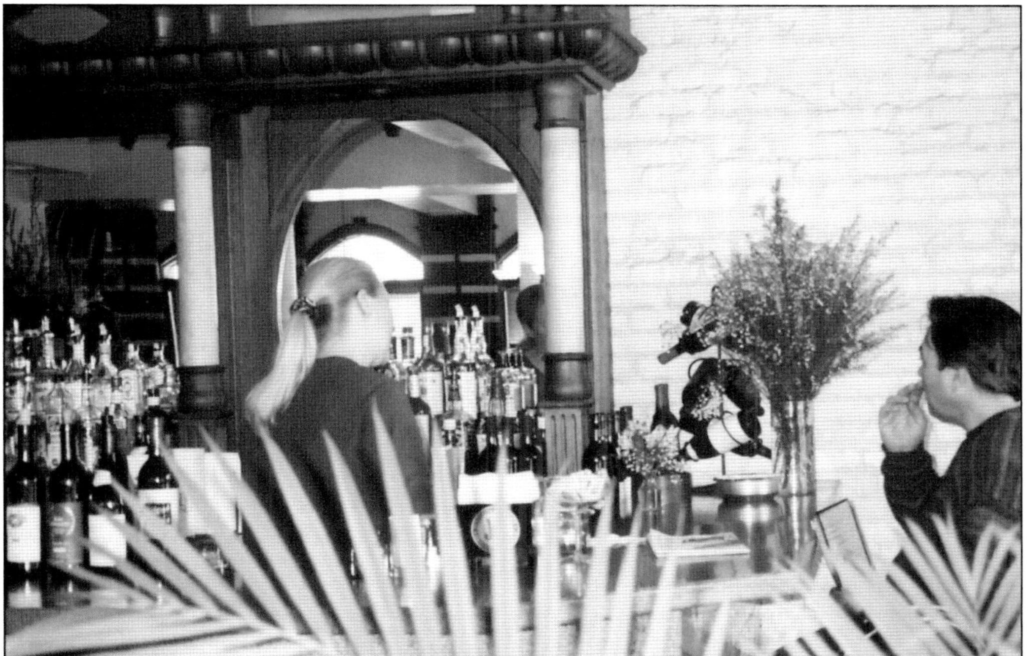

This is a view inside Lucy's, once an Italian cafe called Caffe Verdi and before that a bar. Notice the superb mirror and molding of the centerpiece behind the bar. Patron David Del Bonis seems to be amazed.

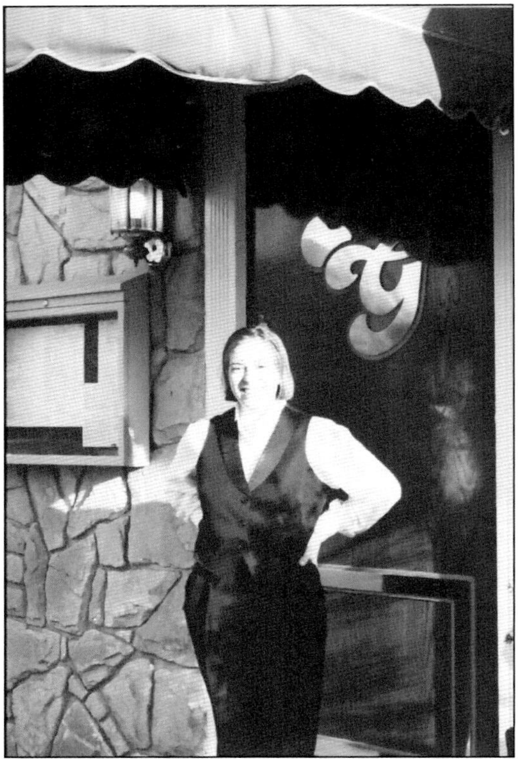

Diane Macera is happy to be on Federal Hill, the owner of the legendary Blue Grotto. Young entrepreneurs are all over the Hill.

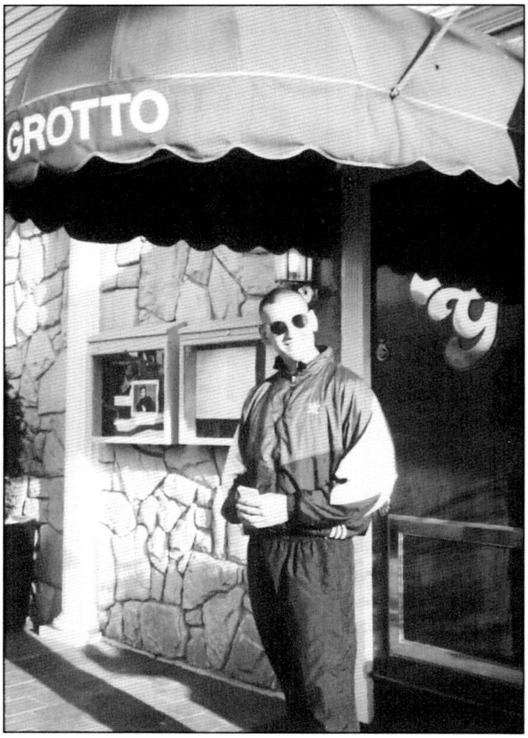

Looking very proud of his job, young Sam Berenson, valet for the famed Blue Grotto, is an example of young people at work on the Hill; for wherever there are great restaurants, there is valet service, and the Hill certainly has that.

How young does one have to be to be owner of a newspaper? This is Robert Salvatore Jr. in his early twenties, owner of the *Federal Hill Gazette*. A dream is fulfilled, and for the first time in nearly twenty years, Federal Hill has its own, very successful newspaper.

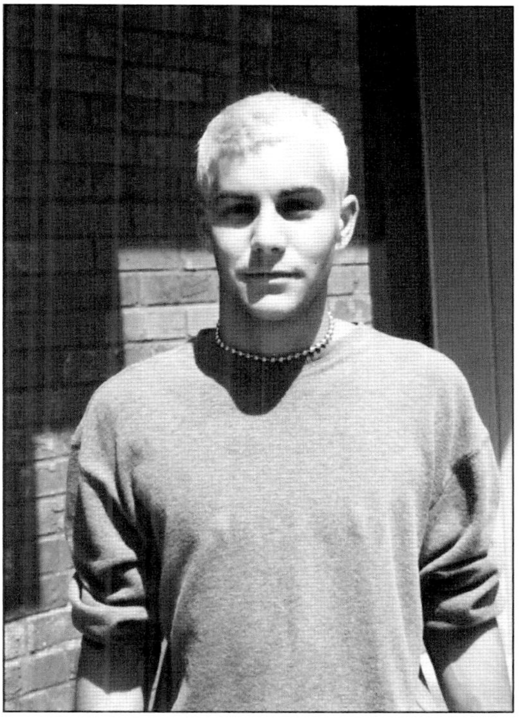

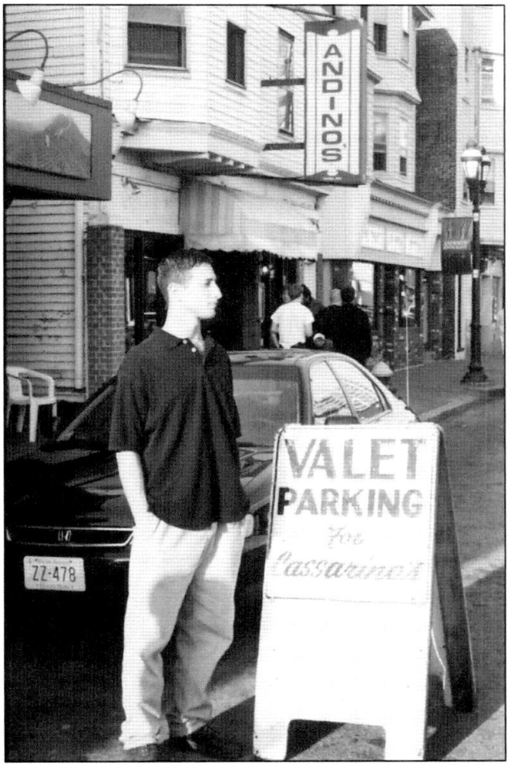

With a superb profile one might find on a Roman coin, James O'Neill epitomizes the new breed of Federal Hill-ites. Hailing from Long Island, James has taken up residence on the Hill while he attends Johnson and Wales University. He buys his goods on the Hill and works on the Hill for two outstanding restaurants. This is the way the young are coming here, and many are staying.

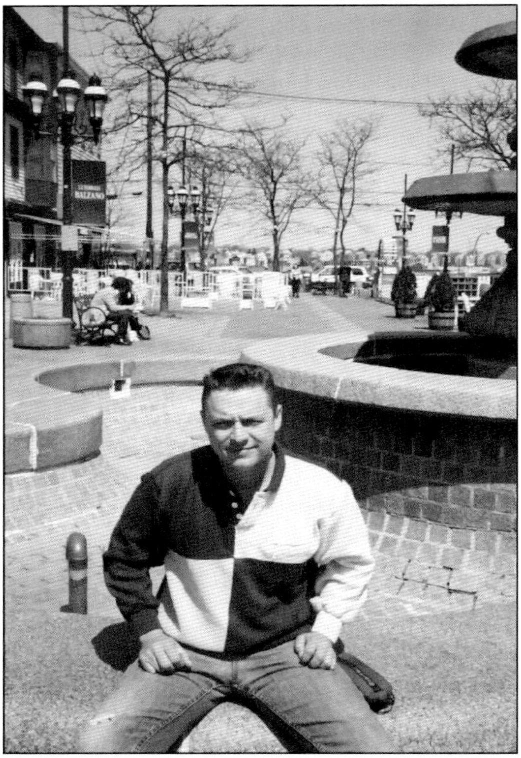

And now the camera is turned on the cameraman. Sitting in famous De Pasquale Square on the rim of the fountain, photographer Al Lothrop, who has been staff photographer for three newspapers and has photographed the rich and famous, is a young man who has been all over the Hill recording it for posterity. He has taken nearly all of the contemporary photos in this book and has contributed to *Federal Hill and Mill Villages*.

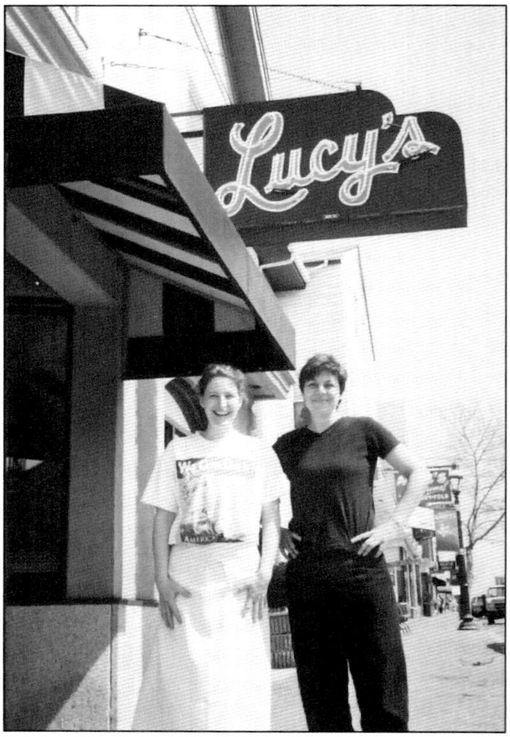

The new owners of Lucy's, Diane Slater (right) with her partner Wendy Davis, have brought a new experience to the Hill. A trendy place, Lucy's is another example of how young people are transforming the terrain, bringing new life to nearly forgotten areas.

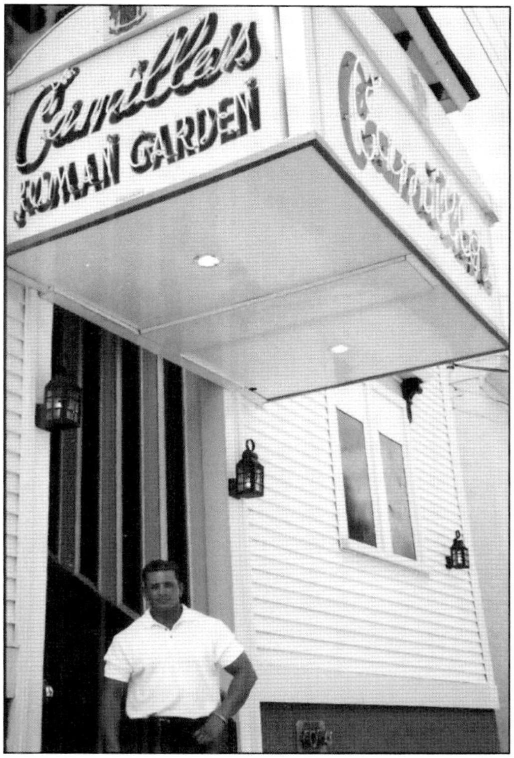

This is the watcher at the gate, so to speak. When he is not serving as valet for the world famous Camille's, Frank Caldarone is ever watchful at the beautiful entrance to this great restaurant.

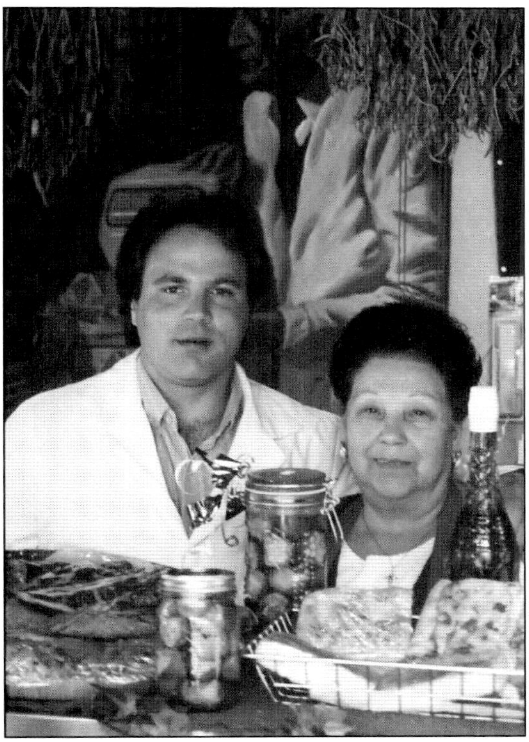

Son-in-law and mother-in-law, Wayne Wheatley and Carmina Conti, carry on the tradition of Wayne's mother and grandfather who started the unique Providence Cheese on the Hill. Wayne is third generation and is the owner.

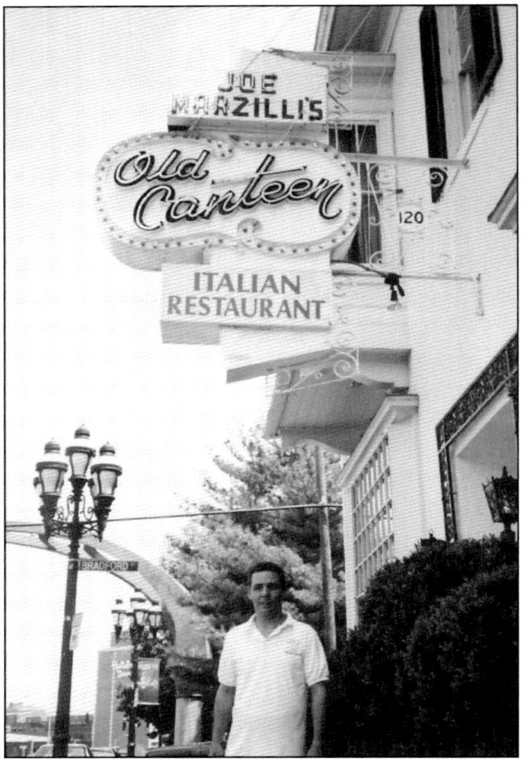

If every famous restaurant in a few blocks is to be represented by service to its customers, then the Old Canteen, Joe Marzilli's marvelous restaurant, has that service in the person of Kenneth Turchetta. He has been there for years and knows the customers on a first-name basis. He is a part of the fabric of Federal Hill.

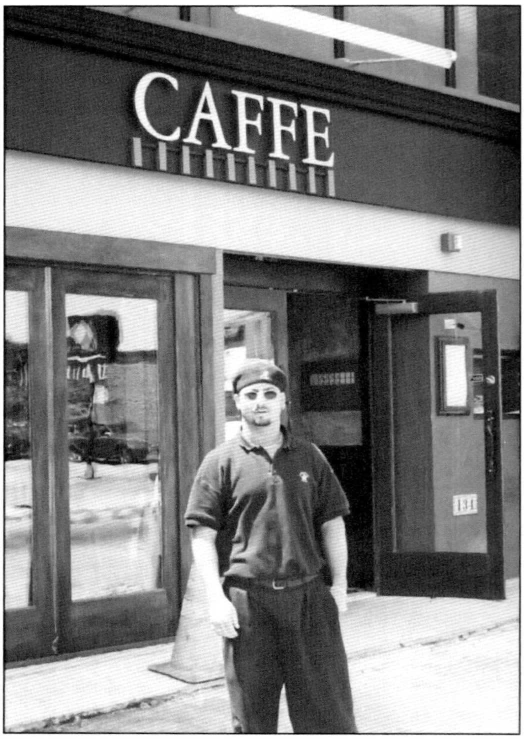

Antonio Sciarra, from Italy, offers just the right cosmopolitan look suited to the Hill. Behind him is the open air Mediterraneo Caffe, a new place on the Hill.

These two young guys, Michael Beaver (left) and Joe Rasso (right), know more about pizza than anybody should know. It is hard to imagine the Hill without them. Young Mike, so much a part of Federal Hill, moved from a small town to the hustle and bustle of this energized place.

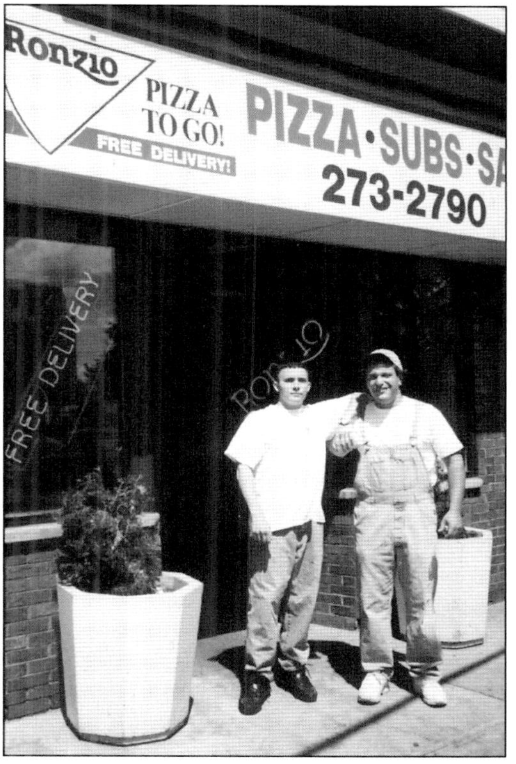

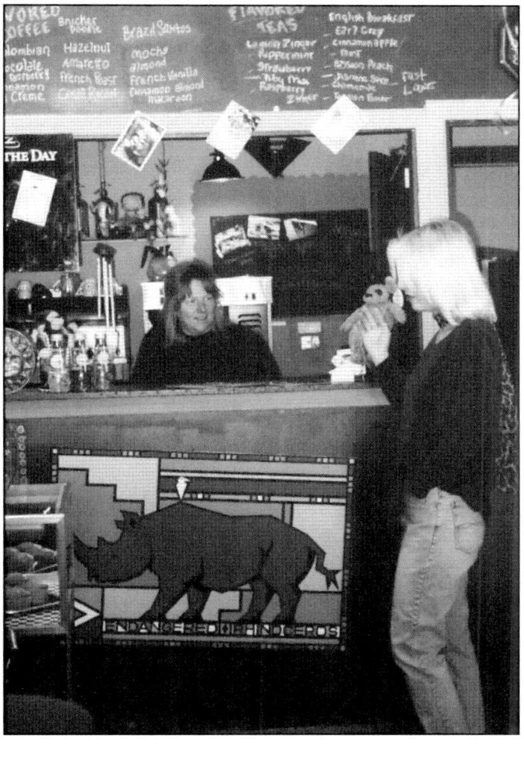

Deborah Tibeault (left) and her partner Laura Sebastian (right) own the very unique, avant-garde restaurant called Caffe Mondo on a corner of Atwells Avenue. They have been on the Hill a few years, starting off as picture framers, then deciding to try something completely new. Art still abounds in the cozy, warm, and very friendly cafe.

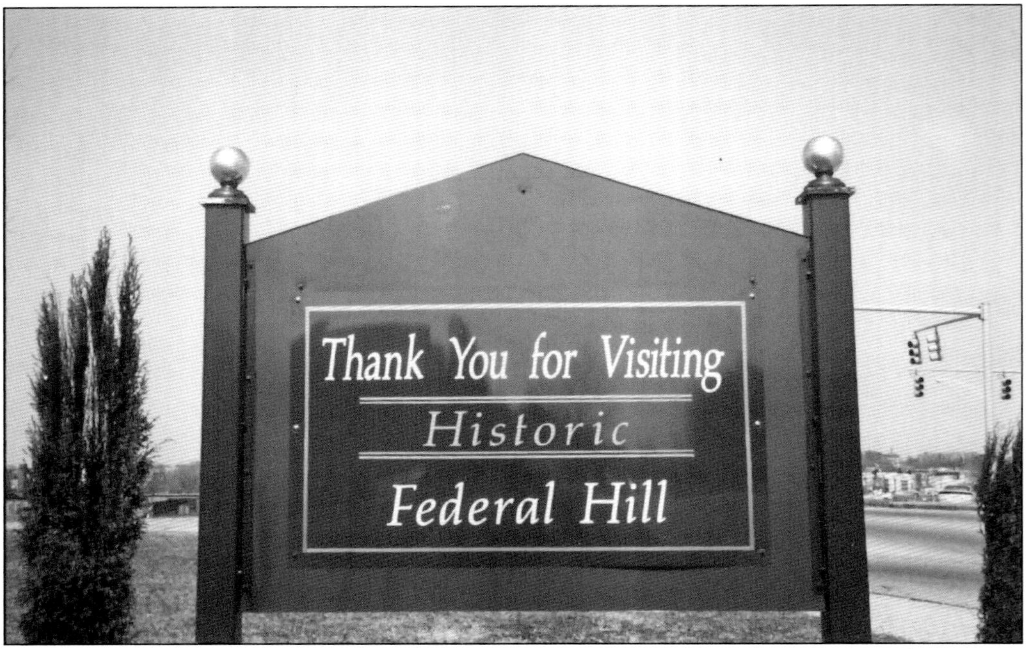

The Hill welcomes and then offer thanks for the visit. This is one of a number of new signs placed on the Hill. Tourists are guided by them to a wonderful experience. This is part of the renaissance of Federal Hill.

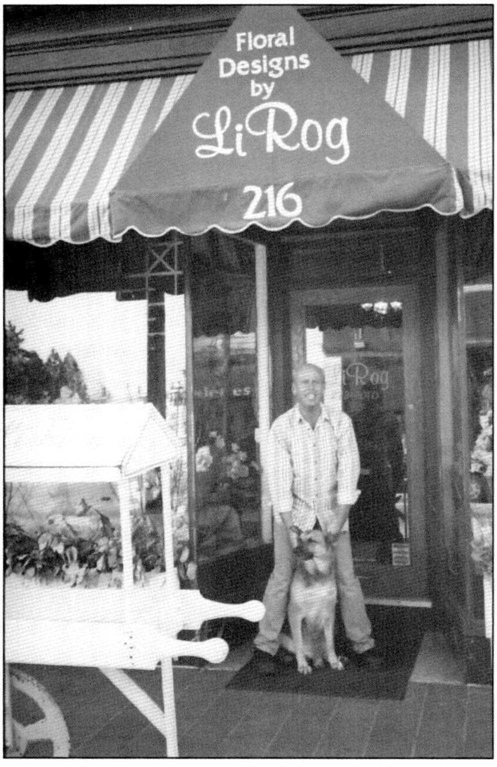

It is safe to say that Roger Lambert decorates the Hill. His amazing designs are seen everywhere. He and his partner Lisa Pratt so love this place that they purchased a two-story historic house on a side street not far from LiRog. They love it here. Even Heidi, the German shepherd, has no complaints.